# Sociology Transformed

Series Editors
John Holmwood
School of Sociology and Social Policy
University of Nottingham
Nottingham, UK

Stephen Turner
Department of Philosophy
University of South Florida
Tampa, FL, USA

The field of sociology has changed rapidly over the last few decades. Sociology Transformed seeks to map these changes on a country by country basis and to contribute to the discussion of the future of the subject. The series is concerned not only with the traditional centres of the discipline, but with its many variant forms across the globe.

More information about this series at
http://www.palgrave.com/gp/series/14477

Stephan Moebius

# Sociology in Germany

## A History

Printed with the funding of the Austrian Academy of Sciences

Stephan Moebius
Sociology
University of Graz
Graz, Steiermark, Austria

Sociology Transformed
ISBN 978-3-030-71865-7     ISBN 978-3-030-71866-4  (eBook)
https://doi.org/10.1007/978-3-030-71866-4

© The Author(s) 2021. This book is an open access publication.
**Open Access** This book is licensed under the terms of the Creative Commons Attribution 4.0 International License (http://creativecommons.org/licenses/by/4.0/), which permits use, sharing, adaptation, distribution and reproduction in any medium or format, as long as you give appropriate credit to the original author(s) and the source, provide a link to the Creative Commons licence and indicate if changes were made.
The images or other third party material in this book are included in the book's Creative Commons licence, unless indicated otherwise in a credit line to the material. If material is not included in the book's Creative Commons licence and your intended use is not permitted by statutory regulation or exceeds the permitted use, you will need to obtain permission directly from the copyright holder.
The use of general descriptive names, registered names, trademarks, service marks, etc. in this publication does not imply, even in the absence of a specific statement, that such names are exempt from the relevant protective laws and regulations and therefore free for general use.
The publisher, the authors and the editors are safe to assume that the advice and information in this book are believed to be true and accurate at the date of publication. Neither the publisher nor the authors or the editors give a warranty, expressed or implied, with respect to the material contained herein or for any errors or omissions that may have been made. The publisher remains neutral with regard to jurisdictional claims in published maps and institutional affiliations.

Cover illustration: © Melisa Hasan

This Palgrave Macmillan imprint is published by the registered company Springer Nature Switzerland AG.
The registered company address is: Gewerbestrasse 11, 6330 Cham, Switzerland

# Acknowledgments

First, I would like to mention and thank in particular Antonia Schirgi and Frithjof Nungesser. From the beginning, they accompanied this book project and were an indispensable help for the translations of the manuscript.

I thank Peter Kenny very much. He proofread the manuscript and greatly improved the readability of the text.

For insightful suggestions and comments on the text and on the history of sociology in Germany in general, I especially would like to thank Lothar Peter, who sparked my enthusiasm for the history of sociology, and Gerhard Schäfer, who shared his encyclopedic knowledge of the history of sociology in Germany. Special thanks also to Frithjof Nungesser, Antonia Schirgi, Andrea Ploder, Christian Dayé, and Tanja Paulitz and to the editors Stephen Turner and John Helmwood for helpful comments and suggestions. However, none of them is responsible for remaining defects. Such defects can, of course, occur, since the history of science is always a kind of self-interpretation of the author, so the author can never completely detach himself from his position in the social and academic field.

I thank Sabine List for her help in compiling the bibliography and Wolfgang Mayer for preparing the index and providing further corrections.

I am also grateful to the Austrian Academy of Sciences (ÖAW) for funding the open access publication of this book.

My special thanks also go to my wife, Julia Schäfer, and my children Caspar and Mira, who in the last years probably learned more about the history of sociology than they wanted to.

# Contents

| | | |
|---|---|---|
| 1 | Introduction | 1 |
| 2 | Sociology in Germany: From the Beginnings to 1945 | 7 |
| | *Sociology in the German Reich* | 9 |
| | *Sociological Pioneers in the German Reich: Tönnies, Simmel, Weber* | 11 |
| | *Sociology Between Explaining and Understanding* | 14 |
| | *The Werturteilsstreit* | 16 |
| | *Social Science Infrastructure Around 1900 (Journals and Professional Organizations)* | 18 |
| | *The "Ideas of 1914" and World War I* | 20 |
| | *Sociology in the Weimar Republic* | 22 |
| | *Sociological Centers and Actors in the Weimar Republic* | 25 |
| |   *Cologne* | 26 |
| |   *Heidelberg* | 27 |
| |   *Berlin* | 30 |
| |   *Hamburg* | 31 |
| |   *Leipzig* | 31 |
| |   *Frankfurt am Main* | 32 |
| |   *Braunschweig* | 34 |
| | *Institutionalization Through Sociological Journals in the Weimar Republic* | 36 |
| | *The Soziologentage and the Sociology of Knowledge Dispute* | 37 |

| | |
|---|---|
| Sociology During the Nazi Regime | 40 |
| "Inner Emigration," Exile, and Sociologies in the Service of National Socialism | 45 |

## 3 Reconstruction and Consolidation of Sociology in West Germany from 1945 to 1967

| | |
|---|---|
| Germany from 1945 to 1967 | 49 |
| *1945–1949* | 50 |
| Re-education and Research Institutions | 53 |
| "Americanization"? | 54 |
| From Re-education to Anti-communism | 56 |
| *1949–1958* | 58 |
| Central Positions and "Schools" | 58 |
| René König in Cologne | 59 |
| Max Horkheimer and Theodor W. Adorno in Frankfurt | 61 |
| Helmut Schelsky in Hamburg and Münster | 63 |
| Social Processes and Problems of the 1950s | 65 |
| Sociological Reflections on Contemporary Problems | 67 |
| The Role Debate | 69 |
| The "Civil War" in West German Sociology | 70 |
| *1959–1968* | 71 |
| Positivism Dispute | 72 |
| Generational Change | 75 |
| The Transformation of the Sociological Field | 78 |

## 4 Ups and Downs of Sociology in Germany: 1968–1990

| | |
|---|---|
| | 85 |
| "1968" | 85 |
| Late Capitalism or Industrial Society? | 88 |
| Critical Theory and the Protests of "1968" | 89 |
| New Research Institutes | 91 |
| New Universities | 92 |
| The Habermas-Luhmann Debate | 94 |
| The Debate on Theory Comparison | 97 |
| Anti-sociology | 99 |
| Social Crises | 100 |
| Differentiation and New (Qualitative) Methods in the "Great Age" of Empirical Social Research | 103 |
| The Establishment of Women's Research and Gender Studies | 107 |

|   | *Historical Self-reflections in the Transition from the 1970s to the 1980s* | 112 |
|---|---|---|
|   | *The Theory Boom of the 1980s* | 113 |
|   | *Processes of Differentiation and Pluralization in the Face of Social Change* | 119 |
| 5 | **Sociology in the German Democratic Republic** | 123 |
|   | *"Sociology—is that really necessary? We have excellent statistics, excellent statistics!"* | 127 |
|   | *Separation from "Bourgeois" Sociology* | 128 |
|   | *The Institutionalization of Marxist-Leninist Sociology* | 129 |
|   | *Marxist-Leninist Sociology on Its Way to a Normal Science?* | 133 |
|   | *The Characteristics and Role of Sociology in the GDR* | 137 |
| 6 | **Sociology in Germany After 1990** | 141 |
|   | *Reflections on Transformations in the Social Sciences* | 145 |
|   | *Why Do We Need Sociology Today?* | 150 |
|   | *The Gender Turn in Feminist Sociology* | 151 |
|   | *The Reception of New Theories of Capitalism* | 154 |
|   | *Key Social Problems in the Early 1990s: Unemployment, Poverty, Right-Wing Extremism, and Racism* | 155 |
|   | *The Red-Green Government and the Political Challenges Around 2000* | 157 |
|   | *Sociology and National Socialism: New Debates and New Research* | 162 |
|   | *Current Trends and Debates* | 163 |

**Bibliography** 173

**Index** 209

# About the Author

**Stephan Moebius** is Full Professor of Sociological Theory and Intellectual History at the University of Graz and full member of the Austrian Academy of Sciences. He is the speaker of the History of Sociology section of the German Sociological Association (DGS).

CHAPTER 1

# Introduction

This book deals with the history of sociology in Germany from late nineteenth century to the present day. Starting with the sociology in the *German Reich*, the processes of institutionalization in the Weimar Republic, and the deep rupture caused by National Socialism, the following history focuses especially on the period after 1945. It presents the intellectual, institutional, and conflict-laden courses and trends of the history of sociology in Germany in its economic, political, social, and cultural contexts.

However, this book presents only a brief history of sociology in Germany. Given the long, complex, and extremely influential tradition of sociology in Germany, it would actually may require a multi-volume project. Therefore, this book provides more of an introductory overview, which nevertheless deals with the most important institutional developments, controversies, actors, theories, and methods of post-war sociology in Germany. Crucially, this book does not deal with "German sociology," a phrase used in the literature to characterize a specific kind of sociology, which has served National Socialism.

My presentation is based on the methodology for the history of sociology developed by Lothar Peter in his 2001 contribution to the *Jahrbuch für Soziologiegeschichte* (*Yearbook on the History of Sociology*). Taking Wolf Lepenies' introduction to the four-volume edition of *Geschichte der Soziologie* (1981; *The History of Sociology*) and Dirk Kaesler's (1984) study of early German sociology as his point of departure, Peter (2001,

2015) outlined a methodological research design geared specifically to history-of-sociology analyses. At the heart of such analyses is the analytical distinction of three major dimensions of research in the history of sociology: the *cognitive* dimension, the *social* dimension, and the dimension of its *history of impact and discourse*. The general framework for research on the history of sociology first of all involves contextualizing, by reference to historical reality and social history, the ideas, theories, methods, instruments, institutions, actors, and history of impact to be analyzed. In other words, the object of research must first be considered in the broader context of the societal (economic, political, social, and cultural) processes at the time of its emergence. This framing is to account for the fact that ideas do not surface in a historical and social void but are historically and socially situated or, rather, because of their "existential determination" (*Seinsverbundenheit*; Mannheim) are only possible at a specific point in time. My own starting point is that I understand sociology as a specific modern response to social problems and crises and thus a scientific and intellectual way of perceiving, interpreting, and solving social problems. Accordingly, a study on the history of sociology or of ideas would have to take contemporary society into consideration as an essential point of reference for the concrete relevance of sociological ideas.

The *cognitive dimension*, as the first level of analysis, therefore consists in exposing the historical contexts of research and in an analysis of ideas, contemporary paradigms, theories, methods, empirical research, and discourses that embed the development of and provide the backdrop to what constitutes sociological thinking. Investigation of the cognitive dimension is followed by examining the *social dimension*. In the *social dimension*, Peter distinguishes between the analysis of actors and the analysis of institutional processes. The analyses of institutionalization can involve several levels: group formation, constellations, schools of thought, specialist journals, or professional organizations. Lastly, analyses at the level of the *history of impact and discourse* inquire how sociological knowledge enters into and is used in social discourse. Which position do theories, methods, controversies, and ideas occupy in sociological discourse, and what role do techniques and relations of power play? Another dimension of Peter's methodology that is often neglected in the study of the history of sociology and closely tied to the history of discourse is sociology's history of impact, particularly its (intended or mostly unintended) impact on the future course of the discipline, neighboring disciplines, and society in general. Investigating the impact and imprint of sociology on discourse in society would merit a study of its own. It is obvious that in a short history of sociology one cannot treat all dimensions exhaustively. Yet an attempt has been made to take them into account as far as possible.

According to the methodology just outlined, each chapter begins with a historical contextualization, in which the central economic, political, social, and cultural processes of German history are described. In Chap. 2 the beginnings of sociology in Germany are discussed, dealing with the pioneers, first professional organizations, and early controversies. Also, this chapter presents both the interwar period, when sociology became established at universities, and the years of National Socialism, which brought sociology as an institutionalized discipline to an end.

Chapter 3 focuses on the two decades after 1945, the period of the "post-war society" (1945–1967). After World War II Germany was undergoing a profound process of change. Just as society as a whole, sociology had to be rebuilt. Journals were refounded or newly founded, the German Sociological Association was restored and sociology was reestablished as a university subject. Different "schools" and regional centers of sociology emerged. By the end of the 1950s, an institutional and generational change can be observed. The so-called "post-war generation" assumed central positions in organizations, editorial boards of journals, and universities.

Chapter 4 discusses the ups and downs of sociology from 1968 to 1990. The student movement brought sociology into the limelight. Some sociological "schools" became closely connected with it. As a university subject, sociology gained enormously in importance, which was connected with a growing need for social reflection in all areas of life. A characteristic feature of sociology in this period was an increased differentiation into specialized subfields. The number of academic positions for sociologists and the number of students increased, partly as a result of the founding of new universities and of reforms in higher education policy. The increasing number of non-university research institutions complemented sociological research at the universities. This expansion, which came together with a highly visible public sociology, also led to counter-movements and anti-sociological effects. The "planning euphoria" of the 1960s and 1970s faded, and many looked at 1968 with disappointment and turned away from sociology. This changed a little bit in the 1980s, which was the heyday of sociological theory in Germany.

Chapter 5 takes a short look at sociology in the GDR (German Democratic Republic). GDR sociology did not emerge until the 1960s and could not develop in the same way as in West Germany, not only because it was largely overshadowed by Marxist-Leninist philosophy and political economy but also because it was in the service of economic policy. The connection to economic policy and historical materialism promoted the tendency to economic reductionism in GDR sociology. Only when the social processes and dynamics could no longer be adequately described within the conventional ideological framework did certain changes occur, as could be observed in the 1980s.

As is shown in Chap. 6, the fall of the Berlin Wall and German reunification shaped the development of sociology in the 1990s. The triumph of capitalist society fostered globalization theories and a brief comeback of modernization theory. But as the system change came along with severe social problems, since the mid-1990s theories and research projects focusing on social exclusion, precarious work, and xenophobia moved more and more to the center stage of sociological thinking. In addition there was a boom of gender studies and of various subfields of cultural studies. The landscape of sociological theories in Germany was changing: Whereas before grand theories were dominant, nowadays we can observe a trend toward rapidly alternating sociological diagnoses of contemporary society.

How do these presentist trends correlate with the history of sociology? Why do we need a history of sociology (cf. in general Dayé and Moebius 2015)? For reasons of identity formation (cf. Lepenies 1981)? Just to inform present and future sociology about its history and, thus, to ensure not to reinvent the wheel? In my opinion, the history of sociology is important because it is a reflection of society and an analysis of society's professional self-descriptions (Nolte 2000, pp. 19–21, 244). It is a critical undertaking because it analyzes the social effects and developments as well as the related ideological perspectives, struggles, and antagonistic power relations within the sociological field. "In this way [...] not only the changes, progress or setbacks inherent in the discipline can be reconstructed in their significance for the further development of sociological discourse, but society itself, to which the theoretical, methodological, and empirical efforts of the discipline in the past referred, can be better recognized in its historical particularity and thus placed in plausible and comparable contexts with the present" (Peter 2001, p. 57). Reconstructing the history of sociology can, thus, "strengthen the capacity for critical sociological analysis of modern contemporary society" (Peter 2015, p. 142). In this way, the sociological analysis of the history of sociology uncovers the dynamics of the social within the science of the social and thus contributes to an increased orientation, self-reflection, and enlightening of the discipline.

**Open Access** This chapter is licensed under the terms of the Creative Commons Attribution 4.0 International License (http://creativecommons.org/licenses/by/4.0/), which permits use, sharing, adaptation, distribution and reproduction in any medium or format, as long as you give appropriate credit to the original author(s) and the source, provide a link to the Creative Commons licence and indicate if changes were made.

The images or other third party material in this chapter are included in the chapter's Creative Commons licence, unless indicated otherwise in a credit line to the material. If material is not included in the chapter's Creative Commons licence and your intended use is not permitted by statutory regulation or exceeds the permitted use, you will need to obtain permission directly from the copyright holder.

CHAPTER 2

# Sociology in Germany: From the Beginnings to 1945

The beginning of sociological thinking in Germany can be traced back to the middle of the nineteenth century. Until then, society had primarily been understood within the framework of contract theory (Thomas Hobbes, John Locke), that is, as something that has to be constructed. Around 1850, the idea arose to characterize "society" more broadly as the "social system constituted by human coexistence" (Nolte 2000, p. 33). This conceptual shift was provoked by social processes and problems similar to those which facilitated the emergence of sociology in England (initiated by Herbert Spencer (1820–1903)) and in France (initiated by Henri de Saint-Simon (1760–1825) and Auguste Comte (1798–1857)). These processes and problems were: the transition from the feudal age to bourgeois society, industrialization and the drastic intensification of the division of labor, the emergence of social classes within a capitalist economic system, and the so-called social question (*soziale Frage*) which resulted from the tensions between the social classes.[1] These developments showed that "society" could no longer be thought of as a freely chosen association of independent individuals, but had to be conceived of as a structured

---

[1] In German, the term *soziale Frage* ("social question") refers to the social grievances, inequalities, and problems that accompanied the transition from an agrarian to an urbanizing industrial society.

entity largely determined by economic dynamics and increasingly "shaped by the political borders" (Nolte 2000, p. 32).

The "social question" was the starting point for both the materialist social theory of Karl Marx (1818–1883) and Friedrich Engels (1820–1895) and for the first steps toward a *Gesellschaftswissenschaft* (the science of society) in the German-speaking world. Around 1850, the first German representatives of such a "science of society" were Lorenz von Stein (1815–1890), who based his concept of society on the analysis of social movements in France, and Robert von Mohl (1799–1875), who wanted to differentiate strictly between the new *Gesellschaftswissenschaft* and the already existing *Staatswissenschaft* (the science of the state). So far, social processes had been the object of investigation primarily in the philosophy of history and the *Staatswissenschaften*. In contrast to these disciplines, von Stein and von Mohl claimed that "society" has to be regarded as an independent social sphere, which has to be strictly distinguished from the state. Furthermore, in contrast to politically active socialists and communists, von Stein and von Mohl wanted to solve the "social question" in a "scientific way" (Mikl-Horke 2001, pp. 40–43).[2] The new *Gesellschaftswissenschaft* was seen as a way to social reforms to avoid a social revolution.

The call for an independent *Gesellschaftswissenschaft*, however, met with little approval within the academic field and was resolutely rejected by the humanities and the *Staatswissenschaften*. This might explain why, some years later, German social scientists such as Ferdinand Tönnies (1855–1936), Georg Simmel (1958–1918), and Max Weber (1864–1920) avoided the notion "*Gesellschaftswissenschaft*." Confronted with the powerful *Staatswissenschaften* and a widespread anti-sociological attitude, which mainly concerned the sociological concepts from France and England,[3] the early proponents of sociology had to struggle to make their voices heard.

Unlike von Stein or von Mohl, and faced with the rapid pace of social and cultural change, extremely concentrated in large cities, the early sociologists were no longer concerned with the emergence of "society" (Nolte 2000, p. 55), but with its cohesion. They saw a particular problem

---

[2] All translations of German texts are by the author unless otherwise indicated. If there are English citations, it will be marked as "English in original."

[3] Significant critics were for example the historian Heinrich von Treitschke (1834–1896) and the philosopher Wilhelm Dilthey (1833–1911).

in the dissolution of traditional worldviews and cultural values. Hence, German society, so the interpretation, not only faced the "social question" but it also had to deal with a "cultural crisis" (Lichtblau 1996). Against this background, the beginning of World War I—which was interpreted as a struggle of German culture against Western civilization—was hailed as an opportunity to leave all the social cleavages, cultural tensions, all the value relativism, and political conflicts behind.

## Sociology in the *German Reich*

The economic, political, social, and cultural developments of the *German Reich*, which had been founded in 1871, were conducive to the emergence, establishment, and institutionalization of sociology, because the now observable dynamics and consequences of condensed and rapid processes of social differentiation, transformation, and modernization lent themselves to a broader analytic perspective—a "sociological optic" so to speak.

The lack of political modernization of the *Reich* was conflicting with the accelerated economic and cultural modernization. Therefore, some social scientists perceive Germany as a "belated nation" (Plessner 1959 [1935]), or they describe the German development as a "special path" (*Sonderweg*) (Wehler 1977, p. 11).[4] The central characteristics of social transformation and modernization were intense industrialization and the rise of the *German Reich* to become the second most powerful industrial nation in the world, the expansion of the monetary economy, massive arms build-up, and an imperialist policy of expansion and for certain time also of colonialism. Society was characterized by an increasing population growth, an intensification of the division of labor, and social differentiation. Rapid urbanization was accompanied by housing and poverty problems. The labor movement grew rapidly, as did the women's movement. Tendencies toward secularization questioned the once binding power of

---

[4] For the reconstruction of the historical processes, I especially refer to Wehler (1977) and Nipperdey (1990). For the special features of the historical development of Germany see Elias (1989/1996). However, some historians contradicted the "special path" thesis, since, on the one hand, it is based on an allegedly "normal" path of other Western countries. On the other hand, with its focus on the state and the unmodern, "belated," "pre-industrial elite," it would neglect the central importance of the successes as well of the capitalist interests of the bourgeoisie, which were easily linked with the authoritarian state, so Blackbourn and Eley (1980); for discussion of the thesis see Kocka (1982).

Jewish, Catholic, and Protestant religion. New technologies and inventions such as electricity, the automobile, and the zeppelin reinforced the impression that this epoch was one of big changes. New scientific disciplines such as genetics, religious studies, and psychoanalysis emerged. The foundation of clubs (*Vereine*) increased and new forms of sociability such as the *Lebensreform* (life reform) movement were formed, which attempted to satisfy the longing for community. This was a concrete reaction to urbanization. Urbanization again facilitated mass culture, which spread through cinemas, penny novels, and the gramophone. The accompanying commercialization of culture led to a proliferation of "objective culture" (Georg Simmel) and to the growth of the advertising industry. Generally, the logic of cultural production increasingly centered on entertainment. With the growth of the social class of salaried employees, a new audience of this mass culture emerged. At the same time, cultural and social criticism was on the rise too, as evidenced by Friedrich Nietzsche's (1844–1900) philosophy, Gerhart Hauptmann's (1862–1946) plays, Heinrich Mann's (1871–1950) novels, and the emergence of satirical magazines. Between 1871 and 1918, many new avant-garde movements emerged in the arts, music, literature, and architecture, often contradictory to one another, such as Impressionism, Expressionism, Futurism, or atonal music.

All these developments deeply shattered old certainties and self-evident schemes of perception, thought, and action. The rapid pace of social change, extremely concentrated in large cities, led many people to experience a kind of emotional and perceptual overload (Ullrich 1997; Radkau 1998). On a general level, this "increase in nervous life" which Georg Simmel (1995 [1903], p. 116) described in his well-known 1903 essay "Die Großstädte und das Geistesleben" ("The Metropolis and Mental Life"), was perceived by bourgeois intellectuals and scientists less as a "social" than as a profound "cultural crisis" (Drehsen and Sparn 1996; Lichtblau 1996). Hence, in their eyes, German society not only had to deal with the "social" but also—and perhaps even more so—with the "cultural question" (Bruch et al. 1989, p. 11, 14).

At the turn of the century, the social conflicts that existed in modern European societies, the socio-cultural experiences of crisis and dissolution of cultural traditions, and the mental and spiritual tensions led to the desire to explain and cope with modern life, which was experienced as fragmented and threatening. The historical situation called for sociology, one could say, even if in the scientific field it was often regarded with hostility or dismissed as an auxiliary science. Nevertheless, from the 1890s onwards sociology began to institutionalize and to offer new and independent observations, explanations, and interpretations (cf. Kaesler 1984; Lichtblau 1996, 2018). Therefore, the establishment of sociology as a scientific discipline was the result of the increased differentiation in the academic field as well as the growing "need for the interpretation" of the rapid and far-reaching changes of the age (Rammstedt 1988, p. 283). These changes were not only understood as economic or political processes, but as genuinely *social* and *cultural* processes.

Hence, the widespread feeling of crisis at the *fin de siècle* stimulated classical sociological reflections and diagnoses of modernity (Frisby 1995; Lichtblau 1996).[5] These attempts to analyze and to solve the perceived crisis took place in Germany in an academic field characterized by historicism on the one hand and an insistent critique of positivism, empiricism, and utilitarianism on the other (Beiser 2015). The early German sociologists like Tönnies, Simmel, and Weber, who by the way were all strongly influenced by Nietzsche (cf. Lichtblau 1996; Baier 1981; Hennis 1987; Partyga 2016; Treiber 2016; only Tönnies later became a sharp critic of Nietzsche), did not share the strong faith in progress that can be found in the writings of Saint-Simon, Herbert Spencer, or Auguste Comte. Instead, in the works of Tönnies (although his sociology was more influenced by Spencer and Comte), Simmel, and Weber we find rather "pessimistic analyses of the fundamental structural problems of modern societies" (Dahme and Rammstedt 1984, p. 459), but also, specifically in the works of Tönnies, sometimes new "utopian" ideas (Cahnman 1968; Liebersohn 1988).

### *Sociological Pioneers in the* German Reich: *Tönnies, Simmel, Weber*

Ferdinand Tönnies, one of the first classic thinkers of German sociology and an internationally renowned Hobbes researcher, reacted to the transformation processes and social tensions of the age in his major work *Gemeinschaft und Gesellschaft* (*Community and Association*, or generally translated as *Community and Society*), published in 1887 (Tönnies 2017 [1887] [1935]). With *Gemeinschaft und Gesellschaft*, Tönnies attempted

---

[5] This, of course, applies not only to sociology in Germany, but also to the sociology of Émile Durkheim (1858–1917) and his disciples in France, even though their sociology, in contrast to that in Germany, was far more oriented towards positivism.

to explain the social changes and struggles in the transition to modernity within an evolutionary framework. Like communitarians today he mourned the decline of community, which was in danger of disappearing in favor of capitalist market society. Although this book addressed urgent questions of the day, initially it went relatively unnoticed. This may be due to the fact that its skeptical tenor did not fit in with the economic boom that began in 1895 (Bickel 1991, p. 46). It was only a few decades later, especially in the 1920s, that Tönnies' work became popular. This delayed reception, however, was often linked to an ideological misreading, which interpreted Tönnies' concept of community as a romantic glorification of the community or even as a proto-fascist propagation of a *Volksgemeinschaft* (people's community). Tönnies' intention, however, was a different one. For him, *Gemeinschaft und Gesellschaft* could serve as a basis for reform proposals to better the situation of the working class. He saw the concept of community in the light of a new society of the future, of a new "social order, one qualitatively different from modern society" (Liebersohn 1988, p. 35), a new social order in a kind of an ethical, German "socialism," whereby Tönnies' was not concerned with the abolition of capitalism, but with the restoring of community, "managing the production of goods," preferably in the form of cooperatives and social democratic reforms (Tönnies 2012 [1919], pp. 215–219; Bond 2013, p. 254).

Georg Simmel devoted himself particularly to the then new phenomena and problems that accompanied the emergence of modern culture (Lichtblau 1996). Although he was also infected by contemporary cultural pessimism, he—more than his colleagues—nonetheless emphasized the ambivalent consequences of modernity. The new monetary culture for example (Simmel 1989 [1900]) provides a drastic example of the contradictory effects modern cultural dynamics can have on the individual: On the one hand, it promotes the conditions for the formation of individuality, more independent relationships, intensified subjective experience, and personal lifestyle; on the other hand, the monetary culture threatens individuality because of its levelling, reifying, and objectifying tendencies. Hence, according to Simmel (1989 [1900]), the formation of modernity results in a tension between the deindividualizing forces of modern monetary culture and the resistance of the subject to counteract these forces. Also, it induces an intensifying conflict between bourgeois culture and mass society. Both of these conflicts, Simmel claims, are linked to a still more fundamental cultural conflict of modern *Vergesellschaftung* (sociation), which Simmel (1987 [1911]) pronouncedly described as the "tragedy of culture."

For Simmel (1987 [1911]) the "tragedy of culture" consists in the contradiction between "objective" and "subjective culture." The sense of the term "objective culture" came from his teachers Moritz Lazarus (1824–1903) and Heyman Steinthal (1823–1899) (Köhnke 1996, pp. 337–355; Klautke 2016, pp. 34–36), the inventors of the *Völkerpsychologie* (folk psychology). With the progressing development of modern society, "objective culture" (e.g., technology, science, rights, and scholarship, but also art works) expanded dramatically so that individuals are less and less able to subjectively appropriate its elements and creatively exploit them as a means of self-realization or for the development of individuality.

Simmel investigated this specific antinomy of modern culture in his 1900 book *Die Philosophie des Geldes* (*The Philosophy of Money*, Simmel 1989 [1900]). The book is not only an analysis of money, or of monetary culture, but also an analysis of contemporary society. In the last chapters of the book, Simmel describes the radical transformation of modern life brought about by modern monetary culture. Characteristics of this transformation are the acceleration of social life, the increasing distancing between people, and a new rhythm of work and life.

Over the years, it became increasingly clear in Simmel's writings that, according to his educated bourgeois background and the reception of Goethe and Nietzsche, he was looking for the solution of the cultural crisis in a "law of the individual," according to which the individual is called on to become and to realize herself/himself (Köhnke 1996, pp. 489–514).

Similar to Simmel's analysis of the relation between subjective and objective culture and to his search for a "law of the individual" (cf. Müller 2020, p. 410; Marty 2020), Max Weber's major work *Die protestantische Ethik und der Geist des Kapitalismus* (Weber 2016 [1904–1905] [1920]) (*The Protestant Ethic and the Spirit of Capitalism*) examined the extent to which the individual conduct of life is related to the so-called Spirit of Capitalism. Like Simmel, Weber was concerned with an analysis of the central ideas that gave rise to capitalism. The sociologist and economist Werner Sombart (1863–1941) as well as Weber's friend and later housemate Ernst Troeltsch (1865–1923) worked on these topics almost simultaneously with Weber. Similar to Weber, they also saw a close connection between religious ideas and the emergence of capitalism.

According to Weber, the conditions that supported modern capitalism's coming into being have to be explained not only by economic factors but also by a particular "spirit of capitalism." Weber understood "spirit" as a certain mental condition, stance, and attitude. For him, the individual mental constitution that was decisive for the formation of capitalism resulted from the "Protestant ethic." By "Protestant ethic," Weber means a principle of strict and godly life conduct and working ethics inspired by the Protestant faith, especially by Calvinism and Puritan sects. According to Weber, the advent of high capitalism forced by the technological transformation of the nineteenth century was accompanied by the secularization of the "Protestant ethic": the religious component increasingly receded, while the profane, worldly side, that is, modern vocational orientation and identification with one's work, remained and became even stronger.

From Weber's perspective, the "Protestant ethic" is only one, albeit important, element of a much broader cultural process of rationalization that occurred in Western societies and which was understood by Weber as the "fate of our time." The process of rationalization, according to Weber, entails a general increase in the systematization, predictability, and effectiveness of *all* social areas, social relations, and actions. Weber described this process of rationalization as the "disenchantment of the world." However, similar to Simmel, he also diagnosed new aesthetic and expressive cultural movements that strived for a "re-enchantment of the world" and that were directed against the process of rationalization.[6]

## *Sociology Between Explaining and Understanding*

One characteristic of sociology in Germany, as we will continue to see throughout this book, is that it is deeply influenced by philosophy. This was already the case with the founders of sociology. Tönnies' work was deeply influenced by Hobbes and Arthur Schopenhauer (1788–1860).

---

[6] There was also international exchange. Tönnies and Simmel had contacts to France (René Worms (1869–1926), Henri Bergson (1859–1941), Durkheim School), Simmel corresponded with Albion Small (1854–1926) and Lester F. Ward (1841–1913) (cf. Simmel 2005), some of his articles appeared in the *American Journal of Sociology*, he even got a call to the USA and became important for the sociology of the Chicago School (Robert Park (1864–1944) was one of his disciples). Max Weber was inspired in his analyses of capitalism by his impressions of the USA, which he collected in 1904 on the occasion of the Congress of Arts and Sciences in St. Louis (Scaff 2011).

The central influence on Simmel and Weber was not only Wilhelm Windelband's (1848–1915) and Heinrich Rickert's (1863–1936) Neo-Kantianism,[7] but also Friedrich Nietzsche and Wilhelm Dilthey's *Einleitung in die Geisteswissenschaften* (*Introduction to the Human Sciences*) published in 1883 (Kaesler 2014, p. 557). Weber and Simmel, who had positively received Spencer until 1892 (Köhnke 1996, pp. 413, 424), both shared Dilthey's criticism of philosophical movements that were committed to positivism, organicism, and historical speculation, and that were dominant in English and French sociology. Dilthey emphasized the differences between the humanities (*Geisteswissenschaften*) and the natural sciences (*Naturwissenschaften*). While the natural sciences strive for the discovery of causal relations that allow for an *explanation* of natural phenomena, the humanities and social sciences try to reconstruct meanings that allow for an *understanding* of cultural phenomena. In a way, Dilthey's approach caught the spirit of the age since, in those days, a central concern was how to interpret and understand the dramatic and pervasive social changes (rather than to explain them) (Acham 2013, p. 164). In a certain sense, the beginning of sociology in Germany, with Simmel and Weber, was "anti-sociological," because it was closely linked with Nietzsche's and Dilthey's criticisms of French and English sociology (Lichtblau 1996, pp. 77–177; 2001).

It was especially Max Weber who promoted the formation of sociology as an independent discipline by attempting to mediate between the two opposing approaches toward investigation, explaining, and understanding (Rossi 1987). Accordingly, he defined sociology as an undertaking that was to combine both understanding and explaining: "Sociology [...] should mean: a science which attempts the interpretive understanding of social action in order thereby to arrive at a causal explanation of its course and effects" (Weber 1988b [1921], p. 542). Furthermore, it was Weber who strongly advocated a new understanding of science and scholarship in general (Kaesler 1984, p. 458). As Weber argues in his famous lecture "Science as a Vocation" ("Wissenschaft als Beruf"), research requires an austere fulfillment of duty and self-critical specialists (*Fachmenschen* as Weber would say) who have to refrain from any "academic prophecy"

---

[7] Windelband, for example, introduced 1894 the distinction between nomothetic and idiographic approaches. Rickert introduced the concept of "cultural sciences," thus distinguishing those sciences from the natural sciences that do not seek general laws, but whose research objects are linked to certain cultural meanings and values.

(Weber 1994 [1917] [1919], p. 23), that is, any claim to be a spiritual leader, prophet, or redeemer. A scholar should devote himself/herself to the cause. He or she should not indulge in sensationalism or self-idolization.

Basically, Weber's focus on pure science and academic specialization can be interpreted as a reaction to a general feeling of uncertainty and crisis widespread among the educated German bourgeoisie (*Bildungsbürgertum*). Due to the rise of mass culture, this class feared for its superior social status as well as for the primacy of its traditional pattern of interpretation that revolved around culture and education (*Kultur und Bildung*) (Kaesler 1984, p. 459; Bollenbeck 1994, pp. 229–268). Trust in science as well as the traditional ideal of self-cultivation (*Bildungsideal*) vanished, thereby questioning the bourgeoisie's self-understanding as culture-defining group. The functional change of science was accompanied by fears of a functional loss of education and self-cultivation (*Bildung*). One the one hand, this led to an appreciation of "culture," as one can see from the establishment of "new" disciplines like "cultural philosophy," "cultural sciences," "cultural history," and "cultural sociology" (Bollenbeck 1994, pp. 257–262); on the other hand, it led to a widespread perception of a prevailing cultural crisis (Lichtblau 1996). This perception of a crisis was caused partly by internal processes in the academic field, such as an increasing criticism of historicism (Kaesler 2014, p. 556), and partly by the expansion of higher education, a "growing numbers of students," and an "increasing specialization" (Nipperdey 1990, p. 589) of the academic field. Many feared that science and scholarship, decoupled from education and self-cultivation (*Bildung*), would no longer be meaningful and prestigious (Nipperdey 1990, p. 591). In these debates around culture and education, Weber adopted a kind of "midpoint in the field of power" between the "Mandarin and modernist positions inside the university social sciences field" (Steinmetz 2009, p. 97).

## *The* Werturteilsstreit

Weber's understanding of social sciences became clear and particularly prominent because of the so-called *Werturteilsstreit*, which can be literally translated as the "value judgement dispute." Although the dispute was initially fought out in the field of economics, it also became central to sociology, which at that time consisted of many economists. In this way it became the first major controversy in German-speaking sociology. The controversy, that continues to this day (see Chaps. 4, 6, and Turner and Factor 1984), started in 1883 as a methodological dispute within German-speaking economics between Gustav Schmoller (1838–1917), representative of the German Historical School of Economics, and Carl Menger (1840–1921), representative of the Austrian School of Economics called *Grenznutzenschule* (marginalist school). At first it was a written dispute, which was then continued orally at meetings of the *Verein für Socialpolitik* (German Economic Association) in 1905, 1909, and 1911, as well as in 1914 (Albert 2010, p. 16). In 1913/1914, the dispute reached its peak. The *Verein für Socialpolitik* was founded in 1873 by members of the German Historical School of Economics. The aim of this association was to contribute to the socio-political improvement of the social situation of industrial workers as well as to provide a scientific analysis of the *soziale Frage* (social question). The association positioned itself between the Manchester School of Economics, which propagated the principle of free competition and laissez-faire economics, and revolutionary socialism or radical social policy.

The focus of the *Werturteilsstreit* was on the question of whether it is scientifically justified to express "evaluative opinions on practical questions, in particular in the field of economic and social policy" (Albert 2010, p. 15). The opponents were Schmoller, Eduard Spranger (1882–1963), and Rudolf Goldscheid (1870–1931), who supported the idea of scholarship openly taking sides, and Menger, Lujo Brentano (1844–1931), Werner Sombart, and Max Weber, who claimed that scholarship should abstain from value judgements. Yet, even though Weber supported the idea of value-neutral scholarship, he made some concessions to the other position. Thus, as the German Historical School of Economics had shown, as cultural beings (*Kulturmenschen*), individuals cannot help but take an evaluative stance toward the phenomena she or he studies. According to Weber, this implicates that the selection of research objects is always guided by a perspective that is influenced by values. But contrary to what the Historical School advocated, Weber argues that the actual research of the chosen phenomenon should, then, ideally be free of value judgements (Weber 1988a [1904]). Thus, Weber challenged the *Kathedersozialisten* (socialists of the chair), as some members of the *Verein für Socialpolitik* were called, with his call for *Werturteilsfreiheit*.

## Social Science Infrastructure Around 1900 (Journals and Professional Organizations)

Sociology did not yet exist as an academic discipline at the universities in the *German Reich*. Those whom we now regard as early sociologists in Germany—including the aforementioned classical authors—studied and worked in disciplines like *Staatswissenschaften*, economics, law, or philosophy before they turned toward sociology. Their concern was initially not so much the training of future students but rather to establish sociology as an academic discipline and to secure a "'niche' within the highly institutionalized academic system of German universities" (Kaesler 1984, p. 251). However, student associations already existed, the largest being the *Social Science Student Association* in Berlin, at which Tönnies, Simmel, and Weber, among others, lectured (Köhnke 1988).

If one wanted to publish sociological ideas in an academic journal in Germany around 1900, this was possible mainly in journals of economics or the *Staatswissenschaften* (Holzhauser et al. 2019). However, genuinely sociological journals did not yet exist. An exception is the *Monatsschrift für Soziologie*, founded in 1909, of which only one volume appeared (Lichtblau 2018, p. 17). Overall, however, there was a broad field of possibilities for disseminating sociological content (Stölting 1986, pp. 145–194; Neef 2012, pp. 229–261). Since 1898 there had been the *Zeitschrift für Sozialwissenschaft* (*Journal of Social Sciences*), to which all disciplines dealing with the "social question" contributed (Stölting 1986, p. 156). Also, in 1902 the *Vierteljahrsschrift für wissenschaftliche Philosophie und Soziologie* (*Quarterly for Scientific Philosophy and Sociology*) was founded. Yet, according to the founders of this journal, sociology was a branch of philosophy, not an independent discipline. Founded by Robert von Mohl in 1844, the *Zeitschrift für die gesamte Staatswissenschaft* (*Journal for the Entire Staatswissenschaft*) developed a social science profile, especially under Albert Schäffle's (1831–1903) editorship. Around 1900 there were, however, two journals that were of particular importance for the institutionalization of sociology in Germany (Lichtblau 2018, p. 18): the *Jahrbuch für Gesetzgebung, Verwaltung und Rechtspflege des Deutschen Reiches* (*Yearbook for Legislation, Public Administration, and Judicature in the German Reich*), published since 1873. This journal was also called "Schmollers Jahrbuch" ("Schmoller's Yearbook"), since Schmoller's editorship. Moreover, there was the *Archiv für Sozialwissenschaft und Sozialpolitik* (*Archive for Social Science and Social Policy*), first published in 1904 by Weber, Sombart, and Edgar Jaffé (1866–1921). It was in this journal that Weber published his already mentioned "Protestant Ethic" and the famous essay on "'Objectivity' in Social Science and Social Policy."

Important collaborators and authors of the *Archiv für Sozialwissenschaft und Sozialpolitik* were also members of the *Verein für Socialpolitik* (Gorges 1980, 2018). As mentioned earlier, the *Verein* clearly aimed at sociopolitical improvements for the working classes. It did so by means of empirical research, through which it became the "center of survey research in Germany" (Oberschall 1997, p. 48).

When in 1878 the then Imperial Chancellor Otto von Bismarck enacted the so called *Sozialistengesetze* (Law against the public danger of Social Democratic endeavors or Anti-Socialist Laws), which banned all socialist associations (with the exception of the Social Democratic parliamentary group in the *Reichstag*), the *Verein für Socialpolitik* shifted its goals. Instead of their earlier focus on the "social question," they now started to investigate the so-called agrarian question, that is, the situation of peasants and medium-sized farmers. Whereas they previously conducted applied research aiming at policy advice, their intention was now to conduct "purely" scientific research (Gorges 1980, p. 158). However, as exemplarily shown by the *Werturteilsstreit*, there were numerous differences within the association and not all members agreed on the political or the methodological issues.

Still before the peak of the *Werturteilsstreit* in 1913/1914, the tensions between the scholars led to the founding of the German Sociological Association (GSA, *Deutsche Gesellschaft für Soziologie*) in 1909 (Honigsheim 1959).[8] The aim of the GSA was explicitly to not pursue "practical" sociopolitical goals, but to pursue a form of scholarship that is committed to *Werturteilsfreiheit*, not influenced by power structures or religion, and, thus, strictly avoids ideological conflicts as far as possible (Dörk 2018a, p. 817). The written invitation to the founding event of the German Sociological Association stated that the new organization not only wanted to raise awareness of sociological issues, but also to promote the establishment of sociological professorships and to create a central office for sociological research (Simmel 2008 [1908]; cf. Dörk 2018a). The invitation also included a long list of sociological

---

[8] In other countries, sociological associations already existed by then: in France the *Institut International de Sociologie* (1893) founded by René Worms, in the USA the *American Sociological Association* (1905), and in Austria the *Wiener Soziologische Gesellschaft* (1907) and the *Grazer Soziologische Gesellschaft* (1908).

problems the association wanted to attend to: methods, the division of labor, ethics, public opinion, sexuality, and "racial issues." In addition to Tönnies, Simmel, and Max Weber, Paul Barth (1858–1922), Georg Jellinek (1851–1911), Karl Lamprecht (1856–1915), Theodor Lipps (1851–1914), Franz Oppenheimer (1864–1943), Werner Sombart, Ernst Troeltsch, Alfred Vierkandt (1867–1953), Alfred Weber (1868–1958), and others signed the invitation.

The official founding of the GSA took place on March 7, 1909, at the Hotel Esplanade in Berlin. The board consisted of Tönnies—who served as chairman of the meeting and later, until 1933, as president of the newly founded association—Georg Simmel, and Werner Sombart. Max Weber took care of the finances (Dörk 2018a, p. 816). In 1912, the GSA already had 334 members (Kaesler 2014, p. 654). The new organization's aim was to foster research, but also to encourage regular exchange between its members. Larger regular meetings with lectures—the so-called *Soziologentag* (literally "Sociologists' Day")—were planned for this purpose.

In October 1910, the first German *Soziologentag* took place in Frankfurt am Main. The expectations were high. At the end of his speech the president, Tönnies (1911, p. 37), stated that his hope for sociology was nothing less than that humankind would recognize itself through sociology and that it would learn to control itself through self-knowledge. But precisely because of a "lack of self-control," the first *Soziologentag* ended in a scandal that was again caused by a dispute about the question of value judgements (Lepsius 2011, pp. 15–16) and which intensified in 1913/1914 the above-mentioned *Werturteilsstreit* (cf. Albert 2010).

## *The "Ideas of 1914" and World War I*

In October 1912, the second *Soziologentag* took place in Berlin. The central subject of the meeting was the nation—a pressing topic with respect to the highly charged political atmosphere of the time. The younger brother of Max, Alfred Weber, delivered the keynote address that discussed the sociological concept of culture. A central topic of his presentation was the distinction between culture and civilization (Loader 2012, pp. 73–80). As his lecture shows, these two terms formed a crucial conceptual opposition already on the eve of World War I. This dichotomy was, as Norbert Elias (1977 [1937] [1939], pp. 1–64) has shown, a widespread pattern of interpretation in Germany and was increasingly used to express a national contrast. Since World War I, this dichotomy has been called the "Ideas of 1914" (Nipperdey 1990, p. 594; Bollenbeck 1994, pp. 268–277). It signifies the construction of a "fundamental contradiction" "between the despised Western 'civilization,'" the Enlightenment, consumption, and merchants on the one hand, and on the other the "German culture" considered as "superior," the realm of heroes, the soul, and the spirit (Nolte 2000, p. 69).

World War I began in August 1914. With respect to domestic affairs, World War I seemed to offer a solution to the internal political and social conflicts. Many contemporaries considered the beginning of the war as a promise for national reconciliation and unity. However, not all sections of the German population were equally keen about the general mobilization. It was above all members of the bourgeoisie as well as the urban and intellectual classes who developed a strong enthusiasm for the war and idealized its beginning as the so-called "August Experience" (*August-Erlebnis*) (Flasch 2000).

Similar to many other intellectuals and scholars, in 1914 the majority of the German sociologists believed that the Germans now had to defend the German "culture" against the French, English, and American "civilization" that was denounced as materialistic. With few exceptions, also the sociologists saw the war as a cultural struggle (Joas and Knöbl 2012, pp. 133–144). Nothing remained from the previously praised *Werturteilsfreiheit*. To the contrary, instead of making the war, militancy, and mass hysteria the subjects of professional and sober sociological analysis, the German Sociological Association decided right at the beginning of the war to put its forces and resources at the service of war propaganda and to "inform foreign countries about the justified 'rational will to win' of the Germans" (Papcke 1985, p. 139). Hence, the same scholars who lamented the social levelling that accompanied the emergence of mass society "hailed the levelling and de-differentiation of society into a nation and *Volksgemeinschaft* (people's community)" (Nolte 2000, p. 66).

In a speech in November 1914, shortly after the beginning of the war, Simmel (1999 [1914]) attempted to found his nationalism on his *Lebensphilosophie* (philosophy of life). For him, new dimensions of experience, new communities, and even a new type of human being could emerge from the war. According to Simmel's vitalistic point of view, the war could not only bring about a solution for the tragedy and crisis of culture and the alienating effects of individualism but also a revival of creative vitality.

In his "nationalist mood" (Nipperdey 1990, p. 814), Max Weber immediately volunteered for military service. In early August 1914, he wrote to his publisher Paul Siebeck that the war was "great and wonderful," a "holy war of defense" (Weber cited by Kaube 2014, p. 350; Kaesler 2014, pp. 737–759). Although Weber's initial enthusiasm for war declined very soon (Joas and Knöbl 2012, pp. 142–143), he did not really develop a scientific perspective on the war. Only Emil Lederer (1882–1939), a cultural sociologist and economist, provided a sober and objective sociological analysis of it. In 1915, he presented an important analysis of the ideological transformation from society to community in all countries involved in the war (Lederer 2014 [1915]).

In its statutes, the German Sociological Association had committed itself to *Werturteilsfreiheit*. Nevertheless, only shortly after the foundation of the GSA this ethos vanished. In the course of World War I, *Werturteilsfreiheit* was no longer existent or of any concern for the German Sociological Association.

## Sociology in the Weimar Republic

The enthusiasm of sociologists about the war declined considerably during the course of the war (Joas and Knöbl 2012, pp. 142–143). Disillusioned and shocked, sociologists criticized the monarchy and Prussian power politics. Tönnies, Max Weber, and Troeltsch all turned into so-called "rational Republicans" (*Vernunftrepublikaner*) (Stölting 1986, p. 71), meaning that they became supporters of the new democratic Weimar Republic, not because they felt very sympathetic with this new form of government, but more due to rational reasons (cf. Mommsen 2004 [1959], pp. 305–355; Wierzock 2017). Alfred Weber became co-founder of the left-liberal DDP (German Democratic Party) (Demm 1990, pp. 256–294). Even Max Scheler (1874–1928), who had praised the "genius of war"—this was the title of his book published in 1915— almost hymn-like while the war was still ongoing, now changed his mind. According to the sociologists, the Monarchy had abdicated, and now it was time to make the most of the new social and political conditions.

With Germany's defeat in the war, not only the war, but also the reign of Wilhelm II ended. In many German cities workers' and soldiers' councils were founded, allowing the hope for a radical democratic council republic (*Räterepublik*). The German Revolution of 1918–1919 took place. However, after bloody battles and numerous deaths, the conservative forces soon regained dominance.

On January 19, 1919, the first elections to the National Assembly took place. For the first time in Germany, women were permitted to exercise an active and passive suffrage. The new republic was faced with enormous tasks and problems (for the following see Ullrich 2009, p. 44): securing the supply of food, repatriation, and reintegration of the millions of soldiers, conversion to a peace economy, reparation payments to the victorious powers, and further burdens from the Treaty of Versailles. Many Germans perceived this settlement as a humiliation. In addition, there was a lack of identification with the Republic and parliamentarianism among the population. In the first phase of the Republic (1919–1923), dissatisfaction became apparent through several attempted coups and the increase in votes for radical parties. Only in the second phase (1923–1929) did the currency reform and the "Dawes" plan, which regulated reparations payments according to economic performance and which led to foreign investment and loans, bring about an economic upswing. Despite these positive trends, the Republic remained economically and politically crisis-prone. There were economic monopolies, an increase in short-term work and unemployment due to the rationalization of work processes, a crisis in agriculture, rural exodus, and the return of the former upper class to power (in 1925, the former monarchist and field marshal Paul von Hindenburg was elected president of Germany). The class of the employees became more and more important, so that it also became the subject of sociological research. This "new middle class" between the proletarian masses and the capitalist elite, however, was deeply unsettled. The combination of upward social mobility and the fear of losing one's social status, as well as the associated uncertainty, led the middle classes to adopt nationalist attitudes (Peukert 1987, p. 161). As sociological analyses at the end of the Weimar Republic showed, there were strong affinities between the "new middle class" and the National Socialists (Geiger 1932).

The term "Golden Twenties" that is commonly used when speaking of the 1920s refers not only to the economic upswing in the mid-1920s, but also to the cultural productivity and creativity of that time. Avant-garde styles and art movements such as Dadaism, Bauhaus, and New Objectivity developed. The Weimar era was a veritable "field of experimentation" and a moment of "culmination of modernity" (Becker 2018). Numerous new technologies and inventions emerged: the expansion of the railway and shipping, the development of the telecommunications infrastructure, the first transmission of images, radio, the relativity theory, and penicillin (Becker 2018). Mass culture and entertainment culture continued to grow, especially in the metropolis of Berlin. Mass media such as film, photography, radio, records, and magazines became increasingly widespread.

In mass culture and economic rationalization, an increasing influence of the USA could be observed. Within sociology, this was reflected in the reception of sociology from the USA that began in the mid-1920s. Only the right-wing conservative forces did not share the enthusiasm for the USA. For them, the USA was the epitome of the hostile Western civilization that was undermining German culture.

Although the "mass culture" generally found acceptance across classes, this should not obscure the fact that Weimar society remained a deeply divided class society (Winkler 2005, p. 296). Not everyone was able to participate in the new entertainment culture. Social reality continued to be characterized by high unemployment, poor provision for war widows, impoverished families, and prostitution. In particular, unemployed youths tended to take radical political positions and to engage in paramilitary combat units.

Nationalist and right-wing conservative positions found intellectual breeding ground in the so-called "stab-in-the-back myth" (*Dolchstoßlegende*) as well as in the "Conservative Revolution" (Breuer 1995). The "stab-in-the-back myth" had been created by the Supreme Army Command. The myth said that Germany had not suffered a war defeat because of its military weakness, but because of social democratic and Jewish activities at home. The myth continued to circulate among large sections of the population until the end of the Weimar Republic. The "Conservative Revolution" was a nationalist current of thought that was anti-republican, anti-liberal, anti-democratic, belligerent, and culturally pessimistic, and aimed at a "new nationalism."

In the third phase (1929–1933), the Republic changed, in particular because of the dynamics of the global economic crisis. Unemployment rose rapidly. In new elections in 1930, besides the KPD (Communist Party of Germany), the National Socialist German Workers' Party (NSDAP, or short Nazi Party) won additional votes. When in renewed elections at the end of 1932 it became apparent that the NSDAP was to receive fewer votes and the KPD more, Hindenburg, the president of the *German Reich*, decided to make Adolf Hitler chancellor in order to avert the danger from the left. This was followed by the Enabling Act (*Ermächtigungsgesetz*) of 1933, bans of the Social Democratic Party of

Germany (SPD) and the KPD, and the dissolution of all parties. The NSDAP became the state party and a period of state terror began. The Weimar Republic no longer existed.

### Sociological Centers and Actors in the Weimar Republic

Simmel had died in 1918, close to the end of the war, Max Weber in 1920. Their respective sociologies continued to play a role but often more subcutaneously or in a one-dimensional way. For example: Although some of the sociologists referred to Simmel by developing a Simmel-oriented "formal sociology," like Leopold von Wiese (1876–1967) with his *Beziehungslehre* (theory of relationships), this was more directed to an ahistorical formalism than toward Simmel's historical theory of modernity. It was only many years after World War II that Simmel and Weber enjoyed a broader reception again. In the Weimar Republic, Tönnies was primarily active as president of the German Sociological Association, and his book *Gemeinschaft und Gesellschaft* received a great deal of attention, especially among those who lamented the decline of Gemeinschaft.

During the Weimar Republic, sociology as an academic discipline began to institutionalize and professionalize itself.[9] This positive development was initially due to Carl Heinrich Becker (1876–1933), a State Secretary and later Minister of Education in the Prussian Ministry of Culture. He promoted the establishment of new chairs of sociology, because he hoped that sociology would be able to create a synthesis between the increasingly differentiated academic disciplines (Becker 1919). His view was fiercely contested (Stölting 1986, pp. 92–101; Loader 2012, p. 102), but finally he won. While there were only three professorships in 1919, further sociological professorships were established at many universities during the Weimar era. However, there was now much sociology, but not the synthesis that Becker had desired.

The first processes of an institutionalization of sociology began at newly founded universities: Franz Oppenheimer began teaching at the first chair of sociology in Frankfurt am Main, and in Cologne Leopold von Wiese was appointed to the chair of economic *Staatswissenschaften* (science of the state) and sociology and Max Scheler to the chair of philosophy and sociology.

---

[9] For a more detailed overview of sociology in the interwar period in Germany see Moebius (2021).

## Cologne

In 1919, the first "Research Institute for Social Sciences" was founded in Cologne (cf. Knebelspieß and Moebius 2019). The foundation was an initiative of the mayor Konrad Adenauer (who became the first chancellor of the Federal Republic of Germany after World War II) (von Alemann 1981, p. 349). The institute had three departments, a sociological, a socio-political, and a legal one. The sociological department was headed by von Wiese and Scheler. However, there was no cooperation between the two of them. Von Wiese devoted himself to the development of his *Beziehungslehre*, Scheler to the sociology of knowledge, phenomenology, and philosophical anthropology. The first sociological assistants were Paul Honigsheim, Anny Ohrnberger, and Maria Scheu (Gorges 1986, p. 101). In 1921, von Wiese founded the *Kölner Vierteljahrshefte für Sozialwissenschaften* (*Cologne Quarterly of Social Sciences*), which was renamed to *Kölner Vierteljahrshefte für Soziologie* (*Cologne Quarterly of Sociology*) in 1923. Nowadays, as the *Kölner Zeitschrift für Soziologie und Sozialpsychologie* (*KZfSS, Cologne Journal of Sociology and Social Psychology*), it is still one of the most renowned places for sociological articles in Germany (Moebius 2017). The founding of this first purely sociological journal in Germany was an important component of von Wiese's efforts to institutionalize sociology in the academic field of the Weimar Republic. He hoped that the journal would unite sociology. However, a large part of the journal was dedicated to his *Beziehungslehre*.

During the interwar period, von Wiese increasingly became an important spokesman of and an "institution builder" (Kaesler 1984, p. 462) in sociology. He was a "gate-keeper," not only because he was in charge of an institute with its own journal, but also because he had great influence on the German Sociological Association as secretary and organizer of the *Soziologentage* (Gorges 1986, p. 97). Although his *Beziehungslehre* was one of the central theoretical positions at the beginning of the 1920s, it did not have a lasting influence. In later generations it had almost no effect—apart from Howard P. Becker (1899–1960), who was temporarily a disciple of von Wiese. It was rather von Wiese's organizational talent that made him an important sociologist in the interwar period.

Max Scheler was central to the emergence of the sociology of knowledge, which he built up parallel to Karl Mannheim (1893–1947). In 1928 Scheler founded Philosophical Anthropology at the same time as Helmuth Plessner (1892–1985). Both had developed this line of thought, which is still a component (and also a unique characteristic) of German-speaking sociology, in very different ways and in a "rival relationship" in Cologne (Fischer 2008, pp. 23–91). The "anthropologization" that could be observed in the interwar period (Rehberg 1981), and to which Scheler and Plessner contributed significantly, was also the result of an examination of the problem of relativism that they saw in historicism (Acham 1998, p. 544). In short, many hoped for an unshakeable basis and a firm foundation in uncertain times.

*Heidelberg*
Another central place of the sociological field of the Weimar Republic was Heidelberg, where the Institute for Social Sciences and *Staatswissenschaften* was founded in 1924 (Blomert 1999). Heidelberg stood for a historical sociology of culture, represented in particular by Alfred Weber (Stölting 1986, p. 106; Loader 2012, pp. 110–143). Characteristic of Alfred Weber's cultural sociology was an appreciation of the cultural as opposed to the process of civilization, that is, in relation to capitalism, urbanization, industrialization, and rationalization (Eckert 1970). Weber distinguished three spheres of historical process: the social process, the civilizational process, and the cultural movement (*Kulturbewegung*). The social process included the social structure, the economy, politics, and the population. The civilizational process designated the area of the means to control nature, that is, technology, inventions, science, and rational thinking. The cultural movement, on the other hand, included ideas, intellectual beliefs, religious convictions, art, and values. Weber saw the main problem of his time in the increasing discrepancy between the cultural and the social-civilizational sphere; cultural sociology he considered as the solution to the problem. Cultural sociology should, with the help of cultural history, record the spontaneous, purposeless, creative, and vital forces of man in a historical manner and bring them to bear again. As was already the case before the war, a normative charging of the concept of culture could still be observed during the Weimar era in Alfred Weber and other scholars of the educated middle classes of his generation, who wanted to enhance their own social status through the valorization of culture. For them, "culture" continued to serve as a tendentious term.

In 1924, Arnold Bergstraesser (1896–1964) became the assistant of Alfred Weber. In Heidelberg, Bergstraesser endeavored to promote international scholarly exchange, especially with France. He became one of the directors of the Academic Exchange Service (now "Deutscher Akademischer Austauschdienst" (*DAAD*), German Academic Exchange

Service), which was newly founded there. It was probably also through the Exchange Service that Talcott Parsons (1902–1979) came to Heidelberg, where in 1926/1927 he obtained his doctorate with a thesis on capitalism in Sombart and Max Weber. Bergstraesser had been close to the "national revolution" since 1933 (Schmitt 1997, p. 173). But after hostilities by Nazi students and the withdrawal of the *venia legendi*, he emigrated to California in 1937. In 1941/1942 and in 1942/1943, he was imprisoned in the USA for several months because he was suspected of collaborating with the Nazis (Liebold 2012, pp. 96–100; Schmitt 1997, pp. 175–176). After World War II, Bergstraesser was one of the co-founders of political science in the Federal Republic of Germany after 1945.

The second director of the institute in Heidelberg was Emil Lederer (1882–1939). He was professor of social policy. He wrote, among other things, about social classes, the social-psychic habitus of the present, the sociology of revolutions, violence, art, public opinion, employees, and unemployment. Among Lederer's assistants was Hans Speier (1905–1990). Other students and participants in Lederer's seminars were among others Albert Salomon (1891–1966), Fritz Simon Croner (1896–1979), who helped to develop Swedish sociology from 1934 (Larsson and Magdalenič 2015, pp. 53–54), Carl Zuckmayer (1896–1977), Svend Riemer (1905–1977), who presented one of the first sociological analyses of National Socialism in 1932 (Riemer 1932; Kaesler and Steiner 1992, pp. 108–111), Hans H. Gerth (1908–1978), and Talcott Parsons (Blomert 1999, pp. 59, 93). Speier's interests included the sociology of knowledge, the role of intellectuals, employees, and propaganda. In the early 1930s, Speier moved to Berlin with Lederer. He also followed Lederer into exile in the USA in 1933, where Lederer became the first dean of the University in Exile at the New School for Social Research.

Just a few short words about the University in Exile (Rutkoff and Scott 1986, 1988; Krohn 1987, pp. 70–104; Fleck 2015, pp. 65–74; Friedlander 2018): In 1933, one of the co-founders of the New School, Alvin Johnson, set up a graduate faculty there consisting of refugee European social scientists (cf. Friedlander 2018). Johnson appointed Emil Lederer as the first dean of this University in Exile. Together they sought out other social scientists. Under the editorship of Lederer and his former assistant Hans Speier, the faculty's journal *Social Research* was published.[10] During these

---

[10] Until 1945, the University in Exile offered a first refuge to more than 180 European social scientists (Krohn 1995, p. 27).

first years, besides Lederer and Speier, Frieda Wunderlich (1884–1965), Carl Mayer (1902–1974), a sociologist of religion who earned his doctorate in Heidelberg, and (since 1935) Albert Salomon were employed. A few years later, Gottfried Salomon (1892–1964), former assistant of Oppenheimer, joined them. The University in Exile offered them a safe haven, when the life-threatening repression of the Nazi regime forced more and more academics to flee Germany.

In 1924, Norbert Elias (1897–1990) came to Heidelberg and became a postdoctoral researcher preparing for his habilitation under Alfred Weber.[11] Elias soon belonged to the inner circle of the institute and later became the "unofficial assistant" (Elias 1990, p. 125) of Karl Mannheim, who had fled the White Terror from Hungary in 1919 together with Georg Lukács (1885–1971). Both, Lukács and Mannheim, were Simmel students. But while Lukács finally detached himself from his life-philosophical phase and became a Marxist, Mannheim developed the sociology of knowledge with numerous contributions and pertinent research. In 1925, he submitted his habilitation on conservatism to Alfred Weber, Carl Brinkmann (1885–1954), and Emil Lederer in Heidelberg, which was written from the perspective of the sociology of knowledge. He taught in Heidelberg from 1926 (Blomert 1999, p. 239). In 1929, the widely received and controversially discussed book *Ideology and Utopia* was published.

---

[11] In order to become a *Privatdozent*, to obtain the formal permission to teach at universities (*venia legendi*), academics had to write a habilitation thesis and to give a habilitation lecture with subsequent discussion before an academic committee (on the history of the *Privatdozent* see Busch 1959). Completing the habilitation is still the precondition for a professorship today, with the exception of the junior professorship introduced in 2002 (on the junior professorship see Chap. 6). Yet, being a *Privatdozent* does not mean being a professor. The habilitation merely enables academics to apply for a professorship, which has its own appointment procedure. Thus, even today, the threat of obtaining professorship (and permanent employment) only late or possibly never that was already described by Max Weber (1994 [1917] [1919]) in *Wissenschaft als Beruf* (*Science as a Vocation*) and experienced by Simmel himself still exists for many *Privatdozenten*. Concerning the assistants: It was not until the 1920s that positions for assistants were established regularly in the humanities. In most cases, they were selected and employed by the professors or the head of the institute personally (cf. Bock 1972). The resulting dependencies promoted the development of "schools." This also perpetuated the dominance of the *Bildungs- und Besitzbürgertum* (the intellectual and economic upper bourgeoisie) in the higher education system (Kaesler 1984; for the *German Reich* see also Mommsen 1994, pp. 70–74). This changed especially in the 1970s (see Chaps. 3 and 5).

Siegfried Landshut (1897–1968) also studied in Heidelberg in the mid-1920s and then continued his work at the university of Hamburg. In 1929, he wrote an interesting critique of sociology (Landshut 1929/1969) in which he argued for a decidedly historical orientation. Together with the SPD-archivist Jacob Peter Mayer (1903–1992) and in collaboration with the archivist Friedrich Salomon (1890–1946), Landshut also published Marx's early writings (almost simultaneously to the publication within the *Marx-Engels-Gesamtausgabe* (MEGA)), which had hitherto received little attention, and thus helped to create new interpretations of Marx's work in the West (Nicolaysen 1997, pp. 132–157, 374–379).[12] After the Second World War, Landshut was a central figure in the development of political science in Germany.

*Berlin*
In Berlin, the new higher education policy of the government, which promoted sociology, had a particularly positive effect. Besides Werner Sombart, at this time Alfred Vierkandt, Kurt Breysig (1866–1940), Richard Thurnwald (1869–1954), Karl Dunkmann (1868–1932), and Goetz Briefs (1889–1974) were in Berlin (see Stölting 1986, pp. 109–110). Alfred Vierkandt was particularly relevant for the institutionalization of sociology there. This, however, was not so much related to his concept of a formal sociology as to the publication of the famous *Handwörterbuch der Soziologie* (1931, *Handbook of Sociology*). With the *Handbook*, Vierkandt wanted to show that sociology was an independent science. The handbook was intended to be a kind of codification of the contemporary state of sociology in Germany. From the table of contents of this book, it can be seen that despite its successive differentiation, German-speaking sociology at that time still understood itself foremost as a cultural sociology. Thus, three of the four parts are dedicated to issues of cultural sociology.

Although there were occasional contacts with foreign sociologists, sociology in Germany remained largely isolated. One of the few exceptions was the ethno-sociologist Richard Thurnwald, who taught in Berlin. He contributed to the internationalization of sociology during the Weimar Republic. He was receptive, for example, to US-American sociology and

---

[12] For example, after World War II, Marx's early writings inspired doctoral theses by later leading German sociologists such as Heinrich Popitz (1925–2002) or Ralf Dahrendorf (1929–2009) (Nicolaysen 1997, pp. 378–388).

cultural anthropology. Numerous foreign researchers participated in the *Zeitschrift für Völkerpsychologie und Soziologie* (*Journal of Völkerpsychologie and Sociology*), which he founded in 1925 and that he edited together with Bronislaw Malinowski (1884–1942). From 1936, however, he adapted to the NS regime and advocated German colonialism (Steinmetz 2009).

In Berlin, there also was Frieda Wunderlich. Since 1930 she was professor of sociology and social policy there at a public institute for vocational education studies, the Staatliches Berufspädagogisches Institut in Berlin (Wobbe 1997, pp. 173). As a Jew, social reformer, and women's rights activist she had to flee Germany in 1933. Through Hans Speier she reached the University in Exile in 1933, where she became the first female dean in 1938/1939, succeeding Emil Lederer.

*Hamburg*
Sociology in Hamburg, represented by Andreas Walther (1879–1960), had a clear empirical orientation. Walther strove for the reception and discussion of Max Weber's work, and he also advocated a close alliance between sociology, ethnology, and historical studies. However, his historical-sociological orientation changed when he studied in the USA. There he published an essay on sociology in Germany and became acquainted with empirical research techniques, which subsequently guided his work. Conversely, he was also one of the first to make US-American sociology known in Germany (Walther 1927) and was therefore an exception among the otherwise anti-American conservative sociologists. From 1933 onwards, he put his empirical sociology at the service of the National Socialist social-hygienic population policy (Waßner 1986, p. 407).

*Leipzig*
Hans Freyer (1887–1960) played an even more active role in the Nazi regime. In 1925, Freyer was appointed to the chair of sociology in Leipzig (Muller 1987, pp. 122–222). There he had a great impact on younger, especially national-revolutionary scholars (Schäfer 1990), so that nowadays sociology under Freyer is referred to as the circle of "Leipzig sociology" (Rehberg 1999). Besides Freyer, Arnold Gehlen (1904–1976), and Helmut Schelsky (1912–1984) were the most prominent representatives of sociology in Leipzig. After 1945, Schelsky was one of the most influential sociologists of the Federal Republic of Germany (FRG). All three allied themselves with National Socialism (Rehberg 1999, p. 73). Other students and collaborators of Freyer's included Gunther Ipsen

(1899–1984), Karl-Heinz Pfeffer (1906–1971), and Karl Valentin Müller (1896–1973), all of whom appeared as "convinced National Socialists" in their academic work and political practice (Schäfer 1990, p. 158). Freyer described "sociology as a science of reality," which was the title of his main work, published in 1930 (*Soziologie als Wirklichkeitswissenschaft*). Initially, Freyer argued in a strictly historical way and in the manner of sociology of knowledge. Since every sociology is historically and culturally bound to a certain social reality (Freyer 1930, p. 67), national sociologies also differ. Therefore, one could not assume ahistorical or anthropological basic forms of the social as formal sociology does. If one followed this historical perspective, for Freyer, the present sociology had to be a different one from that during the period of the emergence of liberalism, bourgeoisie, and capitalism. The result is that every nation has—according to its history—its own sociology. However, it was then highly problematic that Freyer left this historical perspective for a more political one, concluding that the time had come for a "German" sociology to contribute to the process of the Germans "becoming a people" (*Volkswerdung*). In 1931, the book *Revolution von rechts* (*Revolution from the Right*) was published. In this book he affirmed his desire for the process of "becoming a people" (Muller 1987, pp. 186–266) and for the dissolution of society into a "people's community" (*Volksgemeinschaft*) (Stölting 2006, p. 27).

## Frankfurt am Main

Sociology developed quite differently in Frankfurt, which was, alongside Cologne, of central importance for the institutionalization of sociology. Franz Oppenheimer received the first sociological professorship in 1919 (Caspari and Lichtblau 2014). He understood sociology as a historical universal science (*historische Universalwissenschaft*) in which economics, history, ethnology, law, art, and religious studies "merge" (Oppenheimer 1922, p. 134).[13] Oppenheimer's assistants were Fritz Sternberg (1895–1963) and Gottfried Salomon. As of 1926, Salomon (later Salomon-Delatour) published the *Jahrbuch für Soziologie* (*Yearbook for Sociology*), with which he wanted to achieve an internationalization and an alternative to a one-sidedly "German" sociology (Henning 2006, p. 77).

---

[13] In 1936, Oppenheimer was named honorary member of the American Sociological Association and emigrated first to Japan, then to the USA in 1940, where he died impoverished in 1943 (Caspari and Lichtblau 2014).

In 1930, Karl Mannheim succeeded Oppenheimer in Frankfurt. When Mannheim left Heidelberg and went to Frankfurt, some of his students, such as Nina Rubinstein (1908–1996), Kurt H. Wolff (1912–2003), Norbert Elias, and Hans Gerth, followed him. Gottfried Salomon formally became Mannheim's assistant, but the relationship between them was clouded (Henning 2006, p. 81). Others, such as Gisèle Freund (1908–2000), Jakob Katz (1904–1998), and Wilhelm Carlé (1887–?), became Mannheim's students, so that a real "Mannheim circle" (Ilieva 2010) or "Mannheim research group" (Kettler et al. 2008, p. 1) was formed in Frankfurt.[14] Among them were also an unusually large number of female students (Honegger 1993, pp. 185–190; Kettler and Meja 1993; Kettler et al. 2008; Ilieva 2010, pp. 127–135). Besides Freund and Rubinstein there were also Margarete Freudenthal (1894–1984), Frieda Haussig (1903–1982), Käthe Truhel (1906–1992), Toni Oelsner (1907–1981), the sisters (born Seligmann) Evelyn Anderson (1909–1977) and Ilse Ziegellaub (since 1944: Seglow) (1900–1984), Natalie Halperin (1908–1974), and later, in exile in London, Viola Klein (1908–1973), who published in 1946 the feminist book *The Feminine Character: History of an Ideology*, and Charlotte Lütkens (1896–1967), who had previously studied in the classes of Alfred Weber, Emil Lederer, and Franz Oppenheimer. With Frieda Wunderlich, Klein and Lütkens were among the very few women from Germany, who after 1933 were still able to do sociology in the academic field.

In the mid-1930s Elias wrote *Über den Prozeß der Zivilisation* (1979 [1939]), which later became a world bestseller in the second half of the 1970s and which drew on central concepts of Alfred Weber, but turned them in a completely different direction. Gerth, also academically socialized in Heidelberg, had begun a dissertation under Mannheim with a thesis on the socio-historical position of the bourgeois intellectuals around 1800. He completed his doctorate in 1933 under the successor of Karl Mannheim, Heinz Marr (1876–1940) (Gerth 2000, pp. 134–135). Like Mannheim, Lederer, Speier, Elias, Wolff, Gisèle Freund, and many others of Mannheim's circle in Frankfurt, Gerth also had to flee into exile after the NSDAP came to power in 1933. Gerth arrived at New York in 1937 and became later very well known for his translations of Max Weber essays, published with C. Wright Mills (1916–1962).

---

[14] Many of Mannheim's students in Frankfurt were co-supervised by Norbert Elias, as Gisèle Freund (1977, p. 12) put it, Elias "was the link between Mannheim and the students."

At the same time as in Heidelberg, an institute, the Institute for Social Research (IfS), was founded in Frankfurt in 1924 (see Jay 1981 [1973]; Wiggershaus 2001 [1988]; Albrecht et al. 1999; Demirović 1999). The first director was the Austrian Marxist Carl Grünberg (1861–1940). After Grünberg had suffered a stroke in 1928, Max Horkheimer took over as director in the early 1930s. Unlike the economist Grünberg, Horkheimer stood for the connection between Marxism, "bourgeois science," and philosophy (Wiggershaus 2001 [1988], p. 53). In addition, with Erich Fromm (1900–1980), who had obtained his doctorate with Alfred Weber, the institute expanded its orientation toward psychoanalysis and social psychology. The *Zeitschrift für Sozialforschung* (English: *Journal of Social Research*), which first appeared in 1932 and continued to be published in exile until 1941, became the institute's medium of publication. Besides Horkheimer, in the interwar period, the central actors in the sphere of the IfS and the *Zeitschrift für Sozialforschung* were Friedrich Pollock (1894–1970), Erich Fromm, Otto Kirchheimer (1905–1965), Franz L. Neumann (1900–1954), Henryk Grossmann (1881–1950), Herbert Marcuse (1898–1979), Leo Löwenthal (1900–1993), Siegfried Kracauer (1889–1966), Walter Benjamin (1892–1940), and Theodor W. Adorno (1903–1969). The institute was in competition with Karl Mannheim's sociological seminar. According to Horkheimer, Mannheim's sociology of knowledge had both an idealist and a relativist tendency (Barboza 2010, p. 163).

At the beginning of the 1930s, as the National Socialists' seizure of power became increasingly apparent, branches of the IfS were established in Geneva, London, and Paris. This ensured the existence of the IfS. In the summer of 1934, a branch office was opened at Columbia University in New York, which subsequently became the main office of the IfS. In 1940 it moved to Pacific Palisades in California (Wheatland 2009). Horkheimer and Adorno began their work on the *Dialectic of Enlightenment*, while Otto Kirchheimer, Franz L. Neumann, and Herbert Marcuse spent several years producing secret reports on Nazi Germany for the Office of Strategic Services (OSS) to combat fascism (Neumann et al. 2013; Müller 2010).

*Braunschweig*
René König (1906–1992), who studied in Berlin in the 1920s and who became one of Western Germany's leading sociologists after World War II, remarked in retrospect that toward the end of the Weimar era there had been a new, promising wave in sociology, represented in particular by Karl

Mannheim and Theodor Geiger (1891–1952). Part of this "new wave" was the increasing orientation toward US-American sociology, as could be observed with Thurnwald, Walther, Mannheim, and Geiger. In 1928, Geiger had been appointed professor of sociology at the Technical University of Braunschweig on the recommendation of Tönnies and Vierkandt (see Geißler and Meyer 2000, p. 279). In the interwar period, Geiger received broad and international attention because of several publications: the monograph *Die Masse und ihre Aktion. Ein Beitrag zur Soziologie der Revolutionen* (1926, *The Mass and its Action. A Contribution to the Sociology of Revolutions*), articles on community, society, revolution, and leadership, published in Vierkandt's *Handwörterbuch* (1931), and the book *Die soziale Schichtung des deutschen Volkes* (1932, *The Social Stratification of the German People*). In this book, Geiger (1932, pp. 12, 25) used the terms "stratum," "social situation" (*soziale Lage*), "habitus," "lifestyle" (*Lebensduktus*), and "mentality" long before they became commonly used in sociology to analyze social structure. Among sociologists, Geiger was one of the most decisive critics of National Socialism. In *Die soziale Schichtung des deutschen Volkes* (1932), he threw a nuanced glance at the social structure of the Weimar Republic and discovered an increasing popular approval of the policies of the NSDAP. Toward the end of the book, he analyzed the interrelation between the middle classes' fears of relegation and their longings for promotion on the one side and the NSDAP's success in the 1930 elections to the Reichstag on the other (Geiger 1932, p. 111). Geiger advocated for an empirical orientation of sociology. He criticized the speculative, philosophical, and detached style of many colleagues. He recommended them instead to acquire knowledge of statistical methods from the USA (Meyer 2001, pp. 42–71). In September 1933, Geiger was dismissed. Despite certain attempts to adapt to the ruling regime (Geißler and Meyer 2000, p. 280), he was threatened and subjected to spying. He had impeded the planned professorship for "Organische Gesellschaftslehre und Politik" (Organic Sociology and Politics) for Adolf Hitler in Braunschweig and he had already publicly criticized the NSDAP for several years. He emigrated to Denmark, where he first received a scholarship from the Rockefeller Foundation in Copenhagen and finally became the first Danish professor of sociology at Aarhus University in 1938 (Kropp 2015).[15]

---

[15] After 1945, returning to Denmark from exile in Sweden, Geiger participated in the founding of the *International Sociological Association* (ISA) as the representative of the Scandinavian countries.

In addition to the aforementioned centers and actors of sociology during the Weimar Republic, there were further places where sociology was practiced like Aachen, Göttingen, Halle, Jena, Kiel, or Münster. In comparison to those mentioned, however, they were not equally visible.[16]

At the beginning of the 1930s, contemporaries such as Geiger evaluated the epoch of Weimar sociology positively: "Finally, sociology in Germany too has left behind the epoch of the struggle for its recognition as an independent academic discipline" (Geiger 1931, p. 568). However, it was not only in the academic field that things seemed to develop positively for sociology. Besides academic institutionalization, the popular education movement and non-university institutions were also of great importance for the recognition and dissemination of sociology (see Lepsius 2017a [1981], pp. 15–16; Fornefeld et al. 1986).

### Institutionalization Through Sociological Journals in the Weimar Republic

The process of the institutionalization of sociology in the Weimar Republic was advanced by the founding of new journals (for the following see Stölting 1986, pp. 145–194; Neef 2012, pp. 229–261). The central medium for sociological publications in the Weimar period and the first sociological journal was the aforementioned *Kölner Vierteljahrshefte für Soziologie (Cologne Quarterly of Sociology)*. Besides von Wiese, Max Scheler, Ferdinand Tönnies, and Alfred Vierkandt, also Rudolf Goldscheid, Hans Kelsen, Wilhelm Jerusalem, Robert Michels, Richard Thurnwald, Werner Sombart, Andreas Walther, Max Graf zu Solms, Paul Ludwig Landsberg, Friedrich Hertz, Franz Oppenheimer, Carl Brinkmann, Karl Dunkmann, Rudolf Heberle, Theodor Geiger, Othmar Spann, Max Rumpf, Robert E. Park, Pitirim A. Sorokin, Sebald Rudolf Steinmetz, Charles Bouglé, Helmuth Plessner, Howard P. Becker, Johann Plenge, and Karl Mannheim published there. Some women, such as Käthe Bauer-Mengelberg, Maria Steinhoff, Hanna Meuter, Gertrud Faßhauer, and Charlotte von Reichenau, were also among the authors who published in this journal. If one examines the topics of the first issues of the *Vierteljahreshefte* up to 1923 (Gorges 1986), they reveal a predominantly self-referential

---

[16] But see for more details on these places Moebius (2021).

examination of the authors' understanding of science, but no analysis of the immediate social problems of their time.

In 1925, Gottfried Salomon founded the *Jahrbuch für Soziologie*, of which only three volumes were published. It saw itself as a melting pot of different approaches. Among the authors of the *Jahrbuch* were, for example, Celestin Bouglé, Maurice Halbwachs, Robert H. Lowie, René Maunier, Robert Michels, Gaetano Mosca, Pitirim A. Sorokin, Yasama Takata, Tönnies, Vierkandt, but also von Wiese.

Similarly international was the *Zeitschrift für Völkerpsychologie und Soziologie* by Richard Thurnwald and Bronislaw Malinowski, also published since 1925 (as of 1932 it was called *Sociologus*). Not only were William F. Ogburn (1886–1959), Edward Sapir (1884–1939), Pitirim Sorokin (1889–1968), and Steinmetz co-editors of the journal over the years, but from 1932 onwards and under the extended subtitle *A Journal of Sociology and Social Psychology* it was published bilingually.

### *The Soziologentage and the Sociology of Knowledge Dispute*

The first *Soziologentag* (Sociologists' Day) of the German Sociological Association after World War I took place in Jena in September 1922. Ferdinand Tönnies took over the office of president; Leopold von Wiese became secretary (Dörk 2018b). At first, the activities of the GSA were continued as if nothing had happened between 1914 and 1918. Even after the war, the GSA was unable to move toward self-criticism of its war propaganda speeches. Instead of trying to focus on current social problems, von Wiese called for a *Ruhe des Schauens* ("quietness of observation") and urged for caution regarding too much *Weltnähe* ("worldliness") (von Wiese quoted by Papcke 1986, p. 184). Symptomatic of this deliberately unworldly attitude were the *Soziologentage* (Kaesler 1981; Gorges 1986). The third *Soziologentag*, held in 1922, for example, was held under the motto "The Nature of the Revolution." In light of the Russian Revolution in 1917 and the failed proletarian revolution in Germany in 1918/1919, a realistic sociological analysis and discussion of "revolution" would have seemed obvious. However, the conference was less concerned with the essence of the revolution than with "the definition of sociology" (Kaesler 2008, p. 81). Antipodes of this controversy were in particular Leopold von Wiese, who regarded his *Beziehungslehre* as the essence of sociology, and the Austrian Marxist Max Adler (1873–1937), who criticized von

Wiese's keynote lecture as completely unsociological. There were also attacks against von Wiese at other meetings of the GSA.

One of the highlights in the history of the *Soziologentage* in the interwar period occurred at the sixth meeting in 1928, in Zurich, Switzerland. One of the main topics was "competition"; key note speakers were Leopold von Wiese and Karl Mannheim. The subject of Mannheim's lecture was "Competition in the Intellectual Domain" (*Die Konkurrenz auf dem Gebiete des Geistigen*). The lecture was perceived by some as a "spiritual revolution" and "fireworks of stimulating insights" (Elias 1990, p. 145); by others, like Alfred Weber, it was seen as a rebellion within the GSA (König 1987, p. 356; Loader 2012, pp. 149–152).

Mannheim's lecture was the peak in the so-called "Sociology of Knowledge Dispute" of sociology in Germany and made him become the young and heatedly debated "shooting star" in sociology and outside of sociology (Kettler and Meja 1994, p. 284). "Representatives of all generations of German scholars" (Srubar 2010, p. 60), from Alfred Weber and Werner Sombart to Otto Neurath (1882–1945), Max Horkheimer, Ernst Robert Curtius (1886–1956), Max Adler, Ernst Grünwald (1912–1933), Alexander von Schelting (1894–1963), Hannah Arendt (1906–1975), Herbert Marcuse, and Karl August Wittvogel (1896–1988), all discussed Mannheim's theses controversially (Meja and Stehr 1990). They accused him either of sociologism, relativism, sociological materialism, or "submarxism." The sociology of knowledge was also regarded as a rival to Marxist approaches. Conservatives accused Mannheim of being a danger to German youth. The participants in these discussions, however, were not only critical, but also agreed with some aspects and confirmed Mannheim's thesis of the importance of competition in the intellectual and academic field. Some also feared that the sociology of knowledge could play a central role in the academic field in the future (Srubar 2010, p. 61).

Mannheim had in no way intended to provoke such a dispute. With his theses of the existential connectedness (*Seinsverbundenheit*) of knowledge and the competition between intellectual styles, he rather thought to have paved the way to a better understanding between the positions. Like many others of his time, he too was in constant search of a synthesis. In particular, he attributed to the "free-floating intelligentsia," as privileged agents, the ability to take a bird's eye view and to create a relational synthesis between the partial perspectives. Thus, Mannheim too ended up exaggerating the role of the intellectuals and "accepted a view of the intellectual's situation that was tacitly held by many of his more orthodox colleagues" (Ringer 1990, p. 292).

As can be seen from the brief overview of centers, persons, publications, and conferences, a wide range of different orientations existed in the period after World War I. In a retrospective account of sociology in Germany from 1918 to 1933, Mannheim traces this plurality back to the great dynamics of the modern society, which he considered "the most dynamic period in the history of German society" (Mannheim 2013 [1934], pp. 210–211). There was no uniform understanding of sociology, as was still desired in 1919. Sociology had managed to institutionalize itself successfully and to differentiate into various fields. There were different orientations in theory, ranging from Critical Theory (Horkheimer, Adorno, Kracauer, Benjamin) to Philosophical Anthropology (Scheler, Plessner), Phenomenological Sociology (Max Scheler and the Austrian Alfred Schütz (1899–1959)), Formal Sociology (von Wiese, Vierkandt), Marxist Sociology (Wittvogel, Georg Lukács ), and other positions. The field of special sociologies was even more differentiated and diverse. In addition to the dominant cultural sociology, several other fields of research emerged such as economic sociology, the sociology of labor, of companies, of technology, of population, of ethnicity, of law, of politics, of knowledge, of language, of literature, of music, of masses, and of intellectuals. Empirical social research also existed, but in comparison to the USA it was still only in the process of being established (Schad 1972). These different positions in sociology were not very apparent in the public perception of sociology. In the academic field, boundary work and delimitation were pursued. Depending on the perspective, sociology was either criticized as socialist and state disintegrating, as liberalist, or as a foreign import (Stölting 1984, pp. 56–58).

In 1934, Mannheim published the article "German Sociology." In this article he tried to draw a contemporary image of sociology in Germany. For him, the peculiarities of German sociology resulted above all from the thought of Georg Wilhelm Friedrich Hegel (1770–1831), the confrontations with Marx, and the interpretative tradition of Dilthey, Simmel, and Weber (Mannheim 2013 [1934], pp. 213–219). In particular, the interpretative approach in the tradition of the humanities and the related sociology of knowledge and historical sociology of culture were central characteristics of the German sociology. Mannheim also mentions the research on stratification by Theodor Geiger and Emil Lederer as a recent achievement (Mannheim 2013 [1934], pp. 223–224). But what sociology in Germany was still in need of was not a closed system of sociology—as he writes in critical opposition to von Wiese—but "an exact observation of social forces at work" (Mannheim 2013 [1934], p. 218).

Despite all the differences and despite the struggles between the controversial positions about what sociology should "actually" be (Stölting 1984, pp. 55–56)—struggles that were also publicly fought out at the *Soziologentage* of the German Sociological Association (Kaesler 1981)—it is still possible to find common ground between the positions. Dirk Kaesler, for example, identifies links in the "distinct and specific philosophical tradition" (Kaesler 1984, p. 311) of the approaches. By looking at the philosophical background, Kaesler (1984, p. 311) argues, the strong influence of the *Geisteswissenschaften* (humanities) on early German sociology as well as its emphasis on "understanding" as "the dominant methodological orientation" and its cultural criticism can be explained. However, it is noticeable that this cultural criticism did not address the actual social problems and therefore it remained largely ineffective for society. This started to change only toward the end of the Weimar Republic with a younger generation of sociologists, including Mannheim, Kracauer, and Geiger. This generation also had a philosophical background. However, this did not hinder a realistic analysis. At times—especially when it came to a Marxist orientation—the philosophical orientation even urged "sociology to be redefined and to turn to empirical and application-oriented work on the social structure of the present" (Lepsius 2017a [1981], p. 16). If sociology had not been abruptly interrupted by National Socialism in 1933, this new generation might have given sociology in Germany a "development push" (König 1987, p. 356). In any case, the "melodies of sociology" before 1933 were far from being "played through," as Schelsky (1959, p. 37) claimed. Rather, sociology had only arrived at the overture when the piece was violently interrupted and the actors were either murdered or forced into exile.

## Sociology During the Nazi Regime

In the interwar period, most of the sociologists did not anticipate the danger of fascism. National Socialism brought sociology as an institutionalized discipline to an end. Journals were discontinued, the German Sociological Association was closed down, and there was no diploma degree in sociology. The Nazis had no interest in sociology as an independent science. But even though sociology cannot be identified as a discipline in the years 1933 to 1945, there were, as in other academic disciplines, people who worked sociologically. It was in particular their empirical and methodological knowledge that was useful for the Nazis.

On January 30, 1933, Adolf Hitler was appointed chancellor by Reich President Hindenburg. With this appointment, the national-conservative forces surrounding Hindenburg attempted to push back or even eliminate parties and movements that were in favor of the Republic (Herbert 2018, p. 30).[17] They thought they could "tame" Hitler or keep him small. Hitler's election sparked enormous dynamics and mass enthusiasm, so that the other nationalist parties faded into the background. The NSDAP was supported by its own paramilitary organizations—the SA (*Sturmabteilung*, literally "Storm Division") led by Hermann Göring and the SS (*Schutzstaffel*, literally "Protection Squad"). They eliminated opponents of the National Socialists, especially Communists, with brute force. A decisive event for the establishment of the National Socialist dictatorship was the Reichstag fire at the end of February 1933, which the government used to override central basic rights of the Constitution of the Weimar Republic. Up to 20,000 Communists were arrested or abused in "wild camps" by the SA over the course of the weeks that followed (Herbert 2018, p. 33). In the election on March 5, 1933, the NSDAP got 44% of the electoral votes, the 81 seats of the deputies of the KPD were cancelled. So the NSDAP was able to achieve a majority. Within a few weeks after the election, the Weimar Constitution was repealed. Over the following months, the remaining parties were dissolved, trade unions were eliminated, and social institutions such as universities were "brought into line" (*gleichgeschaltet*), if they had not already "brought themselves into line." In addition to opportunism and fear of the brutality of the SA, however, the basic ideas of the "national revolution," "the destruction of Marxism," and the propagation of a *Volksgemeinschaft* ("people's community") were particularly favorable to the spread of National Socialism. These ideas were met with a wide social acceptance. Within the educated bourgeoisie, the anti-bourgeois conduct of the Nazis was rejected, but the common hatred of Marxism, of the Jews, of the republic, and the culture of modernity, together with the common passion for nationalism, *völkisch* rejuvenation, and the hope for a privileged position in the propagated "people's community" outweighed this rejection.

---

[17] For the following reconstruction of the historical processes I rely mainly on Herbert (2018).

Despite the propagation of a uniform "people's community," there was no coherence in cultural policy. Rather, there was a "differentiation according to social strata" (Hermand 2010, p. 61), according to which each social class was culturally addressed. This formed a further building block for the loyalty of those who did not have to flee into exile for political, "racial," or other reasons. That does not imply that everything was possible. The cultural activities had to correspond to certain norms. Thus, Marxist and avant-garde directions in cultural life were suppressed, as were modern abstract or non-objective art.

The image of women was strictly confined to her supposedly "natural" role as a mother and "racial breeder" (*Rassenzüchterin*) and "Mother's Day" was given special emphasis. However, the ideology of women as mothers could not be sustained without contradictions, at least after the war began, when the lack of workers and the increase in arms production meant that an increasing number of women were needed in working and professional life.

Hitler could rely on the loyalty of economic leaders in his power building (Abendroth 1967). Later, some of them were able to make use of the networks they had built up under National Socialism after World War II and were influential as so-called "miracle makers" (*Wundertäter*) in the economic reconstruction of the Federal Republic of Germany (Grunenberg 2007). He could also count on the *Reichswehr* (the national army) and the administration as well as on the growing loyalty of large parts of the population. This resulted partly from the improvement in living conditions. The forced orientation of the economy, of the government spending, and of the finances toward accelerated armament allowed the national economy to strengthen and led to the creation of jobs. It should not be forgotten, however, that the expansion of power was also accompanied and fostered by the violence of the Nazi militias. The establishment of concentration camps and the SS played a central role in the violent suppression of opponents. The SS took over the police force and, as of the beginning of World War II in 1939, as Waffen-SS, it assumed a military function alongside the regular army (now called *Wehrmacht*). Already in 1935 it was certain that political resistance became more dangerous, but did not cease to renew from 1935, new resistance groups of the labor movement, bourgeois, and especially religious groups continued even after 1938 (cf. Herbert 2014, pp. 520–532).

In March 1936, German troops marched into the demilitarized Rhineland. That same year the Olympic Games were held in Berlin, where the regime propagandistically presented itself as a regular country. In the summer of 1936, Germany and Italy supported General Franco's coup against the Republican government in Spain. The march into and the annexation (*Anschluss*) of Austria, which was approved by the Western powers, followed in 1938. Czechoslovakia was next.

With regard to the inner situation of Germany, the anti-Semitic politics toward the Jews peaked in a brutal manner on November 9, 1938. That day, in Germany and Austria, the SS and SA initiated large-scale pogroms against Jewish institutions such as cemeteries, synagogues, and shops. Hundreds of Jews were looted and murdered. A total of 30,000 Jews were taken into so-called "protective custody" and deported to concentration camps. The population largely observed these events passively. But the "raids, arsons, lootings, murders had happened in public, and no one in Germany could henceforth claim not to have known anything about the persecution of the Jews" (Herbert 2018, p. 58). The "November Pogroms" now clearly demonstrated that German policy toward the Jews had taken on a new, cruel dimension. The emigration numbers went up. But as Hitler announced at the beginning of 1939, the regime was now no longer merely concerned with deportation, but with the extermination of the Jews in Europe (Herbert 2018, p. 59).

At the end of August 1939, shortly before the beginning of the war against Poland, the Molotov-Ribbentrop Pact was signed, a non-aggression pact between Nazi Germany and the Soviet Union, with the secret supplementary agreement concerning the destruction of Polish autonomy. On September 1, 1939, the German Wehrmacht invaded Poland. World War II began. A few months later Germany conquered Denmark, Norway, Belgium, the Netherlands, and Luxembourg, and it defeated the French army in 1940. The "trauma of 1918," the Treaty of Versailles, seemed to have been avenged; the population as a whole was enthusiastic, paying homage to its leader, and the cult of Hitler reached its "peak in society as a whole" (Herbert 2018, p. 64).

Great Britain and the Soviet Union were now the remaining enemies of the Germans. According to Hitler's own account, the war in the East was supposed to be clearly different in its severity from that in the West. It was to be a war of annihilation. The battle against the Soviet Union in the summer of 1941, which was already prepared in 1940 and was led despite the Molotov-Ribbentrop Pact, was fought with the utmost brutality (cf. Herbert 2014, pp. 435–445). Famines were systematically taken into account. The cruelest example was the blockade of Leningrad (today Saint

Petersburg). From 1941 to 1944, the German military built a blockade ring around the city in order to systematically starve the population. A mass of deaths began to occur mostly due to starvation. In addition, the population was bombed by the German *Luftwaffe* (air force). More than a million people were killed. As a comparison, these are twice as many deaths as those that occurred in all air raids on Germany. The scale of the planned mass of deaths among the Soviet prisoners of war was also immense; the number of deaths already amounted to 600,000 at the end of October 1941 and over time increased to millions (Herbert 2018, pp. 81–82). The brutal "anti-Russian campaign" was ideologically highly charged. The idea of "living space in the East" was also a driving force. Communism was considered as a creation of the Jews. Right at the beginning of the invasion thousands of Jewish and communist men were murdered, and the extermination was then extended to women and children.

In addition to the atrocities mentioned, systematic "racial hygiene" (*Rassenhygiene*) was pursued as a social policy and a population policy measure toward the sick, the elderly, and the disabled. With regards to these social groups, the mass killings by using gas were already being tested, and became, from 1941 onwards, the daily routine for the systematic mass murder of the Jews (Herbert 2018, p. 75). Hundreds of thousands died in the ghettos and prisoner-of-war camps or died of hunger. Between June 1941 and March 1942, the Waffen-SS, police, and Wehrmacht shot more than 600,000 Jews in the occupied territories of the Soviet Union (Herbert 2018, p. 89). On January 20, 1942, in Berlin at Wannsee, the organization of the deportation actions and systematic mass murder was discussed. It was decided to deploy the Jews who were able to work for forced labor and to murder the rest in the concentration camps. About 6 million Jews were murdered during the war. The total number of deaths during World War II exceeded 50 million people. The Soviet Union had to mourn the highest number of deaths—over 26 million.

In December 1941, the USA entered the war. As a result, between 1942 and 1943 the war turned in favor of the Allies. The war ended with the Battle of Berlin in April 1945 and Hitler shot himself in his air-raid shelter (*Führerbunker*) near the Reich Chancellery on April 30.

## "Inner Emigration," Exile, and Sociologies in the Service of National Socialism

Already in 1933, many professors were dismissed or fled into exile abroad. Even after 1933, sociology continued to be taught at some universities and doctorates and habilitations were awarded (Lepsius 2017b [1979], p. 87; Rammstedt 1986, p. 14). In some places, such as Leipzig, there was no interruption of sociology, but rather continuity. Statistically speaking, the discontinuation was far more significant than the continuity (Holzhauser 2015). In particular, those positions such as *völkische Soziologie* (*völkisch* sociology), which were already in circulation in the 1920s and were oriented toward the *Volksgemeinschaft*, were continued. Sociology was not abandoned per se—except for its (supposedly) "Jewish" and Marxist variants, which were marked as "misguided"—but in principle was considered compatible with National Socialist ideologies and objectives. As already mentioned, Hitler himself almost accepted a sociological professorship which was offered to him at the University of Braunschweig (Dahrendorf 1965, p. 109; Rammstedt 1986, p. 12). Hence, in general, the Nazis did not at all fear that sociology would be ideologically disintegrating. However, the regime generally did not seek special proximity to sociology either, unless it matched its political goals (Turner 1992, p. 8). Applied social research was best suited to these goals.

After 1933, the personnel and profile of sociology in Germany changed.[18] Many sociologists were forced into exile due to "racially" and politically motivated persecution. Some sociologists went into a kind of "inner emigration," as it was called at the time. Some sociologists sympathized with the Nazi regime or even worked for the objectives of the Nazi regime (Klingemann 1996). Three kinds of sociology that existed during the Nazi era can be differentiated (Kaesler 1984, pp. 528–529; Lepsius 2008, p. 37): "inner emigration," exile, and sociologies in the service of

---

[18] For the analysis of sociology under National Socialism, one can draw on numerous studies that have been carried out since the 1980s (see Lepsius 2017b [1981], 2017c [1979]; Papcke 1980, 1986; Bergmann et al. 1981; Klingemann 1981, 1986, 1990, 1992, 1996, 2008, 2009; Urs Jaeggi et al. 1983; Dirk Kaesler 1984; Kaesler and Steiner 1992; René König 1987; Stölting 1984; Rammstedt 1986; Weyer 1984a, 1984b, 1984c, 1984d; Cobet 1988; Breuer 2002; Turner 1992; Turner and Kaesler 1992; Schäfer 1990, 1997, 2014, 2017). Earlier analyses were conducted by Riemer (1932), Maus (1959), and Dahrendorf (1965). For recent studies see among others the contributions in Christ and Suderland (2014) as well as Becker (2014), Dyk and Schauer (2015), Schnitzler (2018), and Schauer (2018).

National Socialism. The latter can be divided into several orientations (Schauer 2018, pp. 135–136) like, inter alia, *völkische Soziologie* (*völkisch* sociology), *Gemeinschaftssoziologie* (sociology of community), and social science contract research for the Nazi regime.

Inner emigration is the attitude of those persons who were either adversely critical of or distanced themselves from the Nazi regime, but who nevertheless remained in Germany. Examples of "inner emigrants" are Ferdinand Tönnies, Alfred Weber, Alfred von Martin (1882–1979), and Alfred Vierkandt. The systematic persecution and murder on racist and political grounds forced most sociologists into exile, a fact that weakened sociology in Germany (as well as in Austria) lastingly. Amongst the German exiled sociologists were: Theodor Geiger who fled to Scandinavia; Karl Mannheim and Norbert Elias, both of whom fled to Great Britain; and many others who fled to the most commonly chosen country of destination, the USA, including sociologists such as Emil Lederer, Max Horkheimer, Theodor W. Adorno, Friedrich Pollock, Siegfried Kracauer, Paul Honigsheim, Hans Speier, Alfred Schütz, Carl Meyer, Franz Borkenau (1900–1957), Franz Neumann, Erich Fromm, Franz Oppenheimer, Arnold Bergstraesser, Ernest Manheim (1900–2002), Hans Gerth. In the USA, the New School for Social Research in New York in particular offered an academic space where the exiles could work and survive.

While in the 1920s many US-Americans still considered it attractive to study in Germany, central ideas of sociology from Europe were now available in the USA and were in part further developed there. As the names testify, sociology had not already reached its intellectual end in 1933. Rather, it had developed a wide range of themes and topics in the interwar period, a variety of special sociologies had developed, which now also became victims of National Socialism.

Sociologists who advocated a sociology of *Volksgemeinschaft* (people's community) or a "völkische sociology" were mainly Max Hildebert Boehm (1891–1968), Max Rumpf (1878–1953), and Hans Freyer, with whom Arnold Gehlen, Helmut Schelsky, Gunther Ipsen, and Karl Heinz Pfeffer studied in Leipzig—one of Freyer's doctoral students, Gerhard Krüger, was the main initiator of the Nazi book burnings—Franz Wilhelm Jerusalem (1883–1970), the "racial scientist" Hans K. Günther (1891–1968), the NS pedagogue Ernst Krieck (1882–1947), and the Hamburg sociologist Andreas Walther. Leopold von Wiese too tried to serve the regime opportunistically. Although he was not a committed National Socialist, he "did not shy away from offering sociology, and especially his at the time influential *Beziehungslehre*, to the National Socialists" (Dyk and Schauer 2015, p. 47). However, von Wiese's formal sociology was considered impractical by the National Socialists and therefore it was hardly noticed.

The German Sociological Association was "closed down" in 1934 (Schnitzler 2018, p. 849). Just before the closing, Hans Freyer had been elected as the new chairman, now called "Führer." Only after World War II did the association become active again, with von Wiese as chairman. However, for the National Socialists, the mostly non-university institutions in which research was conducted with practical application of social science knowledge, such as population sociology, urban sociology, and agricultural sociology, were far more important than the theorists and the German Sociological Association (see the list of institutions in Klingemann 1986, pp. 263–279).

The initial position from which sociology in Germany after 1945 started to re-develop was a particularly difficult one. It was no longer possible to immediately build on the sociology of the Weimar Republic, not only because the staff had been murdered or fled into exile, but also because the social problems and challenges after 1945 were completely different from those before.

**Open Access** This chapter is licensed under the terms of the Creative Commons Attribution 4.0 International License (http://creativecommons.org/licenses/by/4.0/), which permits use, sharing, adaptation, distribution and reproduction in any medium or format, as long as you give appropriate credit to the original author(s) and the source, provide a link to the Creative Commons licence and indicate if changes were made.

The images or other third party material in this chapter are included in the chapter's Creative Commons licence, unless indicated otherwise in a credit line to the material. If material is not included in the chapter's Creative Commons licence and your intended use is not permitted by statutory regulation or exceeds the permitted use, you will need to obtain permission directly from the copyright holder.

CHAPTER 3

# Reconstruction and Consolidation of Sociology in West Germany from 1945 to 1967

Frankfurt, September 19, 1946: The *Deutsche Gesellschaft für Soziologie* (German Sociological Association, GSA) held its first *Soziologentag* ("Sociologists' Day") after the end of World War II. The GSA was the first academic society to be re-established in Germany after 1945. The topic of the meeting was "The Current Situation, from a Sociological Point of View." One was eager to hear what the sociologists had to say about the past years of the National Socialist dictatorship, the war that had been started by Germany, the Holocaust, and the unimaginably high number of deaths. More than 50 million people died during World War II, including more than 26 million from the Soviet Union. Approximately 5.7 million Jews had been killed—for the most part systematically. A total of "about 12 to 14 million people died outside of combat" (Herbert 2018, p. 95). But not only the killings, atrocities, and the war suggested themselves as issues to be addressed at a *Soziologentag* immediately after the end of the Nazi regime. Also, the question of how it was at all possible that the Nazi dictatorship came about would have been a relevant topic for sociological analyses in 1946. One could have taken up existing studies here, such as Theodor Geiger's analyses of the middle class. As early as 1932, he analyzed the social structure of the Weimar Republic in *Die soziale Schichtung des deutschen Volkes* (1932; *The Social Stratification of the German People*)

© The Author(s) 2021
S. Moebius, *Sociology in Germany*, Sociology Transformed,
https://doi.org/10.1007/978-3-030-71866-4_3

and discovered an increasing consent of the population to the policies of the NSDAP (National Socialist German Workers' Party or Nazi Party). A number of analyses by emigrants dealing with National Socialism or totalitarianism in general had appeared even before 1945, especially in American exile. Consider, for example, the following: *State of the Masses: The Threat of the Classless Society* (1940) written by Emil Lederer, who fled from Berlin and was later dean of faculty at the University in Exile; Franz Borkenau's *The Totalitarian Enemy* (1939); Fritz Sternberg's *Der Faschismus an der Macht*; Ernst Fraenkel's *The Dual State* (1941); Erich Fromm's *Escape from Freedom* (1941); Eduard Heimann's *Communism, Fascism, and Democracy* (1938); *The End of Economic Man. A Study of the New Totalitarianism* by Peter Drucker; Max Horkheimer and Theodor W. Adorno's *Dialektik der Aufklärung* (1944, *Dialectic of Enlightenment* 1972); Adolph Lowe's *The Price of Liberty*; Karl Mannheim's *Diagnosis of Our Time* (1943); Sigmund Neumann's *Permanent Revolution* (1942); Franz L. Neumann's *Behemoth* (1942); and Joseph A. Schumpeter's *Capitalism, Socialism, and Democracy* (1942). After all, what was said at the *Soziologentag* about the dictatorship, the millions of deaths, the Holocaust, and the guilt of the Germans?

## 1945–1949

The first president of the re-established German Sociological Association after 1945 was Leopold von Wiese. He was still in good contact with his former student Howard P. Becker (1899–1960) as well as with Edward Y. Hartshorne (1912–1946), an officer of the US Army and an expert regarding the German higher education system. Hartshorne had a close cooperation with the sociologist René König (1906–1992) and helped to reopen the universities (Tent 1998). He also was responsible for the denazification and initiating of processes of democratization. His consent was necessary for the re-establishment of the GSA.[1]

The Allies regarded German sociology as a victim of the Nazi regime and as an unencumbered science for two reasons: firstly, because of the high number of emigrated sociologists and secondly, because of the narrative spread by von Wiese that there had been no official sociology in Germany after 1934. However, sociology was not the victim that it

---

[1] Hartshorne had already conducted research on German universities in the 1930s. In August 1946, he was shot dead on a highway.

presented itself to be. German sociologists such as Andreas Walther and Hans Freyer, who were not forced into exile and who were closely associated with the Nazi regime, had continued to teach and publish. Furthermore, the Nazi regime itself was not anti-sociological: Remember that—as already mentioned in the previous chapter—Hitler almost accepted a sociological professorship in Braunschweig (Dahrendorf 1965, p. 109). In general, however, the regime did not seek particularly close relations to those sociologists who remained in Germany, unless their ideas, theories, and/or empirical results served the political cause of the regime and matched with the political objectives (Turner 1992, p. 8). This was particularly true of applied social research.

Some sociologists used their empirical research skills to advance the regime's population policy and Nazi eugenics (*Nationalsozialistische Rassenhygiene*) (Klingemann 1996). Others did not emigrate physically, but went into a form of "inner emigration." Ferdinand Tönnies and Alfred Weber belonged to this group of sociologists in "inner emigration." Von Wiese emigrated in neither way. During the Nazi regime, von Wiese had behaved opportunistically. However, by the end of World War II, he understood how to take the chance and present himself as a liberal sociologist of the Weimar Republic.

That the GSA was reactivated immediately after World War II was also due to the fact that the Americans considered sociology important for the re-education, reorientation, and democratization of the Germans. Whether their expectations would be fulfilled was uncertain, since the new president of the association had nothing more to say about the past years of dictatorship, the Holocaust, and the crimes against humanity as: "And yet the plague came on the people from outside, unprepared, as an insidious raid. This is a metaphysical secret that the sociologist cannot touch" (von Wiese 1948, p. 29). The years of the Nazi dictatorship should not be addressed explicitly. They could not even be analyzed because they were—according to von Wiese—metaphysical. Like many other Germans after 1945, von Wiese followed the narrative that the Germans had been "seduced" or "raped" by Hitler (Frei 2012).

Apart from Heinz Maus (1911–1978), nobody dared to object. Maus, who was close to the Frankfurt School and who was later one of the first Germans to write about sociology under National Socialism (Maus 1959),[2]

---

[2] Outside of Germany, there were studies on sociology under National Socialism very early by, for example, Don Hager (1949).

criticized the silence of the official sociology. At the *Soziologentag* he read a letter from Max Horkheimer, who wrote from exile that a sociology of terror was what was needed now (Greven and van de Moetter 1981, p. 19). This proposal ebbed away and found no support. Maus' plan to do his habilitation with von Wiese was then no longer feasible. He was henceforth regarded as someone who fouls his own nest (*"Nestbeschmutzer"*) (Papcke 1985, p. 194).

The members of the GSA were not prepared to deal with the past (van Dyk and Schauer 2015, p. 143). This they shared with the majority of Germans at that time. The GSA was not even prepared to readmit their former colleagues who were forced into exile. The new statutes of the GSA denied "leading figures from abroad" full membership. In contrast, people with a National Socialist past were to be treated "as liberally as possible" (Borggräfe and Schnitzler 2014, p. 461). Their attitude toward Marxists was not equally liberal; this can be seen from the case of Georg Lukács, whose membership was decisively rejected.

At the time of its re-establishment, the GSA had nothing substantial to say, neither about the National Socialist past, the war crimes, and crimes against humanity, nor about the then "present situation": the chaotic, miserable, and disastrous conditions in Germany after 1945 (Bessel 2009; Reichardt and Zierenberg 2009). In the destroyed cities, the infrastructure was ailing, the black market and crime flourished, there was a housing shortage and starvation, expellees, displaced persons (former forced laborers, prisoners of war, and survivors of the concentration camps) traversed the country, more than 10 million people fled to West Germany, 9 million forced laborers moved to their respective territories, several million German soldiers were taken as prisoners of war, families were divided. In short, the general conditions as well as the living conditions were catastrophic and anomic; consequently, there was a real need for social planning. Consequently, there were indeed sufficient problems that would have offered themselves for sociological research. But the GSA preferred to deal with "formal-theoretical questions" (van Dyk and Schauer 2015, p. 148) and as an academic circle it remained relatively distanced from the reality of ordinary Germans.

The Allies were confronted with enormous challenges and unfathomable atrocities. The liberation of the concentration camps revealed the full and horrific extent of the Nazis' extermination policy. How could one re-educate a population capable of such practices to democracy and humanity? Furthermore, the majority of Germans did not see the Allies as liberators. Most Germans experienced liberation as defeat. Official sociology, as it was represented by the GSA, did little to improve the situation. It supported the Americans neither in the process of re-education nor in simply integrating sociology into teacher training (van Dyk and Schauer 2015, p. 148).

## Re-education and Research Institutions

Re-education and democratization, therefore, had to rely on sociological expertise other than that of the GSA. Universities and, even more so, non-university research institutions offered alternative sources of expertise. Many newly or re-established institutions and universities, often supported and driven by the US military government, devoted themselves to practice-oriented teaching and research on social processes. Immediately after the war a number of new institutions were founded; for example, the *Akademie für Gemeinwirtschaft* (Academy of Public Economics) in Hamburg and the *Hochschule für Arbeit, Politik und Wirtschaft* (University of Labor, Politics, and Economics) in Wilhelmshaven, both served the trade unions to train the next generation. In the French occupation zone there was the *Höhere Verwaltungsakademie* (later *Verwaltungshochschule*; Higher Academy of Administration) in Speyer. The first post-war appointments of sociologists took place in these institutions, including professors with a Nazi past (Arnold Gehlen 1947 in Speyer, Helmut Schelsky 1948 in Hamburg).

A number of new research institutes were established, some of them connected to the universities, others not. In 1946, Otto Neuloh (1902–1993) founded the *Sozialforschungsstelle* (Social Research Centre) at the University of Münster, which was based in Dortmund. The Social Research Centre was the largest institution of its kind in the 1950s and 1960s. Neuloh saw the Social Research Centre as a kind of clinic for social issues and the researchers as "doctors of social life" (Adamski 2009; Neuloh et al. 1983). The institution benefited considerably from the teaching of empirical methods developed in the USA (Kändler 2016, p. 129), but also from US-American group sociology and urban sociology. From the early 1950s onwards, the Social Research Centre gained considerable attention due to its research on technical developments as well as its sociology of labor, work, organizations, and industry. In addition, a form of municipal sociology, inspired by US community studies, was conducted (Weischer 2004, p. 67).

In 1947, the *Forschungsinstitut für Sozial- und Verwaltungswissenschaften an der Universität Köln* (Research Institute for Social and Administrative Sciences at the University of Cologne) was re-established. The sociology department was headed by Leopold von Wiese, who, however, did not conduct any empirical research. Also in Cologne, the *Wirtschaftswissenschaftliche Institut der Gewerkschaften* (WWI; Institute of Economics of the Trade Unions) was founded in 1946. From 1951 to 1958, the UNESCO Institute for Social Sciences existed in Cologne. From 1953, it was headed by Nels Anderson (1889–1986), another important university officer, and devoted itself to community studies and population surveys. In addition to the institutions located in Cologne, the Institute for Social Sciences in Darmstadt, initiated by Nels Anderson in 1949, and the Institute for Social Research (IfS), reopened in Frankfurt am Main in the early 1950s, should also be mentioned.

Besides these research institutes, in the different Western occupation zones there were also institutions that were particularly devoted to opinion polls. As early as 1945, the Office of Military Government for Germany, United States (OMGUS) began to conduct numerous opinion polls (OMGUS Surveys 1945–1949, later HICOG-Surveys). Subsequently, opinion research institutes such as EMNID in Bielefeld, Infratest in Munich, the German Institute for Surveys of the People (DIVO), and the Institute for Public Opinion Research in Allensbach, established in 1947 by Erich P. Neumann (1912–1973) and Elisabeth Noelle-Neumann (1916–2010), were founded.[3]

## *"Americanization"?*

All of these institutions and activities promoted the implementation and application of empirical methods. In this respect, empirical research was

---

[3] Noelle-Neumann had become acquainted with opinion research in the USA at the end of the 1930s and used it for her doctoral thesis. As, among others, Leo Bogart (1991) stresses, Noelle-Neumann had written anti-Semitic articles in the National Socialist newspaper *Das Reich*, where Erich Neumann also worked, and was a member of the Working Group of National Socialist (female) Students. After World War II, she became head of the Institute for Public Opinion Research in Allensbach (incidentally, the place where the author of this book comes from). The "Allensbach Institute" was close to the party Christian Democratic Union of Germany ("CDU"). Erich Neumann was a PR specialist for CDU politician and Chancellor Konrad Adenauer; also, Elisabeth Noelle-Neumann advised Adenauer and later the German Chancellor Helmut Kohl, who supported her to get a professorship in Mainz.

closely linked to political practice (Kern 1982, p. 233). Since this research was either funded financially and/or supported by methods and methodological consultants from the USA, it was later often referred to as the "Americanization" of post-war West German sociology (Weyer 1986);[4] some even referred to it as a "successful mission" (Schelsky 1959, p. 55) or a "secular mission" (Plé 1990). However, it is often forgotten that there was a long tradition of empirical social research in the German-speaking countries before World War II (cf. Kern 1982, pp. 19–216). Empirical social research was also pursued under National Socialism (Klingemann 1996), although the protagonists of this empirical "sociology of the people" (*Volkssoziologie*) often remained in the tradition of the humanities-oriented German sociology before 1933 (Nolte 2000, pp. 131–132). Important empirical sociologists such as Theodor Geiger or the Austrian Paul F. Lazarsfeld (1901–1976) were forced into exile. After this detour, empirical social research returned to Europe, enriched with knowledge from US-American social research (Fleck 2011).

It is evident that the development of sociology and the shift toward practical social research, as can be observed after 1945, could not have taken place without American support. This is even more so the case since the GSA could not have been relied upon in this respect. Just like the GSA, the old and newly founded journals, the *Kölner Zeitschrift für Soziologie* (formerly *Kölner Vierteljahrshefte*), republished by von Wiese in 1948/1949, and the *Soziale Welt* (*Social World*), founded in 1949, were initially not oriented toward empirical research. In addition to American support of empirical research, some of the sociologists who returned from exile saw social research as a tried and tested means of "applied enlightenment" (Dahrendorf) for the democratization process in Germany.

The re-education by the Allies was not only aimed at denazification, but furthermore to educate the Germans to become democrats (Wehler 2010, p. 960). Higher education policy and science policy were different in the American, British, French, and Soviet occupation zones (Gerhardt 2006, pp. 38–75; Duller et al. 2019, p. 73). It was only when the Federal Republic of Germany was founded in 1949 that the three Western zones

---

[4] On the fear of "Americanization," which was not only found among sociologists, but was also particularly widespread among conservative as well as communist intellectuals, see Schildt (2011). On criticism of the historiographical usage of the term "Americanization" see Doering-Manteuffel (2003). On the simultaneous and politically fomented fear of communism see Biess (2019, pp. 122–133).

became one. Science and university policy became the responsibility of the ministries of education of the federal states. "By the midst of the 1950s the West German university system had reobtained stability" (Duller et al. 2019, p. 73).

Immediately after the war, also the students were occupied with their very survival; most of them had been actively involved in World War II. "This accumulation of formerly active officers and reserve officers at the universities, on the one hand, was seen as a potential threat to the security interests of the victorious powers; on the other hand, the universities were one of those environments where the success or failure of their 'denazification and democratization policies' could best be observed" (Fichter and Lönnendonker 2018, p. 31). However, the attitudes of students in the 1950s were predominantly apolitical, with 60% of them saying in a survey that they had "had enough of political sentiments and no longer wanted to know about worldviews" (Jarausch 1984, p. 223). This would change again only in the middle of the 1960s.

### *From Re-education to Anti-communism*

The first phase (1945–1949) of the history of sociology in Germany after World War II was marked by the re-establishment of the GSA, the establishment of social science institutes with empirical orientation, and a scientific policy that focused on re-education (Gerhardt 2006, p. 35). The revival of sociology immediately after the victory of the Allies led to the reactivation of professors from the Weimar Republic (Lepsius 2017d, pp. 92–94): In addition to von Wiese, also Alfred Vierkandt, Alexander Rüstow, Richard Thurnwald, Carl Brinkmann, Alfred von Martin, and Alfred Weber returned to their former positions. However, with the exception of Alfred Weber and a short-term "reprise of Heidelberg sociology" (Lepsius 2017d, p. 93), their activities had little impact. In the following years, neither Alfred Weber nor Alfred von Martin influenced the subsequent discourse; even Karl Mannheim played hardly a role anymore, he died in January 1947, shortly after having appointed as UNESCO representative for the reconstruction of sociology and democracy.

German sociology broke with the history and tradition that it inherited from the times of the Weimar Republic (Kruse 1998, pp. 155–193; Steinmetz 2010)—a break that at the same time meant a turning away from the hitherto powerful historical sociology, especially represented by the sociological tradition of Heidelberg. The strong historical orientation that had been characteristic of sociology in Germany until then (Steinmetz 2017) could not be re-established after 1945 (Steinmetz 2007). Those who were involved in the refoundation of sociology regarded historically oriented sociology as a backward-looking, idealistic undertaking or as a form of philosophy of history. Like most Germans, sociologists did not want to look back, but rather to leave their history behind as far as possible.

There were also continuities with the personnel of the Nazi era, as Klingemann (2009) especially has shown. During the first 15 years after the war, there was a "quantitative balance" (Rehberg 1992, p. 36) between "sociologists who had returned from exile or to whom 'internal emigration' can really be attributed" (Rehberg 1992, p. 36) and those who were close to the Nazi regime. René König returned from Swiss exile to Cologne, Max Horkheimer (1895–1973) from the USA to Frankfurt (both in 1949), Helmuth Plessner (1892–1985) from the Netherlands to Göttingen (1951), Arnold Bergstraesser (1896–1964) from the USA to Freiburg (1954), to name but a few.[5] Sociologists who held positions during the Nazi regime and now taught again were Arnold Gehlen (1947 in Speyer), Helmut Schelsky (1948 in Hamburg), Hans Freyer (1952 in Münster), Karl Valentin Müller (1955 in Nuremberg).[6] Other former supporters of the Nazi regime initially also found employment at the aforementioned Social Research Centre at the University of Münster in Dortmund (Rehberg 1992, p. 37; Lepsius 2017d, pp. 94–96). The laws that the government under Federal Chancellor Konrad Adenauer had enforced immediately after the founding of the state benefited many of those who were formerly engaged with the Nazi regime. These were laws that granted former supporters of the Nazi regime impunity and interpreted the legal status of former officials generously (Frei 2012). This contributed to the fact that a number of people who had already made a career during the Nazi regime held high positions, especially in industry, the judiciary, the military, and medicine, but also at universities (Frei 2007).

For the Americans, their general goal was to change soon. Denazification and education for democracy were increasingly replaced by the "primacy of education for anti-communism" (van Dyk and Schauer 2015, p. 148). The foundation of the Freie Universität (Free University; FU) Berlin

---

[5] For more details on the history of sociology in Göttingen see Römer and Alber-Armenat (2019), for Freiburg see Bröckling (2014).

[6] For more details on the close relations of these thinkers to the Nazi regime see Schäfer (1990, 2014, 2017).

(1948), a counter-establishment to the traditional Humboldt University, which was then located in the Soviet sector of the city, also fell into this phase. The founding of the FU was a first sign in the institutionalized academic field of the increasing conflict between East and West, which was to have a major impact on Germany.

## 1949–1958

Crucial for the further course and the second phase (1949–1955) of sociology in West Germany were the sociologists returning from exile; alongside the former NSDAP member Helmut Schelsky, they became the "figureheads of post-war sociology" (Gerhardt 2006, p. 105), who received international recognition, too. This development helped the university-based sociology to reorient itself and to restart successfully. It came to a real "re-establishment" (Lepsius 1978/2017c, 1979/2017d, pp. 94–111), often with support from the USA, which affected personnel, studies, the establishment of research institutes, the formation of the first post-war generation, as well as the differentiation and professionalization of sociology (Gerhardt 2006, pp. 75–101).

### *Central Positions and "Schools"*

It was a new generation that determined the institutionalization and the further course of sociology in Germany. In particular, three central positions or "schools" emerged (Lepsius 2017c, p. 81; Sahner 1982; Moebius 2018a),[7] each with its own institutes and journals: René König was appointed professor in Cologne, succeeding Leopold von Wiese, Max Horkheimer was appointed professor of sociology and philosophy in Frankfurt am Main, and Helmut Schelsky became professor of sociology at the *Akademie für Gemeinwirtschaft* in Hamburg, which was founded after the war. Cologne, Frankfurt, and Hamburg, these three locations determined the sociological field of the post-war period until the 1960s, even though sociologists were also appointed elsewhere.[8] The three

---

[7] On the formation of the sociological "schools" based on a quantitative analysis of articles and dissertations, see Sahner (1982).

[8] Helmuth Plessner was appointed in Göttingen, Arnold Bergstraesser in Freiburg, Otto Stammer in Berlin, Emerich K. Francis (1906–1994) in Munich, Arnold Gehlen in Speyer, and Gerhard Mackenroth (1903–1955) in Kiel. Gehlen (1947) was the first to be appointed

positions of this "initial constellation" (Lepsius 2017c, p. 82) were quite contrary (also in their political orientations), although all three emerged out of the tradition of a philosophical and humanities-oriented sociology of the 1920s.

## René König in Cologne

René König, who had returned from exile in Zurich, represented a decidedly empirical sociology, which he positioned in the tradition of Auguste Comte and Émile Durkheim.[9] For him, applied sociology was a critical and enlightening tool for the formation of a liberal and democratic society. According to König, "sociology should be nothing but sociology" (1967, p. 8). With this dictum he distinguished his position from the other dominant positions at the time: Sociology was not social philosophy or cultural criticism, as it was for Horkheimer and Adorno (1903–1969), nor was it a philosophical-anthropological meta-perspective and interpretational science, as it was for Schelsky. For König, sociology is "the scientific-systematic treatment of the general orders of social life, their laws of movement and development, their relations to the natural environment, to culture in general and to the individual areas of life, and finally to the social-cultural person of mankind" (König 1967, p. 8). As Clemens Albrecht (2013, p. 387) has pointed out, König's sociology moved between structural-functionalist ethnology, French theory of the Durkheim School, American social research, and the analysis of social problems; in addition, it was influenced by the broad tradition of German sociology of the interwar period that had become visible in Alfred Vierkandt's famous *Handwörterbuch der Soziologie* (*Concise Dictionary of Sociology*) of 1931. However, it was König's orientation of sociology as an empirical-analytical and independent discipline that was crucial for the further course of sociology in West Germany. This orientation found many disciples and supporters and prevailed over time, so that today this empirical orientation belongs to the general compulsory program in sociological studies (Moebius and Griesbacher 2019).

It was also König who made sociology in Germany international again. He was one of the co-founders of the International Sociological Association (ISA), and, as secretary of the ISA, he organized the World Congress in

---

for sociology in Germany after 1945, Mackenroth (1948), a former NSDAP member, the second, and Schelsky the third (1948).

[9] For the following I refer back to my book about René König, see Moebius (2015).

Zurich in 1950. From 1962 to 1966 he served as president of the ISA. In the early 1950s, König intensified his American contacts while on a trip to the USA financed by the Rockefeller Foundation. And he urged his students too, to internationalize. Although König himself did not conduct empirical social research, he was its main supporter. He himself had written his doctoral dissertation on realistic literature in France, and worked on sociology of the family, on community sociology, and on fashion. In 1952, with the help of Paul F. Lazarsfeld and Robert K. Merton (1910–2003), he published a reader on interviews. Thanks to the support of his co-workers Erwin K. Scheuch (1928–2003), Dietrich Rüschemeyer (*1930), and Peter Heintz (1920–1983), this was later extended to two much-read volumes on applied social research (König et al. 1952, 1956). In 1958, König published a dictionary of sociology that was translated into many languages (König 1967). Over 400,000 copies were sold. The book became one of the best-selling academic books and contributed significantly to the popularity of sociology from Cologne. Since 1962, König also published a multi-volume handbook on empirical sociology (*Handbuch der empirischen Sozialforschung*, 14 volumes), which itself very well demonstrated an increased professionalism and differentiation of sociology. Furthermore, in 1955, König succeeded von Wiese as editor of the renowned *Kölner Zeitschrift für Soziologie*, which he renamed to *Kölner Zeitschrift für Soziologie und Sozialpsychologie* (*KZfSS, Cologne Journal of Sociology and Social Psychology*). In particular, the special issues of the journal were to pave the way for a further differentiation of sociology into specialized sociologies or so-called *Bindestrichsoziologien* ("hyphen-sociologies").[10] This differentiation also had an impact on the GSA. It led to the establishment of various sections of the GSA and was thus also crucial for the institutionalization of sociology.

All these endeavors, especially the quantitative empirical social research and the positivist orientation promoted by König, contributed to the consolidation of sociology in West Germany and defined what in the next

---

[10] The first issue dealt with municipal organization (1956), then the following (I will only list those up to 1979) with juvenile delinquency (1957), sociology of medicine (1958), sociology of school (1959), social stratification and social mobility (1961), sociology of religion (1962), Max Weber (1963), sociology of the GDR (1964), sociology of election (1965), small groups in sport (1966), sociology of law (1967), sociology of the military (1968), sociology of development (1969), sociology of family (1970), sociology of language (1971), sociology and social history (1972), sociology of artists (1974), sociology of science (1975), social policy (1977), sociology of everyday life (1978), German sociology since 1945 (1979).

decades professionalism in sociology should mean. With his empirical orientation, the *Zeitschrift für Soziologie und Sozialpsychologie*, and with the support of his students, who further developed and strengthened this orientation in the sociological field (for instance Scheuch, Peter Atteslander (1926–2016), or the sociologist of family Rosemarie Nave-Herz (*1935)[11]), König formed what was later called the Cologne School of sociology. It was this kind of sociology that then later prevailed in the sociological field as the mainstream of sociology (Moebius 2015; Moebius and Griesbacher 2019). But what were the alternatives?

*Max Horkheimer and Theodor W. Adorno in Frankfurt*
A second thought collective was the Frankfurt School. In 1949, Horkheimer was appointed to a dual chair of philosophy and sociology in Frankfurt am Main, and in 1953 Adorno was appointed associate professor of philosophy and sociology. After 1945, the central representatives of the Frankfurt School and its principal concept of "Critical Theory" were Horkheimer and Adorno, but also the exiled Herbert Marcuse, with whom there were still contacts to the USA, and Jürgen Habermas (*1929), who in 1956 became an employee at the Institute for Social Research (IfS) and assistant to Adorno (Müller-Doohm 2014, p. 103; Wiggershaus 2001, p. 597).

After Horkheimer and Adorno had returned from exile in the USA, they rebuilt Critical Theory in Frankfurt. On the theoretical side, the *Dialectic of Enlightenment*, written by these two sociologists in California, was central. The book was inspired by Georg Lukács' analysis of the downside of Enlightenment, which he described as the rule of instrumental reason. This meant, for example, increasing formalization, quantification, and mathematization, but also the degeneration of culture and art to mere entertainment, a process that was induced by the culture industry (*Kulturindustrie*). Still in the process of working on the *Dialectic of Enlightenment*, the multi-volume *Studies in Prejudice* was developed. The volumes edited by Horkheimer and Samuel H. Flowerman (1912–1958) and financed by the American Jewish Committee (AJC) were published in 1950. They introduced the Institute for Social Research (IfS), which reopened in 1951, to the American methods of empirical social research

---

[11] Together with Renate Mayntz, Helge Pross, and Regina Becker-Schmidt, Nave-Herz, who became professor of sociology in Cologne in 1971, belongs to the first generation of female professors in sociology in Germany.

and fostered Horkheimer's hope for a "combination of European ideas and US-American methods" (Wiggershaus 2001, p. 456). The Institute for Social Research (IfS) endeavored to conduct empirical social research in West Germany, and carried out research on opinions and the atmosphere in organizations. One common feature of the Cologne School and the Frankfurt School was the attempt to help shape the social culture of the young Federal Republic through sociology and empirical social research. Horkheimer even tried to persuade König to cooperate with the IfS and in the "development of research methods" (Albrecht 1999, pp. 157 f.). König, in turn, praised the Institute's major empirical study on the *Gruppenexperiment* (group experiment) (Pollock and IfS 1955). This study aimed at ascertaining the attitudes of Germans on the persecution of the Jews, German guilt, occupying powers, and democratic forms of government through group discussions. The result was depressing and alarming. Most of the Germans largely tried to deny their complicity in the Nazi regime. This coincided with measures taken by the newly elected government under Konrad Adenauer that, for example, granted a broad amnesty to Nazi perpetrators. The group experiment, which was a further development of the group discussion by Kurt Lewin (1890–1947), later became a widely used method in qualitative social research in Germany.

At the beginning of the 1950s, there was a proximity between König and the sociologists in Frankfurt, motivated by a joint effort to come to terms with the past in a critical manner. In the early 1950s, Adorno still proposed that sociology should no longer stick to its orientation toward the humanities, but that it should finally turn into an empirical science (Nolte 2000, p. 264). In contrast to König, however, at the end of the 1950s this interest of the Frankfurt School in empirical research increasingly gave way to a social-philosophical, Marxist-inspired analysis of social conditions, which increasingly saw empirical research as a positivist reification, as it had been criticized in the *Dialectic of Enlightenment*. Initially latent differences between the Cologne School and the Frankfurt School eventually turned into struggles for the power of definition and of representation in the sociological field.

In addition to the Frankfurt School, there was another Marxist-oriented branch of the social sciences in Germany, the so-called Marburg School (Peter 2019). The head of this school was Wolfgang Abendroth (1906–1985), who had been in resistance during the Nazi regime. Besides Abendroth, Heinz Maus (since 1960) and Werner Hofmann (1922–1969) (since 1966) determined the character of the neighboring Institute for

Sociology and contributed a lot to the formation of this school. In contrast to Frankfurt, in Marburg the focus was not on the manipulation of consciousness, but on political-economic analyses of the antagonistic class structure and the labor movement as a constructive factor and oppositional force in the process of promoting democracy. Also in contrast to Adorno and Horkheimer, in Marburg the proximity to the labor movement was explicitly sought (Peter 2019, pp. 66–81).

*Helmut Schelsky in Hamburg and Münster*
Besides König and Adorno and Horkheimer, it was especially Helmut Schelsky (1912–1984) who was an important figure in West German sociology, especially with respect to its public perception. Schelsky, a former member of the NSDAP (see Schäfer 2017, p. 25), became a kind of "star" and "public intellectual" (Schäfer 2015) of the FRG. Now, after World War II, he fully committed himself to the democratization of Germany (Schäfer 2017, p. 56). He also coined the central terms by which the Germans formed their conception and perception of their own society. One of these concepts was, for example, the thesis of a *nivellierte Mittelstandsgesellschaft* (leveled middle-class society) that was first put forward in 1953 (Schäfer 2000). It was directed against Marxist interpretations of society as a class society and suggested both that more and more people were rising from the lower classes to the middle class and that an increasing number of people were descending from the upper class to the middle class. Even though the thesis was controversial, and after all turned out not to be true, it shaped the self-image and perception of the German society (Schäfer 2000). Other research in the 1950s dealt with sociology of youth, family, generations, and sexuality. In 1955, together with Gehlen, Schelsky published the first sociological textbook in the Federal Republic of Germany, titled *Soziologie. Ein Lehr- und Handbuch zur modernen Gesellschaftskunde (Sociology. A Text- and Handbook on Modern Social Studies)*. Some of Schelsky's books were particularly well received; among them were *Die skeptische Generation* (1957, *The Skeptical Generation*), *Soziologie der Sexualität* (1955, *Sociology of Sexuality*), and *Ortbestimmung der deutschen Soziologie* (1959, *Localization of German Sociology*) (Schäfer 2015, p. 2; Wöhrle 2015).

> Without having to abandon his conservative roots, he [Schelsky] participated in a creative way in the founding of institutions (Bielefeld University, Centre for Interdisciplinary Research/ZIF) and for almost three decades

proved to be a key contributor to the debate in the social sciences. Until the 1970s he was present in the feuilleton and in political discourses, but then lost the openness and tolerance he had shown during the first two decades of his career. [...] His polemical interventions put him on the track of 'anti-Sociology,' without him stopping the pursuit of sociology himself. (Schäfer 2015, p. 2)

In Hamburg, Schelsky developed his research on the empirical sociology of the family, youth, education, and organizations. Immediately after the war, he had acquired extensive knowledge of the state of research in the USA and UK at the *American Reading Room* (Karlsruhe), which was of benefit to his interpretations. As a university lecturer, Schelsky was influential due to the numerous habilitations and doctorates which he supervised (Schäfer 2015, pp. 20–21). Since 1961 he had been editor of the journal *Soziale Welt (Social World)*. Many of those he supported also later became professors, among them Lars Clausen (1935–2010), Ralf Dahrendorf (1929–2009), Hans Paul Bahrdt (1918–1994), Heinrich Popitz (1925–2002), and Niklas Luhmann (1927–1998). Schelsky's appointment to a professorship at the University of Münster in 1960, a position involving the management of the *Sozialforschungsstelle an der Universität Münster zu Dortmund* (Social Research Centre at the University of Münster in Dortmund), contributed significantly to his role as an academic mentor (Wöhrle 2019).

At the beginning of the 1950s, the different perspectives, power relations, and conflicts were still not really pronounced. The predominant focus was on joint efforts to establish and reorient sociology and to analyze social problems. Academic cooperation was formed between Cologne and Frankfurt as well as with political interest groups. König, Horkheimer, and Adorno, for example, shared their experiences of exile and were interested in a critical reappraisal of the past (Moebius 2015, p. 13).

The coalitions between the three "schools" often shifted. Nevertheless, one consensus prevailed until the mid-1950s: All shared their appreciation of empirical social research and attributed a central role in the democratization of Germany to empirical research. The common hopes were not only academically but also politically motivated. These hopes were directed at employing sociology to prevent a relapse into totalitarianism and to modernize Germany. König and the Frankfurt-based sociologists in particularly criticized the restorative policies of Chancellor Adenauer.

## Social Processes and Problems of the 1950s

In the 1950s, there was a kind of "generation consensus" (Bude 2002, p. 413). This "consensus" was partly the result of a similar perception of social processes and problems, which had to be reflected and analyzed sociologically. Which processes and problems were these? Initially, these were the industrial and social structural changes that were now noticeable, as well as political change. In 1949, a "foundation of two states" took place (Wolfrum 2006a, p. 11): In the West, the first elections to the German *Bundestag* were held in August, and in the Soviet occupation zone the German Democratic Republic (GDR) was founded in October 1949. Konrad Adenauer became Chancellor of the Federal Republic of Germany (FRG) and Bonn its capital. The High Commissioners of the three Western Allies, who had replaced the previously ruling military governors and who held control rights until 1955, were based on the opposite side of the Rhine to Bonn, on the Petersberg. In addition to rebuilding the political system of the Federal Republic, it was also important to revive the economy. This happened in such a successful manner that it was later referred to as *deutsches Wirtschaftswunder* (German Economic Miracle). The "miracle" of the economic boom, observable not only in Germany, was based on various preconditions (for the following see Wolfrum 2006a, pp. 71–74): As early as 1948 there had been a currency reform in the Western zones. The starting point of the economy too was not as bad as one might think. The collapse of the economy in 1945 had primarily been due to the "paralyzed transport sector" (Abelshauser 2011, p. 68). The fixed assets of the industry, however, had not really been affected in its substance; in fact, it had grown till 1945 (Abelshauser 2011, pp. 68–69). In addition, there was the American Marshall Plan. The Marshall Plan, officially called the European Recovery Program, was a major economic recovery program consisting of loans, raw materials, food, and goods. The Korean war was also a contributing factor. Since the USA could no longer sufficiently supply the world markets due to its own increased demand, Germany, among others, was able to fill this gap and expand its export power. Between 1950 and 1955, the gross national product grew by about 9% annually (Recker 2009, p. 32). In addition, work was restructured. Since the mid-1950s, so-called *Gastarbeiter* (guest workers) were recruited from Italy, and later from other countries such as Turkey, Portugal, and Yugoslavia, in order to counter the shortage of personnel in the labor market (Herbert and Hunn 2003). The incipient *Wirtschaftswunder* further led to an increase in consumption and leisure behavior. The symbol of this "miracle" was the successful VW Beetle, which was sold for the millionth time in 1955.

The economic boom was also praised as an achievement of the concept of the "social market economy" (*Soziale Marktwirtschaft*), introduced by Ludwig Erhard, the Minister of Economic Affairs, who was inspired by the economist and sociologist Alfred Müller-Armack (1901–1978) and the so-called Freiburg School of ordoliberalism. Material prosperity grew faster than expected. This contributed to the stabilization of the new political system. The victory at the 1954 FIFA World Cup, the so-called Miracle of Bern, strengthened the spirit of optimism as well as a new "sense of unity" among the Germans. However, despite these positive developments, Germany was not a society of the "leveled middle class" (Schelsky), because the income and lifestyle of the various classes still varied very considerably (Wolfrum 2006a, p. 74).

In 1955, Germany joined NATO. There were controversial debates about Western integration and remilitarization. The government of Adenauer took the criticism of the Communist Party of Germany (KPD) as an occasion to lead a trial against the party. In 1956, the KPD was banned. A "bipolar party system" (Recker 2009, p. 27) established itself. The CDU (Christian Democratic Union of Germany) and the SPD (Social Democratic Party of Germany) then set the tone. Of the small parties, only the liberal-oriented FDP (Free Democratic Party) was able to assert itself, and over the following years, it formed alternating coalitions with both of the major political parties. The first elected government of the FRG, led by Adenauer (CDU), was a coalition government with the FDP. Adenauer's way of governing the new Federal Republic, rigidly according to his interests, soon led to the label "Chancellor Democracy," and his extended period in office—from 1949 to 1963—came to be known as the "Adenauer era."

Socially and culturally, the 1950s was a controversial era (for the following see Wolfrum 2006a, p. 103–107). On the one hand, old elites, strongly conservative values, and old-fashioned moral beliefs still prevailed, which were later identified with the restorative "Adenauer era"; but on the other hand, there were already sporadic cultural innovations in film, art, and music. In particular, the "American way of life" conveyed by the mass media provoked fascination among young people. Nevertheless, in most people, as well as in some sociologists such as Adorno or Gehlen, the new "mass culture" provoked cultural criticism and cultural pessimism.

World War II had brought about a structural change in the family, many men were dead, the women on their own. "The experiences of fleeing, expulsion, everyday hardship, and deprivation, of death, injury, rape, and the loss of relatives and friends shaped at least an entire generation" (Wolfrum 2006a, p. 103). In the 1950s, displaced persons and refugees could still be seen in the streets. There was also still a shortage of housing and fields of debris in the cities. Industrialization led to increasing urbanization and changes in the communities. As far as the former Nazi regime was concerned, there was "communicative silence" (*kommunikatives Beschweigen*, as the philosopher Hermann Lübbe said in 1983) and a general mood of repression (not only in the psychological sense) of National Socialism, which was furthered by the Adenauer government both politically and legally (cf. Frei 2012).

## *Sociological Reflections on Contemporary Problems*

While social processes such as industrialization or the structural change of the family were considered relevant by all sociologists, their reflections on and analyses of these phenomena were quite diverse. For example, the protagonists of the "schools" (König, Horkheimer, Adorno, and Schelsky) were equally interested in the sociology of the family as well as in industrial sociology and municipal sociology. "Family" was a socially highly relevant topic after the war because, on the one hand, families were threatened by the war and the death of many men, and on the other hand, they were perceived by many as one of the few spaces of "retreat and reconciliation" (Conze 2009, p. 187). Even if they shared their perception of the family as highly relevant, there were significant differences in the sociologists' evaluation of this relevance of the family. König and Schelsky, for example, regarded the family as a force for social integration, while Adorno considered it as an institution for internalizing authoritarian behavior.

Concerning the general orientation of sociology in the 1950s, many lamented a "lack of theory" (Dahrendorf 1974, p. 112). There were certainly theoretical positions: König was oriented toward Durkheim and Parsons, Schelsky toward philosophical anthropology, and the Frankfurt-based sociologists toward Marx, Weber, and Lukács. But these orientations were not of primary importance and only gained importance in the following years. Not the theory, but issues such as family, youth, social stratification, and municipal organization were in the foreground.

However, even more than these topics, industrial sociology was at the center of sociological research in the 1950s (Dahrendorf 1974, p. 106; Schmidt 1980).

Due to the rapid process of industrialization after 1945, industrial sociology experienced a veritable boom. Three research groups stood out (Kern 1982, pp. 236–237): (1) In 1957, two studies were carried out at the Social Research Centre Dortmund, theoretically based on phenomenology and philosophical anthropology and methodologically based on qualitative research. These were the studies *Technik und Industriearbeit* (*Technology and Industrial Work*) and *Das Gesellschaftsbild des Arbeiters* (*The Social Image of the Worker*) by Heinrich Popitz, Hans Paul Bahrdt, Ernst August Jüres (1920–2012), and Hanno Kesting (1925–1975). Their main focus was on questions about the change in industrial work through new mechanization and on whether workers think of themselves as members of a common class. Already some years before, studies on collieries had been carried out by the Social Research Centre Dortmund. (2) At the Institute of Economics of the Trade Unions, a quantitative study on worker participation by Theo Pirker (1922–1995), Siegfried Braun (1922–2002), and Burkart Lutz (1925–2013) was carried out in 1955. (3) Also in 1955, at the Institute for Social Research in Frankfurt, Ludwig von Friedeburg (1924–2010), Manfred Teschner (1928–2019), and Friedrich Weltz (*1927) used group discussions and interviews to examine the atmosphere in companies. These research projects have established an independent industrial sociology in Germany. As Gert Schmidt (1980) pointed out, this kind of industrial sociology differed from the studies conducted in the USA, for example, by focusing less on a microanalysis of "human relations"—a kind of sociology of business. Instead, by concentrating on the tradition of Max Weber and Karl Marx, these research groups focused on processes of rationalization, technical progress, and structural change and they took a historical-interpretative perspective (Schmidt 1980, p. 268).

It was such research in which the next generation of sociologists acquired its methodical skills and trained as sociologists. One of the members of this next generation, Ralf Dahrendorf, however, criticized this predominant orientation of sociology toward areas such as industry, businesses, families, youth, and municipal organization. He asked whether this was not a renunciation of the idea of creating a more comprehensive picture of society, an "anxious withdrawal from the unresolved whole of the society we are living in?" (Dahrendorf 1974, p. 116)

## The Role Debate

It was also Dahrendorf who, at the end of the 1950s, provoked one of the first major controversies within "German post-war Sociology" (Fischer 2010; Moebius 2018b) and thus brought theory back into the focus of sociological attention. This controversy became known as the Role Debate. In 1958, with the support of Schelsky, Dahrendorf became professor in Hamburg. That same year, the 29-year-old professor Dahrendorf published a text entitled "Homo sociologicus" in the *Kölner Zeitschrift für Soziologie und Sozialpsychologie*. Thereby, he caused a long-lasting controversy within sociology. Central in this controversy was a critique on Talcott Parsons. Dahrendorf (1958/2017) criticized the image of humans and of society that was inherent in the structural functionalist's version of the *homo sociologicus* and that—according to Dahrendorf—did not take into account social change and conflicts. Beyond his critique on Parsons, he also sharply attacked role theory and in this way made role theory known in Germany. He claimed that this sociological view reduces human beings to their roles. Although humans are alienated by society, beyond society humans are still free. Dahrendorf's thesis, which is reminiscent of Georg Simmel, is that individuality cannot be entirely reduced to social processes, there's always a non-sociated part of the individual. During the following years, the debate revolved around the relationship between society and individual freedom. König ([1961/1962] 2002, p. 24), for instance, turned against the mutual maneuvering-out of individual freedom and society. According to König, the individual can only become free through living together with others. Other critics of the controversy, which lasted into the mid-1970s, were Arnold Gehlen, Helmut Schelsky, Helmuth Plessner, Heinrich Popitz, Hans Paul Bahrdt, Dieter Claessens (1921–1997), Friedrich Tenbruck (1919–1994), later on Peter L. Berger (1929–2017) and Thomas Luckmann (1927–2016), Frigga Haug (*1937) as well as Hans Peter Dreitzel (*1935), and Hans Joas (*1948) (Fischer 2010, pp. 80 f.). None of them agreed with Dahrendorf's position. Through the role debate, sociological pioneers such as Simmel or George Herbert Mead (1863–1931) were (re)discovered within German-speaking sociology, and the reception of Erving Goffman (1922–1982) began. The debate also had an effect on society. The role concept was widely received and enabled sociology to connect with a broader non-academic public (Fischer 2010, p. 82).

### The "Civil War" in West German Sociology

The aforementioned consensus between König, Schelsky, Horkheimer, and Adorno, the "founding constellation" (Lepsius 2017c, p. 83), dissolved at the end of the 1950s (Nolte 2000, pp. 264–267). Field-specific dynamics increasingly picked up speed. Attempts to demarcate, secure, and expand one's own position as well as the associated distinctions became increasingly apparent (Rehberg 1986, pp. 11–22; Schäfer 1996, pp. 385–387). Academic *and* political disagreements alternated. To put it simply, there were three political positions: left (Horkheimer/Adorno), liberal (König, Plessner), and conservative (Schelsky). The slumbering, latent lines of conflict between the leading sociologists now broke out openly. As Gunther Ipsen referred to it, there was a veritable "civil war" in sociology (Weyer 1986, p. 287).

Already in 1950/1951, but increasingly in 1958/1959, there were intense conflicts (Weyer 1984a, pp. 79–87; Weyer 1986). The most severe conflict revolved around the question of which organization should represent sociology in Germany. On the one hand, there was the German Sociological Association (GSA), which belonged to the International Sociological Association (ISA). On the other hand, there was the German section of the *Institut International de Sociologie* (IIS), founded in 1893 by René Worms and revived in 1949 by the Italian fascist Corrado Gini (1884–1965). The IIS understood itself as opposed to the ISA and as the only legitimate professional representation. The German section of the IIS was founded in 1951 and right from the beginning it housed sociologists who had been active in Germany during National Socialism (Weyer 1986, pp. 292–297). Even if in the GSA, too, there were people who had been active during the Nazi regime, the German section of the IIS understood its role more and more as a reservoir of sociologists who had been committed to the "Third Reich." Present at the founding meeting were, for example, Gunther Ipsen, Arnold Gehlen, Karl Valentin Müller, Helmut Schelsky, Kurt Stegmann (1901–1962), and Wilhelm Brepohl (1893–1975). Hans Freyer became their speaker (Weyer 1984a, pp. 81–82). Their aim was to oppose the "Americanization" of sociology. They also wished for a conservative turn in the GSA, which, however, did not occur. On the contrary, due to the change of the executive board of the GSA in 1955, when Helmuth Plessner was elected as the new president, a conservative turn of the GSA seemed increasingly unlikely (Weyer 1986, p. 298).

The conflict became even more serious when the German section of the IIS wanted to hold a congress in Nuremberg in 1958, in competition with the GSA. Against the objection of Schelsky, Plessner and König tried to prevent the congress. Schelsky then withdrew from the GSA. Furthermore, he was disappointed because he himself had ambitions of becoming president of the GSA. He openly broke with König. Students of König, in turn, accused Schelsky of a continuing influence of NS ideologies in his work. König also criticized Schelsky for opening the Social Research Center to *völkisch*-sociologists such as Ipsen, Müller, and Karl-Heinz Pfeffer. The escalation of the dispute and the end of the former cooperation, at least at a personal level, between König and Schelsky, was prompted by the appointment of Karl-Heinz Pfeffer to Münster (Weyer 1984a, p. 85). Even Schelsky had previously referred to Pfeffer as a "convinced Nazi," but nevertheless supported his appointment. König tried to prevent the appointment, but failed.[12]

The controversy described above shows that the debates of those engaged in the process of refounding sociology after 1945 revolved not only around the institutional development of sociology. It was not only about science policy, organizations, or chairs. Behind this was "usually also a dispute about the intellectual profile of the discipline" (Nolte 2000, p. 240) and a conflict about coping with the past. Thus, the "civil war" was also of crucial importance for the question of how West German sociology dealt with the role of sociology in National Socialism (Nolte 2000, pp. 239–244.).[13]

## 1959–1968

What remained of the controversy over GSA and IIS? The GSA was eager to take the conflicting political and ideological ideas to another level. The hope was to mitigate the political and methodological contrasts and to lead them in a scientific direction that would be beneficial for the further institutionalization of the GSA. Attempts were made to "objectivize the

---

[12] To some extent, the conflict between Schelsky and König goes back to the 1930s. Most likely it was Schelsky who had criticized a book by König in a National Socialist student magazine in 1935 and thus put his life at risk. For many decades König did not know who the author was (Neumann and Schäfer 1990, p. 238).

[13] These debates on the reappraisal of the past continue to this day (Christ and Suderland 2014) and will be taken up in Chap. 6.

conflicts at the level of a theory of science and an internal workshop of the GSA was convened in Tübingen in October 1961 that initiated the so-called Positivism Dispute" (Weyer 1984a, p. 86).

## Positivism Dispute

A result of the "civil war in sociology" was the Positivism Dispute (Dahms 1994, pp. 320–403; Ritsert 2010).[14] The beginning of the dispute goes back to a workshop in March 1957 (Link 2015; Demirović 1999, pp. 761–770), to which Adorno had invited outstanding social scientists. "The persons who met in Frankfurt on March 1, 1957 represented the difficult social constellations in the West German social sciences of the post-war period, with two conflicting parties particularly noteworthy: those returning from exile, such as Adorno, and those 'left at home' during the Nazi regime, such as Elisabeth Noelle-Neumann. Some of them had become involved with the regime or had come to an arrangement with it, others had been persecuted by the Nazis. Both knew about the past of the other group" (Link 2015, p. 103). The meeting in Frankfurt marked the break with the "empirical consensus" of the consolidation phase of sociology in West Germany, because now "past political differences as well as the profound epistemological differences between the individual actors resurfaced" (Link 2015, pp. 126–127).

The successor of Plessner and newly elected president of the GSA in 1959, Otto Stammer (1900–1978) from Berlin, wished to overcome the conflicts. He invited leading representatives of the various positions to a further meeting in October 1960 (cf. Demirović 1999, p. 799): Adorno and Horkheimer, König, Freyer, Gehlen, Schelsky, Dahrendorf, and Carl Jantke (1909–1989), as well as Bergstraesser, Wilhelm Emil Mühlmann (1904–1988), and Plessner. However, also this meeting was not a success and fully revealed the dissent (cf. Demirović 1999, pp. 799–804). In addition to the political disagreements, there were also methodological points of conflict. The question was, whether sociology should rather have a philosophical or empirical character (Strubenhoff 2017, p. 6). Although most of the sociologists of that generation were also philosophically trained and continued to pursue philosophy (Plessner, for example, was

---

[14] However, the "civil war" was only the immediate manifestation. The real conflict goes back to controversies between the Frankfurt School and the logical positivists of the Vienna Circle in the 1930s and 1940s, see in detail the first part of the book by Dahms (1994).

also president of the German Philosophical Association in 1950), others, like König, endeavored to detach sociology strictly from its philosophical roots and to bring it closer to economics.

Finally, it was agreed to hold a meeting in Tübingen in October 1961. Dahrendorf was to lead the discussion. He chose his former teacher from the London School of Economics (LSE), Karl Popper (1902–1994), as the main speaker, who was to give a lecture on the "Logik der Sozialwissenschaften" ("The Logic of the Social Sciences"). The co-lecture was to be given by Adorno. Dahrendorf held the slightly "fanciful" assumption that moral and political differences could be dealt with by a discussion of methods (Dahms 1994, p. 323). Positivism was primarily understood as the orientation of the social sciences toward scientific methods. Already in earlier years, Adorno and Horkheimer had criticized these methods as "objectification." The dispute itself, however, was less about positivism per se. Popper himself was not even a positivist but a Critical Rationalist (Dahms 1994, pp. 325–337). In fact, Popper explicitly opposed positivism and the idea to model the social sciences after the natural sciences (Dahms 1994, pp. 341–343). According to him, science starts off from problems, not from collecting data.

The dispute was rather about fundamental problems of a theory of science and *Werturteilsfreiheit* (freedom from value judgements). So, a controversial point was that Adorno did not want to limit critique to methods alone, but also wanted it to be understood as a critique of society. Popper and Adorno also differed in their theoretical argumentation: Popper defended deduction as the principle of theoretical statements, Adorno the principle of dialectic (Ritsert 2010, p. 113). However, the positions between Adorno and Popper were not so far apart. They agreed in their critique of Mannheim's sociology of knowledge as well as of scientism. Nevertheless, they did not get along. Actually, they talked past each other.

It was only afterwards that the lectures were perceived as a dispute and a controversy over the relationship between theory and emancipatory practice (Demirović 1999, p. 810). On the one hand, this was related to the publication of the lectures in 1969: Adorno wrote an excessively long introduction that annoyed Popper. On the other hand, the next generation, students of Popper and Adorno, joined in: Hans Albert (*1921) and Jürgen Habermas. Habermas described Popper as a positivist; Adorno followed him in his introduction and criticized that the positivists would only describe the status quo of society and thus affirm it. He argued that this was also ideological, even if Critical Rationalism actually claimed that it was not ideological. According to Adorno, it was not enough to establish facts; one had to interpret them and reflect upon them philosophically. Therefore, society cannot be explored by scientific methods alone. Society was not so unanimous, was not a thing, but contradictory, always to be seen in larger contexts. Adorno shifted the debate: If it was initially about the relationship between theory and practice, now the focus was on the distinction between theory and empirical research. The positions of Popper and Habermas, in turn, were not as far apart as Habermas' statements suggested (Giddens 1985, p. 99; Strubenhoff 2017).

As a result, the Positivism Dispute led to the peculiar effect that sociologists working in behavioral theory tried to refer to Popper, something that proved not only untenable but also relatively fruitless (Schmid 1993, p. 53). Other approaches that argued in Popper's "line" (Schmid 1993, p. 54), such as rational choice theory, were more successful. Sociologists that focused on empirical social research, in particular the Cologne school, were more likely to support positions they associated with Popper. The sociologists in Frankfurt, especially Adorno, who had also pushed empirical research in the 1950s, turned their attention increasingly to theory and philosophical reflection of society as an antagonistic totality.

The differentiation between theory and empirical social research forced by the Frankfurt School revealed new similarities between the left and conservatives: Interestingly, a similar shift from empirical social research to theory could also be observed in Schelsky's conservative position. He used this theoretical position to highlight the specific approach of German sociology. Thus, he demanded more theory in the tradition of German philosophy against an "American-Austrian" analytical and logical-empiricist style. Referring to Kant, he described his orientation as a "transcendental theory of society" (Schelsky 1959, p. 95). By this he understood a kind of meta-perspective, which was not in opposition to other theories or to empirical social research, but was intended to be a kind of instance of meta-reflection (Wöhrle 2019, pp. 252–253). He vehemently opposed the accusation that German sociology would become provincial if it did not orient itself toward developments in American sociology. For him, emulating the USA would implicitly recognize its dominant model character and thus lead to an explicit provincialism of sociology in Germany (Schelsky 1959, p. 26).

The controversies described were key moments in the consolidation of sociology in Germany and of a "process of self-understanding in German sociology" (Matthes 1978, p. 19; Schmid 2004, p. 24). They shaped a good part of the discussions over the following decades and demonstrated that the sociological field continued to differentiate itself. In 1959, in an analysis of the state of sociology, Schelsky concluded as follows: "There is no common, binding scientific basis for the discipline [...] in the German sociology of today [...]. It is therefore understandable that today every sociologist in Germany would soon regard every other sociologist as 'not a real sociologist'" (Schelsky 1959, pp. 24–25).

As we shall see, the Positivism Dispute led to further major controversies which shaped the sociological field since the end of the 1960s (Moebius 2018b): first the debate carried out under the headline "late capitalism or industrial society?" (*Spätkapitalismus oder Industriegesellschaft?*), later the "Habermas-Luhmann debate," and subsequently the "debate on theory comparison" (*Theorienvergleichsdebatte*) in the mid-1970s (Kneer and Moebius 2010). The effects of these debates can still be observed today (Greshoff 2010, p. 210; Greshoff et al. 2007), as we will see at the end of this book.

## Generational Change

As the *Role Debate* and the *Positivism Dispute* had already shown, by the end of the 1950s and the beginning of the 1960s, an institutional and generational change could be observed. This generational change in the 1960s (Siegfried 2003) was accompanied by a profound change in the education system (Kenkmann 2003), especially with respect to higher education. New universities were founded and others re-established. Whereas there were 14 universities in 1949, there were 62 universities in Germany in 2000 (see Lundgreen et al. 2008, p. 69). In the Western European and North American countries, the number of students increased considerably. In Germany, too, this was due to the economic upswing and educational reforms. These developments brought about significant changes in West German sociology: Together with the changing spirit of this time, sociology experienced a tremendous boom. At some universities, sociology could be studied as a major or a separate diploma for the first time. The first diploma course in sociology took place in Frankfurt in 1954/55 and shortly afterwards in Berlin in 1956. More and more students wanted to study sociology, so that it became a hugely popular fashion subject, a so-called *Massenfach* in the 1960s (Lepsius 2017d, p. 120). The number of sociology chairs rose from 12 in 1955 to 25 in 1960 (Nolte 2000, p. 251). Between 1961 and 1969 the number tripled (Bude and Neidhardt 1998, p. 405).

In 1960, sociology was taught at 17 universities and there were about 150 academic sociological positions, by 1970 there were already 900 positions (Lepsius 2017e, p. 197). On the one hand, this boom was advantageous for the discipline. It spurred differentiation and specialization. On the other hand, the boom brought about problems. The development and expansion of the discipline required a considerable amount of time and resources for organization and administration (Lepsius 2017e, p. 198; 2017d, p. 119), at the expense of research.

The number of assistant positions grew, too, so that sociology was no longer only marked by the full professor (*Ordinarius*) of sociology at a university. The role of the professor, the "German Mandarin" (Fritz Ringer), was transformed from that of a scholar (*Gelehrter*) to a mere expert (*Fachmensch*) in sociology. Sociology was transformed due to the increasing demand for empirical social research.

The GSA also changed. This became evident at the 14th *Soziologentag* in Berlin in 1959. The meeting of the GSA was no longer a discussion group of scholars, but a congress of specialists, focusing on specific fields of sociology. Already in the mid-1950s, "expert committees" had been founded, which were called "sections" (*Sektionen*) from the 1970s onwards. In addition to industrial sociology, sociology of religion, and issues of education and training, a committee for ethnosociology was also involved in the congress. Further committees that were founded in the 1950s and 1960s dealt with methods of empirical social research, the family, youth, organizations, Eastern Europe, and mass communication (Borggräfe 2018). The foundation of these expert committees or sections entailed a further differentiation, specialization, and professionalization of the discipline.

The congress offered the next generation of sociologists a stage. Some of the members of this generation were elected to the executive board of the GSA: Hans Paul Bahrdt, Ralf Dahrendorf, and Heinrich Popitz. "The transition from the 'founding generation' to the 'post-war generation' was thus initiated" (Lepsius 2017d, p. 111). In addition to Dahrendorf, Popitz, and Bahrdt, Erwin K. Scheuch, Renate Mayntz (*1929), Jürgen Habermas, and Niklas Luhmann should also be mentioned as important figures of the new generation.[15]

Ralf Dahrendorf studied in Hamburg and at the London School of Economics (LSE). He obtained his first PhD with a thesis about Marx,

---

[15] Mayntz, Habermas and Luhmann will be discussed in more detail in the next chapter. Therefore, they are not yet introduced here.

supervised by Josef König (1893–1974) and Siegfried Landshut, and his second PhD at the LSE (Meifort 2017, pp. 50–57), studying with Thomas H. Marshall (1893–1981) and completing his degree with his study *Unskilled Labour in British Industry* (1956). Dahrendorf attended the seminars of Karl Popper with great intensity. Together with a fellow student at the LSE, David Lockwood (1929–2014), a prominent theorist of social stratification, he became more and more interested in conflict theory.

Dahrendorf's rapid career accelerated in 1958 when, at the age of 29, he received a call for a chair in sociology at the *Akademie für Gemeinwirtschaft* in Hamburg. One year later, he was on the board of the GSA (1967–1970 its president). In 1960, Dahrendorf was appointed to a chair in Tübingen, and in 1966 he received a call to a professorship at the University of Konstanz, which he had co-founded. He then entered politics and became a member of the liberal Free Democratic Party (FDP). From 1974–1984, he was director of the LSE. He was awarded numerous prizes and honorary titles, including the English nobility title of "Lord." In addition to role theory, one of Dahrendorf's main focuses was conflict theory. He was also one of the central mediators between Anglo-Saxon and German sociology. His book *Gesellschaft und Demokratie in Deutschland* (1965; *Society and Democracy in Germany*, 1967) became a sociological bestseller. Dahrendorf was also actively involved in education policy. In 1965, he entered in the discussions about expanding the education sector and pleaded for education to be acknowledged as a civil right.

Heinrich Popitz had initially worked at the Social Research Centre Dortmund, where, in the 1950s, Popitz and Hans Paul Bahrdt produced the much-respected publications in industrial sociology mentioned above. Popitz became professor in Basel (Switzerland) in 1959 and in Freiburg in 1964 (cf. Bröckling 2014). The main focus of his work was then no longer sociological research on industry, but rather norms, roles, and phenomena of power. His sociological perspective was founded in philosophical anthropology and shaped the profile of sociology in Freiburg for many decades (Eßbach 2014, p. 63).

Bahrdt was Plessner's successor in Göttingen in 1962. In addition to industrial sociology and sociology of bureaucracy, his main areas of research were urban sociology and sociology of science. He also made insightful contributions to the sociology of culture, everyday life, the family, and the environment. Bahrdt became president of the *Soziologisches Forschungsinstitut Göttingen* (SOFI, Sociological Research Institute Göttingen), which was founded in 1968. The institute was increasingly dedicated to industrial sociology, sociology of work, and educational sociology (Baethge and Schumann 2018; Brückweh 2019). From this research context, further classics of industrial sociology in Germany emerged: *Industriearbeit und Arbeiterbewusstsein* (1970, *Industrial Work and Worker Consciousness*) as well as *Das Ende der Arbeitsteilung?* (1984, *Limits of the Division of Labour?*) by Horst Kern (*1940) and Michael Schumann (*1937).

Erwin K. Scheuch, previously professor at Harvard, was appointed professor in Cologne in 1964 and from that time onwards increasingly influenced sociology there (Knebelspieß and Moebius 2019). It was he who further expanded quantitative social research in West Germany. At the same time, however, significant conflicts between Scheuch and König arose that intensified in 1968 due to their different assessments of the student protests. In the following years it was not so much König's wide and diversified understanding of sociology, but rather Scheuch's liberal-conservative view of sociology as a positivist, and in particular, quantitatively oriented science that for a long time shaped the perception of the Cologne School (Moebius 2015).

## The Transformation of the Sociological Field

The sociological field of the 1960s, and even more so of the 1970s, was increasingly shaped by the generation just mentioned—by sociologists who had been students, assistants, or staff members of König, Schelsky, Adorno, Horkheimer, Stammer, Abendroth, or Plessner after 1945.[16] The sociological "schools" became more differentiated and diversified, sociology as a whole more institutionalized and academicized. The "schools" were not so strongly divided in this generation of the so-called Forty-fivers themselves (Moses 2007, p. 55; Bude and Neidhardt 1998, p. 408). At the end of the war, the members of this generation had been between 15 and 25 years old. Most of the younger ones still had to go to war as anti-aircraft auxiliaries (*Flakhelfer*). They were already old enough to come

---

[16] In 1955, Stammer took up the chair of sociology and political science in Berlin. From 1959 to 1963, he was chairman of the GSA. One of Stammer's greatest achievements for German sociology was the establishment of political sociology, of which he was the leading representative. Stammer, who held a guest lectureship at Columbia University in New York in 1954, was very familiar with political sociology in the USA and brought this knowledge to Germany. His students include Renate Mayntz, Karl Dietrich Bracher (1922–2016), Peter Weingart (*1941), Wolfgang Schluchter (*1938), and Christian Ludz (1931–1979).

face-to-face with the horrors of war, but still young enough to actively shape the new beginning of Germany (Moses 2007, p. 57). What the sociologists of this generation had in common, despite all their differences, was that they saw sociology as a means of social self-orientation and enlightenment. They had often acquired sociological knowledge and practice individually, coming from disciplines like philosophy or economics. Interestingly enough, despite ideological differences, their education often started with Marx. However, it was not a matter of neo-Marxism, but of a kind of "de-dramatization" of Marx (Bude and Neidhardt 1998, p. 409), of working out the sociological content of Marx (Lepsius 2017d, p. 120). Among other things, the potentials of conflict theory and the theory of alienation were elaborated.

International exchange programs that allowed this generation to gain experience abroad, mostly in the USA, were also of crucial importance (Gerhardt 2006, p. 77). It was René König, in particular, who sent his students to the USA, where they came in contact with new theories, such as structural functionalism, and with new methods. The younger generation turned its attention primarily to empirical research. The focus was less on general interpretations of the world or utopian ideologies than on specific objects and problems. The position was described by many of this generation as a "need for reality" and "applied enlightenment" (Bude and Neidhardt 1998, p. 410; Sahner 2000). As a result, sociology became increasingly involved in political processes such as educational reform. It acted as a consultant to politics and institutions and often provided data and vocabulary for the interpretation of social processes (Bude and Neidhardt 1998, p. 410).

The market for sociological publications was also changing. In addition to the journals *Kölner Zeitschrift für Soziologie und Sozialpsychologie* and *Soziale Welt*, other journals and handbooks were published (or re-launched): the journal *Sociologus*, originally founded by Richard Thurnwald (starting in 1951); the series *Frankfurter Beiträge zur Soziologie (Frankfurt Contributions to Sociology)* (from 1955 on); the *Lehr- und Handbuch der Soziologie (Text- and handbook of Sociology)* edited by Gehlen and Schelsky (1955); the special issues of the *Kölner Zeitschrift für Soziologie und Sozialpsychologie* (since 1956), *Soziologie (Lexicon of Sociology)* by König (1958), the multi-volume *Handbuch der empirischen Sozialforschung (Handbook of Empirical Social Research)*, also published by König (starting in 1962); various other book series and periodicals of individual institutes and expert committees

(Holzhauser et al. 2019). The world of publishing also began to focus on sociological publications. The Luchterhand publishing house in particular should be mentioned here. Between 1959 and 1977, Luchterhand published the series *Soziologische Texte (Sociological Texts)*, edited by Heinz Maus, Friedrich Fürstenberg (*1930), and Frank Benseler (*1929). In this series, numerous translations were published that made German sociologists familiar with the work of international sociologists, such as Émile Durkheim, Maurice Halbwachs (1877–1945), Lucien Goldmann (1913–1970), Talcott Parsons, C. Wright Mills (1916–1962), and George H. Mead. In the 1960s, Marxist authors such as Abendroth, Lukács, and Marcuse were increasingly published here, as were other writings that became central to the protests of 1968 (Römer 2018, p. 491). In the 1960s, the Suhrkamp publishing house also began publishing sociological books, which had a decisive influence on the intellectual debates in the Federal Republic of Germany and which rose to become one of the most renowned German publishing houses in the social sciences and humanities.

As mentioned, for many members of the new generation, their first contact with sociology was with industrial sociology. At the beginning of the 1960s, other topics emerged and became important, too. This was also a result of social developments: Between 1963 and 1969 there were political turbulences and several changes of government. In October 1962, the magazine *Der Spiegel* had reported that in the case of an attack by the Warsaw Pact, West Germany could not defend itself and that the strategy of the Minister of Defense, Franz Josef Strauß (CSU), was going in the wrong direction. The Minister of Defense then ordered the arrest of the journalists as well as the occupation and search of their office by the police. The protests against this attack on the freedom of the press led to a crisis in the government. Ludwig Erhard (CDU) became the new Chancellor. The protests also led to an increasing politicization of the youth, which I will discuss in more detail in the next chapter. In 1966, Kurt Georg Kiesinger (CDU) was elected Chancellor by 340 of 447 members of the *Bundestag*, in a grand coalition of CDU and SPD, and Willy Brandt (SPD) became Vice-Chancellor. Thus, a former member of the NSDAP (Kiesinger) and a resistance fighter (Brandt) faced each other. As a result of the grand coalition, the opposition had hardly any significance in parliament. Especially the academic youth, the students, expressed unease about this situation. Together with pacifist, Christian, and socialist groups, they formed a movement that considered itself an "extra-parliamentary opposition" (*Außerparlamentarische Opposition*, APO) and made itself increasingly heard, especially in the years around 1968.[17]

The economic upswing, which lasted until 1966, had visible consequences for the social mobility and the purchasing power of large groups of the West German population. One sign of the new prosperity was, for example, the incipient growing popularity of individual tourism. West Germany was in transition toward a service economy. It was increasingly integrated in the international Western community (Conze 2009, pp. 227–330; Wolfrum 2006b, pp. 97–101). Consumption and youth were significantly influenced by this. Commerce and counter culture merged at times (Schildt 2007, p. 53). Western-inspired youth cultures, such as the hippies, and the reception of rock and pop music developed. The Beatles' performance in Hamburg's "Star Club" in 1962 was legendary. In the field of art as well as in film, new developments began, see for example the New German Cinema (directors were among others Alexander Kluge, Wim Wenders, and Rainer Werner Fassbinder). Inspired by the historical avant-garde (Dada, Surrealism), protest art was developed; but there was also the revaluation of "mass culture," Pop Art, and Fluxus. Germany also grew on the whole: There was a veritable baby boom, so that in the 1960s Germany grew by 5 million people to 61 million.

The education sector had also undergone changes. These changes were stimulated by the increasing economic demand for scientific and technical knowledge. However, an OECD study confirmed that in international comparison in terms of its education policy Germany was a developing country. Critics like Dahrendorf, for example, declared that in Germany there was an "education catastrophe" (Picht 1964; Kenkmann 2003, pp. 403–407). In particular, children from working-class families, children from the countryside, and girls were disadvantaged. At the heart of the debates was also the justified assumption that education increasingly determined the social status of individuals. Discussions about education were not only about improving the education system; rather, some debates were concerned more with economic growth and a victory in the Cold War, also in the field of education. Still others linked the "educational revolution" with a reform of the entire society.

The number of students doubled between 1965 and 1975. From 1965 onwards, the higher education system expanded increasingly. The

---

[17] This will be discussed further in the next chapter.

expansion of the education sector was also motivated by the idea that social development could be the result of scientific and rational planning (Ruck 2003, pp. 376–378). There was a real "planning euphoria" (Herbert 2014, pp. 805–809; Ruck 2003), which also led to the expansion of academic institutions. "The belief in progress based on science and technology was a strong bond between East and West. That the future could be planned, that prosperity could be increased indefinitely, and that the prospects were bright, were widespread certainties both here and there, albeit under the condition that the respective model of order would gain the upper hand" (Herbert 2014, p. 825).

The expansion of the education system led to a veritable expansion of higher education that again led to the founding of numerous new universities (Kenkmann 2003) and also boosted sociology of education.[18] Furthermore, the expansion of education (*Bildungsexpansion*) had an impact on the publishing field, the number of inexpensive study books and textbooks, now often available in paperback format, rose rapidly (Römer 2018, p. 493). The expansion of education benefited especially children of employees and women of the middle classes. The proportion of female students grew successively: in 1960 their proportion was 28%, in 1970 36% and in 1989 41% (Wolfrum 2006b, p. 101; see also Frevert 2003, p. 650).

For the majority of the new generation of sociologists the preferred topics were now in line with social developments: social stratification and social inequality (with a focus on unequal educational opportunities), social mobility, public opinion, education, social policy, social planning, conflict, leisure and consumption, youth, and urban life (Nolte 2000, p. 267).

Until 1965, full employment prevailed in West Germany. In 1966/1967, however, there was an economic downturn. The prime objective of the grand coalition formed in 1966 was to overcome the economic crisis. Economic growth, to which citizens had already become accustomed, declined due to a lack of private and public investment. The unemployment rate increased. Industrial work increasingly became a field of political action that required sociological analysis. As a result, industrial sociology experienced a comeback that lasted well into the 1970s (Schmidt 1980, p. 271).

---

[18] One result of this new attention regarding education was among others the foundation of the Max Planck Institute for Human Development in 1963 on the initiative of Hellmut Becker (1913–1993). Its initial aim was to develop methods of educational research and to advice education policy scientifically.

From the mid-1960s onwards, as Paul Nolte has shown, alongside the already mentioned industrial sociology it was political sociology, sociological theory, and the "rediscovery" of the pioneers that became central sociological topics (Nolte 2000, p. 268). Concerning the pioneers: Max Weber in particular experienced a renaissance, which has made him the central figure of German sociology up to this day: In 1963, there was a special issue of the *Kölner Zeitschrift für Soziologie und Sozialpsychologie* on Weber. Books on Weber were published. The *Soziologentag* of 1964 in Heidelberg was held in honor of Weber's 100th anniversary. Speakers included Parsons, Ernst Topitsch (1919–2003), Raymond Aron (1905–1983), Herbert Marcuse, Reinhard Bendix (1916–1991), Georges Friedmann (1902–1977), and Adorno, who had been elected as the new president of the GSA in 1963. The "Forty-fivers" were also actively involved in this.[19]

One topic that was not, or only marginally, dealt with in the 1960s was still National Socialism. Nevertheless, it would have seemed quite obvious to deal with the Nazi past. There would have been occasions to do so: In 1961, the internationally noted trial of Adolf Eichmann, a key figure in the organization of the Holocaust, took place. 1963 saw the Frankfurt Auschwitz trials against former personnel of the Auschwitz concentration camp. However, the majority of Germans were not interested in coming to terms with the past; parts of the judiciary had delayed the trials, and dealing with National Socialism was seen as a kind of "disturbance of the peace." Far-right philosophy was still widespread and provided the breeding ground for the founding of the neo-Nazi party NPD (National Democratic Party of Germany) in 1964. This was directed against the *Gastarbeiter* (guest workers) brought into the country, but also against communism and "Americanism." The increasingly politicized students were also detested by the right-wingers. The past of the Nazi regime and the lack of *Vergangenheitsbewältigung* would have been sufficient material for sociological research. However, a sociology of National Socialism remained absent, although the student movement and the university

[19] Subsequently, it was in particular Wolfgang Schluchter, M. Rainer Lepsius (1928–2014), Reinhard Bendix, Friedrich Tenbruck, Wolfgang J. Mommsen (1930–2004), Johannes Winckelmann (1900–1985), Eduard Baumgarten (1898–1982), and Wilhelm Hennis (1923–2012), and later among others Dirk Kaesler (*1944), Johannes Weiß (*1941), Klaus Lichtblau (*1951), Hartmann Tyrell (*1943), Hubert Treiber (*1942), Stefan Breuer (*1948), and Hans-Peter Müller (*1951), who made Weber's work known and discussed it in Germany.

reform brought the discussion about the Nazi regime and the Nazi past into focus. But other important events did not come into sociological focus either, such as the separation of Germany, which was literally cemented by the construction of the *Berliner Mauer* (Berlin Wall) in 1961.

However, the common orientation of sociologists toward the "applied enlightenment," the renaissance of the founders and pioneers of sociology, and the further differentiation into special sociologies should not obscure the fact that the sociological field at the end of the 1960s was still permeated by struggles and tensions. Everyone agreed that sociology had an enlightening role. But their understanding of enlightenment differed significantly. While theoreticians such as Jürgen Habermas associated the enlightenment with a decidedly critical and emancipatory perspective on society, others, such as Niklas Luhmann, saw the enlightenment as observation and self-reflection, as an enlightenment of the enlightenment. Moreover, the tensions in the sociological field that came to light again openly toward the end of the 1960s were not only related to the increasing differentiation and the struggles for interpretative power, but also to the increasing politicization of students (Siegfried 2018, p. 17)—a politicization that found its visible expression in the protests around 1968.

**Open Access** This chapter is licensed under the terms of the Creative Commons Attribution 4.0 International License (http://creativecommons.org/licenses/by/4.0/), which permits use, sharing, adaptation, distribution and reproduction in any medium or format, as long as you give appropriate credit to the original author(s) and the source, provide a link to the Creative Commons licence and indicate if changes were made.

The images or other third party material in this chapter are included in the chapter's Creative Commons licence, unless indicated otherwise in a credit line to the material. If material is not included in the chapter's Creative Commons licence and your intended use is not permitted by statutory regulation or exceeds the permitted use, you will need to obtain permission directly from the copyright holder.

CHAPTER 4

# Ups and Downs of Sociology in Germany: 1968–1990

## "1968"

Despite an economic prosperity phase that was only interrupted for a very short time, the 1960s saw political and cultural transformations (see in general Schildt et al. 2003). It was mainly adolescents and students who intended to start a revolt in 1968. The protest concerned many issues: The protest movement demanded a reform of education, and at the same time, the adolescents wanted to counterbalance the weakness of the parliamentary opposition through an *Außerparlamentarische Opposition* (APO, extra-parliamentary opposition). The movement also protested against the Vietnam War and for the civil rights movement in the USA. This, the West German protests had in common with the protests in the USA. For the West German 1968 generation, though, there was an additional decisive factor, namely the demand for a rigorous historical reappraisal of the Nazi regime. Many were opposed to the generation of their parents, who remained silent regarding the past. This became evident at school: Even history lessons often ended with the Weimar Republic and left out the Nazi era. The youth also demanded a condemnation of the numerous Nazi criminals who still held high-ranking positions. Many adolescents tried out alternative ways of life—they called for a more liberal sexuality as well as for women's emancipation and they held to post-materialist values that had already gained ground since the first halve of the 1960s. Moreover,

© The Author(s) 2021
S. Moebius, *Sociology in Germany*, Sociology Transformed,
https://doi.org/10.1007/978-3-030-71866-4_4

the protest movement criticized the alliances of the German government with dictatorships. In particular, the movement wanted to prevent the German Emergency Acts drafted and implemented by the grand coalition in Germany, which also contained a restriction of basic constitutional rights (cf. Borowsky 1998, p. 14). And some feared that the Emergency Acts would mean a new Enabling Act.

Numerous events contributed to giving the protests a "dynamic of their own" (Siegfried 2018, p. 9): During a demonstration against the visit of the Shah Mohammed Reza Pahlavi, the student Benno Ohnesorg was shot dead by a policeman on June 2, 1967, at the West-Berlin opera. This led to a new dynamic and an expansion of the wave of protest. Hence, regarding the FRG, the year 1967 must be considered as "the actual date" of the student protests (Frei 2008, p. 118). The protests intensified when the policeman who had shot the student was acquitted. As a result, some media, such as *Der Spiegel*, took sides with the protesters (Frei 2008, pp. 126–127). In addition, in April 1968 the sociology student Rudi Dutschke, a well-known spokesman for the students, became victim of a serious assassination attempt. The press that belonged to the Springer publishing house, above all the populist newspapers *BILD* and *WELT*, was held responsible for the attempted assassination because it had been harassing the students since 1967 and had stylized Dutschke as the "public enemy number one." Thereafter, in many cities violent anti-Springer demonstrations were held. One month later, in May 1968, the government issued the controversial German Emergency Acts. The protests of the extra-parliamentary opposition (APO) were at their peak.

The situation was extremely tense, above all in Berlin and Frankfurt, but also in other cities. The core of the extra-parliamentary opposition (APO) was the *Sozialistische Deutsche Studentenbund* (SDS, Socialist German Student Union), which had been part of the Social Democratic Party (SPD) until 1960 (cf. Fichter and Lönnendonker 2018). The SDS had initially demanded equality of education, a reform of education, and democratization of the universities—decisions should not only be made by professors. In the late 1950s, it had also been actively opposed to the rearmament of Germany with nuclear weapons. The fact that the SDS was expelled from the SPD increased its attractiveness for critical, left-wing students to get involved in the activities of the SDS throughout the 1960s. Many of the 68ers were students of the social sciences and later were to become professors of sociology or political sciences (especially at the universities of Bielefeld, Bremen, Frankfurt, Göttingen, Hanover, Kassel, Münster, or Osnabrück).

The 1968 student movement brought sociology into the limelight. As a subject of study, sociology gained enormously in importance, which was connected with the growing need for social reflection in all areas of life. Parts of the SDS considered themselves to be part of the international labor movement; this was in particular the stance taken by the Marxist social scientist Wolfgang Abendroth in Marburg. The other part, which was closer to the Critical Theory of Frankfurt, saw itself more as part of the "emerging New Left" in Western Europe (Demirović 1999, p. 889), which distinguished itself from both the anti-communism of the West and the so-called real socialism of the East. The students read anarchist literature as well as Marx, Leon Trotsky, Rosa Luxemburg, Sigmund Freud, Wilhelm Reich, Georg Lukács, and authors of Critical Theory, whose writings were perceived as the "theoretical superstructure" of the protest movement (cf. Demirović 1999, pp. 856–910). They were particularly enthusiastic about Herbert Marcuse and his books *Der eindimensionale Mensch* (1964, *One-Dimensional Man*, 1967) and *Eros and Civilization* (originally published in English, 1955), as well as pirate copies of the *Dialectic of Enlightenment* by Horkheimer and Adorno.

New journals and book series were established. The concept of culture was expanded. Pop culture and everyday culture underwent a revaluation; the then prevailing "legitimate culture" (Bourdieu) was revealed as a mere ideology and the separation between high and low culture was deconstructed. It was not only the "Summer of Love," but also the "long summer of theory" (Felsch 2015). The youth read and discussed much more than the generation before. According to the historian Detlef Siegfried, "1968" was also a "reading movement" that created a veritable "market for Marx" (Siegfried 2018, pp. 66–69). This benefited the publishing industry too. The production of sociological books increased. The Rowohlt publishing house with its series "rowohlts deutsche enzyklopädie" (rde) had dominated the academic reading public in the 1950s and 1960s. It was being replaced by the so-called Suhrkamp-culture (especially the "Regenbogen-Reihe" (rainbow colored books) of the "edition Suhrkamp," later the famous "Suhrkamp Taschenbuch Wissenschaft" (stw)) since the beginning of the 1960s.

New journals were established, such as the social science journal *Leviathan* that was founded in 1973 (Blomert 2018) and the *Soziologische Revue*, founded in 1977, in which new books were presented and discussed (Hartmann 2018). Sociological topics were also discussed in the general public. Sociology had become a fashion, indeed an "existentialist" academic discipline, which was studied for reasons of political self-realization and because of the possibility of discussing one's own social future against a theoretical background. "In the student movement, 'society' was not only discovered as an analytical category, but even more so as an existential category" (Bude 1994, p. 246). As studies from the 1960s show, most students of sociology as well as most participants of the student movement in general came from the milieus of those who experienced upward mobility (cf. Reimann and Kiefer 1969). As historiography has demonstrated on many occasions, in times of movements of cultural and social transformation, such as the avant-garde around 1920, those who are most anti-bourgeois are often themselves part of the bourgeoisie. This seems to be partly the case in Germany in 1968 too. Perhaps it was also a kind of class struggle between the upwardly mobile and the established, in which the social sciences were the "vehicle for the upwardly mobile" (Bude 1994, p. 249).

## Late Capitalism or Industrial Society?

From April 8 to April 11, 1968, the 16th German *Soziologentag* was held in Frankfurt am Main on the theme of "Late capitalism or industrial society?" This was right at the heart of the wave of the student movement. Adorno and Ludwig von Friedeburg had prepared the congress, Dahrendorf had been president of the GSA since 1967. First and foremost, this *Soziologentag* was concerned with the question of whether the term "industrial society" or, rather, the term "late capitalism" would be better suited to capture the current social development. Adorno stated that the two were dialectically interwoven. This expressed precisely the contradictory character of contemporary society; "according to the state of its productive *forces* it is an industrial society, in its *relations of* production it is capitalism" (Adorno 1969, p. 18; emphasis in original).

However, this question was subsequently discussed only rarely. Instead, the controversy between Dahrendorf, Adorno, and other members of the Institute for Social Research flared up again. The contentious issues included the question of the necessity of domination, the connection between theory and critique, as well as the relationship between theory and practice (cf. Demirović 1999, pp. 837–844). In his lecture, Adorno made it clear that the capitalist system had spread in such a way that "no location outside of the gears can be obtained from which the spook can be named; the lever can only be applied to its own inconsistency" (Adorno 1969, p. 25). Adorno did not see this as a renunciation of political practice. And it was the role of sociology to point out the inconsistencies. Adorno's hypothesis, however, was strongly refuted by Dahrendorf in his opening speech. He objected that an overly radical critique of society would not lead to emancipatory change, but would rather block the path to practice. Basically, however, the dispute was again about the confrontation between positivism and dialectical sociology, as some observers soon noticed (Demirović 1999, p. 844). Thus, during this *Soziologentag*, too, Critical Theory was attacked: "It was a matter of excluding it from sociology because of it being unscientific and not empirical, a matter of disavowing it politically as totalitarian or rejecting it as impractical and pessimistic" (Demirović 1999, p. 849).

Dahrendorf soon resigned from his presidential office in 1969 because he changed to the sphere of federal politics. First, he became a deputy Secretary of Foreign Relations within the federal government, followed by his membership in the European Commission 1970–1974. He later became director of the London School of Economics (1974–1984) and professor of Social Sciences at the University of Konstanz again.[1]

## CRITICAL THEORY AND THE PROTESTS OF "1968"

The *Soziologentag* that took place in April 1968 was experienced as a disappointment by many students. There was a partial alienation between the students and sociology, and the relation to Critical Theory was ambivalent. At the beginning of the 1968 movement, Critical Theory at first seemed to remain no longer "just" theory, but seemed to become a "practical" venture. In the early days of the protests, the Frankfurt School, especially Adorno, Marcuse, and Habermas, had become political and moral authorities with a public impact and they had become important suppliers of theory for the revolt of the youth. There were numerous attempts to derive a political practice from Critical Theory. In the further course of the protests, however, the relation between the students and Critical Theory ended in a disagreement. There were diverging

---

[1] He was in the 1960s co-founder and has already been professor of the University of Konstanz, see Chap. 3. From 1987 to 1997 he was Warden of St Antony's College at the University of Oxford.

assessments of theory and practice. Adorno warned against pointless actionism. Habermas even accused parts of the student movement of being "left fascists" because of their provocation of manifest violence (Habermas 2008, p. 148; Demirović 1999, p. 920). The accusation of "Leftist Fascism" was undifferentiated and was taken up all too readily by the conservative forces and the government (cf. Abendroth 1968, p. 133). An expert on Critical Theory, Alex Demirović (1999, p. 934), has summarized Habermas' position as follows: Habermas accused the students of completely misinterpreting the social situation. The situation was not revolutionary, although many students believed it was. In Habermas' view they suffered from a delusion; after all, neither did the broad masses of the population share the students' indignation, nor was there any unity between students and workers, so that it was only a *Scheinrevolution* (pseudo-revolution). Since then "Habermas's name [...] was taboo because of his criticism of tendencies toward a 'Leftist Fascism' in the student movement. Whoever mentioned his name, nevertheless, as I did, had to reckon with the same fate of being shunned. In other classes, the exegesis of Marx's texts dominated over all substantial problems" (Joas 2005, p. 163).

The students, on the one hand, began to disrupt the lectures and wanted to politicize the universities, while Adorno, on the other hand, emphasized the autonomy of academia as an area of freedom. Finally, activists accused Critical Theory of being authoritarian and elitist itself. They called for a reorganization of the Institute for Social Research so that students could organize their studies themselves. Finally, in December 1968, students occupied Adorno's Sociological Seminar (Demirović 1999, pp. 941–946). Adorno called the police, who cleared the Institute. He criticized the "pure nonconceptual practicism" of the students (Demirović 1999, p. 916). In the further course of events, the students demanded a public self-criticism of Adorno. In a lecture with 1000 listeners, they shouted "*Nieder mit dem Denunzianten-Ordinarius*" ("Down with the denunciator-professor"). Female students from the *Basisgruppe Soziologie* ("action group sociology," a political student's group), with bared breasts, tried to kiss Adorno (Demirović 1999, p. 947). On the blackboard they wrote: "*Wer nur den lieben Adorno läßt walten, der wird den Kapitalismus ein Leben lang erhalten*" ("Whoever lets dear Adorno rule, will keep capitalism alive") (Siegfried 2018, p. 97). Adorno left the lecture hall and cancelled the lecture until further notice. Four months later he died of a heart attack. But Critical Theory continued to have an effect elsewhere. It had a broad impact, be it in other disciplines such as education, in shared student flats, or in the feuilleton or radio (cf. Boll 2004, pp. 159–187).

The protest movement was at its peak in May 1968, but at the same time its "decay" started to become apparent (see Borowsky 1998, p. 20). Neither could the trade unions be persuaded to go on strike, nor could a broader mass of people be won over to a far-reaching change. After the attempted assassination of Dutschke, the leftist movement had begun to split up more and more into different groups. Some parts radicalized and founded the terrorist organizations "2 June Movement" (that carried out bank robberies, kidnappings, and assassination attempts until 1980, and especially the "Red Army Faction" (RAF, more on that below). In 1970, the SDS disbanded. The larger part of the APO set out on the "long march through the institutions" propagated by Dutschke. What was meant by this was to bring about social change from within, through the influence in institutions. The APO continued to live on not only in the institutions, but also in the social movements of the 1970s and 1980s, the women's movement, anti-nuclear movement, environmental movement, and peace movement, as well as in the political party *Die Grünen* (The Greens), founded in 1980.

## New Research Institutes

As of the mid-1960s, numerous new research institutes were founded. They were, among other things, concerned with peace research, education, and Eastern Europe, although most of them focused on industry and labor. In Munich, for example, the Institut für Sozialwissenschaftliche Forschung (ISF, Institute for Social Science Research) was founded in 1965 (cf. Sauer 2018), the Institut für Arbeitsmarkt- und Berufsforschung (Institute for Employment Research) in Nuremberg in 1967, the Institut für Marxistische Studien und Forschungen (IMSF, Institute for Marxist Studies and Research) in Frankfurt and the Soziologische Forschungsinstitut (SOFI, Sociological Research Institute) in Göttingen both in 1968 (cf. Baethge and Schumann 2018; Brückweh 2019), 1969 the Wissenschaftszentrum Berlin (WZB, Berlin Social Science Center) (cf. Knie and Simon 2018). While the topics of work and industry were on the decline at the beginning of the 1960s, they gained importance again at the end of the 1960s due to a rise in unemployment. In addition, the SPD-led government that was newly elected in 1969 promoted and funded social research and hoped to gain insights into long-term technical and economic change (cf. Kern 1982, pp. 239–246). This was beneficial for empirical social research in general. In 1970, a study was conducted at the SOFI in Göttingen which led to a veritable renaissance of and to an "independent profile of German industrial sociology " (Schmidt 1980, p. 272): *Industriearbeit und Arbeiterbewußtsein (Industrial Work and Worker Consciousness)* by Horst Kern and Michael Schumann. The book dealt with the question of the interrelation of technology, development, new forms of work, and the consciousness of the workers.

Initiated by members of the German *Bundestag*, the *Wissenschaftszentrum Berlin* (WZB, Berlin Social Science Center) was founded in 1969. It was intended to provide a counterweight to Marxist currents and to serve as a center for social science planning and policy advice (cf. Knie and Simon 2018).

## New Universities

The number of students had increased immensely since the 1950s. This also increased the need to establish new universities and to reform the Higher Education system (Kenkmann 2003, pp. 415–423; Rohstock 2010). Moreover, Germany also wanted to remain competitive and not lose ground to the USA or the USSR in the field of science and research. The goal was "research *and* mass education" (Wehrs 2014, p. 41; emphasis in original). The expansion of education brought with it the establishment of numerous new universities and universities of applied sciences (*Fachhochschulen*). In 1962, universities were founded in Bochum and Regensburg. In addition, the so-called reform universities were established: In 1966 a university was founded in Konstanz, in 1969 in Bielefeld, and in 1971 in Bremen. As the new universities needed personnel, the number of professorships and other academic positions increased. "In the following decades, the habitus of the professoriate became more informal and permissive. Several of the [student] movement's spokespersons became professors at a very young age because the expansion of the HE [Higher Education] system needed personnel. Thus the professoriate moved politically to the left for the first time since 1848 revolution" (Duller et al. 2019, p. 77). Often these new positions were no longer powerful and almost independent chairs, but less well-equipped professorships, and in some cases the assistants and students had more and more say in the decision-making processes. However, the increase in participation also meant more work in administration and commissions, at the expense of research and career. "Many a young post-Sixties sociologist who believed in democracy and decision participation got caught up in the jungle of committees and paragraphs, only to reemerge too late for the pursuit of sociological excellence and perhaps even the advance of a career" (Knorr-Cetina 2005, p. 191).

The founding of new universities, the "boom in education" (Raphael 2003, p. 218; Kenkmann 2003), the opening of the universities to young people from the lower social classes, and the general political mood benefited most social sciences, including the institutionalization of sociology. In 1960, it was still possible to study sociology as a major at around 20 universities. By 1970, this number had increased to 60 universities. The number of sociology students increased, reaching its peak in the period 1969–1974 (Siefer and Abrahams 1994, p. 293). The number of classes also increased in line with the number of students (cf. Weischer 2004, pp. 247–250).

Society expected sociology to provide interpretations and advice. This also affected the market for and the style of sociological books. There was a "great demand" for social science literature, encouraged by the "growing educated knowledge" (Raphael 2003, p. 222). Publishers hoped to profit from the sociological diagnoses and promoted the spread of sociology, especially in the form of paperbacks. Some historians of sociology in Germany, such as Oliver Römer (2019), even assume that "1968" was only made possible by a sociology strengthened by the publishers. In any case, sociologists increasingly composed books that explicitly addressed a broader public (cf. Neun 2018). At the same time, the expansion of sociology at the universities led to the founding of new journals (see Römer 2018, p. 496): in 1972 the *Zeitschrift für Soziologie* and the already mentioned journal *Leviathan*, in 1973 the journal *Soziologie* of the GSA, and in 1978 the *Soziologische Revue*). Sociology was now firmly established at the universities and had consolidated as an academic subject. Similar to the field of history, the expansion and growth led to a decline of the weight of "personal acquaintance" and of the "influence of individual powerful professors" and thus to a weakening of the "tendency towards conformity" (Raphael 2003, p. 219). This was another element on the path to a further pluralization of the discipline.

When the new universities were founded, some experimentation was also undertaken (cf. Kruse and Strulik 2019). The sociologists Dahrendorf and Schelsky were the leading figures in this. Dahrendorf was involved in the planning of the University of Konstanz in 1966. There he wanted to establish a pure research university, a "Princeton at the Lake of Konstanz." A novelty in Konstanz was the establishment of a Faculty of Social Sciences.

The foundation of Bielefeld University in 1969 was based on plans by Schelsky. He advocated a research university too. Every second year was to be a sabbatical year. In addition, interdisciplinary exchange was to be massively promoted. The dominant model was Wilhelm Humboldt's educational ideal, that is, to regard education not primarily as training, but as the development of personality and self-development of the person. In 1970, Schelsky became professor in Bielefeld. However, as the university did not develop as he had intended and as the ministry of education and cultural affairs, too, had reservations regarding his reform ideas and the special treatment of a university, he left Bielefeld disappointed after three years (cf. Bock 1986).

A unique feature of Bielefeld (to this day) was the establishment of a faculty that comprised only sociology, as was pushed by Schelsky, and which heralded a new level of professionalization (cf. Kruse and Strulik 2019). The founding of the *Zeitschrift für Soziologie* was also started by people from the faculty. "Bielefeld had sociology in its genes, one might say, and this translated into the faculty's considerable size, rich course offerings, and manifold activities," remembers Karin Knorr-Cetina (2005, p. 189). The Faculty of Sociology in Bielefeld was largely staffed by sympathizers of Schelsky. One of these sociologists, who was strongly supported by Schelsky and who received a professorship at the newly founded faculty, was Niklas Luhmann.

## The Habermas-Luhmann Debate

Jürgen Habermas and Niklas Luhmann both belong to the same generation. Both developed the basic principles of their grand theories in the 1970s; in the early 1980s, their respective major work *Soziale Systeme* (Luhmann 1984, *Social Systems*) and *Theorie des kommunikativen Handelns* (Habermas 1981, *The Theory of Communicative Action*) emerged from these theories.

Luhmann was initially an administrative official. Thanks to a scholarship to Harvard he had met Talcott Parsons in 1960 (cf. Horster 2005, p. 33). He was particularly interested in Parsons' structural functionalism. After the encounter with Parsons, Luhmann wrote a study on the sociology of organizations , which applied Parsons' theory to organizations and which at the time was highly innovative for this field of sociology. Schelsky invited Luhmann to give a lecture at the Social Research Center Dortmund and began to support him. Luhmann was given a position for sociological theory and sociology of law at the Social Research Center—or rather: He was "parked" in this position, as Luhmann himself described it (cf. Horster 2005, p. 38). In 1966, within one year, Luhmann completed his doctorate and habilitation with Dieter Claessens and Helmut Schelsky. In the meantime, he was already initiated into the plans for the foundation of Bielefeld University. Luhmann, too, gave a lecture at the 1968 *Soziologentag*. "Moderne Systemtheorien als Form gesamtgesellschaftlicher Analyse" ("Modern Systems Theories as a Form of Analysis of Society as a Whole") was the title of his lecture, which was only poorly attended. Initially, he was perceived only as a sociologist of organizations, of law and politics, not as a theorist, although he had already published several articles on the theory of social systems in journals in the late 1960s.[2]

The recognition of Luhmann as an independent theorist only really gained momentum through the so-called Habermas-Luhmann debate, especially through the book *Theorie der Gesellschaft oder Sozialtechnologie* (1971, *Theory of Society or Social Technology*), which emerged from this debate (Joas and Knöbl 2009, p. 251). The controversy was also a consequence of the students' disagreement with Critical Theory. After the eviction of the students from the Institute for Social Research by the police, initiated by Adorno, and the accusation of "Leftist Fascism" made by Habermas, many students were in search of theoretical alternatives. "In 1969, when students attempted to annul Critical Theory with Luhmann's systems theory, this developed into a seminar to which Habermas invited Luhmann" (Rammstedt 1999, p. 18).

Habermas had a fast career. As with most major theories originating in Germany, a close connection between sociology and philosophy can be found in his work (cf. Müller-Doohm 2014, pp. 55–96; Yos 2019). He wrote his doctoral thesis on the idealistic philosopher Friedrich Wilhelm Joseph Schelling (1775–1854) under Erich Rothacker (1888–1965), a philosopher and former NSDAP member. At the young age of 24, Habermas became known to a wider public because of a critique of the

---

[2] Karl Hermann Tjaden (1935–2021), professor in Marburg, since 1974 in Kassel, disciple of Abendroth, was one of the first who recognized the theoretical weight of systems-theoretical approaches and dedicated to them a criticism unsurpassed until today (Tjaden 1969; Tjaden 1971).

philosopher Martin Heidegger (1889–1976). This also marked the beginning of his career as a public intellectual (Müller-Doohm 2014, pp. 87–96; Yos 2019, pp. 102–112). Among his intellectual influences at that time were hermeneutics and Marxism as well as democratic liberalism (Joas and Knöbl 2009, pp. 202–207); later on he was also influenced by pragmatism, philosophy of language, and developmental psychology. In the 1950s, Habermas became a faculty member at the Institute for Social Research in Frankfurt. In 1961, still without a habilitation, he was appointed to a professorship of philosophy in Heidelberg. Since he seemed too Marxist to Horkheimer, Habermas could not habilitate in Frankfurt (Joas and Knöbl 2009, p. 201). Horkheimer tried more and more to detach himself and the Institute from Marxism. For Horkheimer, Habermas was too leftist. After unsuccessful inquiries with Schelsky, Plessner, and Arnold Bergstraesser, Habermas finally habilitated in 1961 with the Marxist social scientist Wolfgang Abendroth in Marburg (Müller-Doohm 2014, p. 129). The habilitation thesis dealt with the *Strukturwandel der Öffentlichkeit* (*The Structural Transformation of the Public Sphere*, published in 1962). In 1964, Habermas followed Horkheimer, who had refused to habilitate him, as professor of sociology and philosophy in Frankfurt. Increasingly, Habermas then began to stylize himself as a representative of Critical Theory (Joas and Knöbl 2009, p. 208) and took the first steps toward his seminal *Theory of Communicative Action*.

The controversy between Habermas and Luhmann revolved primarily around the issue of social criticism. Habermas' accusation against Luhmann was that systems theory assumed the function of legitimizing domination. Instead of solving political and practical questions with the help of discourse, systems theory recommended a social-technological analysis: "This theory represents, so to speak, the high form of a technocratic mind, which today allows defining practical questions from the very beginning as technical ones, thus withdrawing them from public and informal discussion" (Habermas 1971, p. 145). Luhmann, on the other hand, accused Habermas of simplifying the complexity of society by drawing contrasts that were too plain—such as those between practice and technology (Luhmann 1971, p. 399).

The fact that the students had called for an engagement with the theory of Luhmann was further evidence of the alienation between Habermas and the left-wing students. In Frankfurt he remained unpopular and was increasingly detested by the students because of his accusing them of being "Leftist Fascists." In 1971, he decided to go to Starnberg as co-director of the renowned *Max-Planck-Institut zur Erforschung der Lebensbedingungen der wissenschaftlich-technischen Welt* (Max Planck Institute for the Study of the Scientific-Technical World). As in the Positivism Dispute, the Habermas-Luhmann controversy again showed a tendency for theoretical controversies to move further and further away from the analysis of concrete social conditions.

## The Debate on Theory Comparison

The Habermas-Luhmann controversy left a deep dissatisfaction among sociologists and the public. Until the end of the 1980s, it led to new discussions about the relationship between theory and practice and to debates about the use of sociological knowledge (see Beck and Bonß 1989; Wingens 1988). In the sociological field, the controversy had also led to further divisions and confrontations. Now Habermasians and Luhmannians were facing each other. Further positions also emerged.

The sociologists were irritated by the multitude of available theories and positions. The 17th *Soziologentag*, held in Kassel in 1974, was intended to provide some clarification. The meeting was to deal with a comparison between leading theoretical positions. This led to a further debate that did not come to an end until the early 1980s. The comparison of the theories was accompanied by the expectation of transforming diversity into a "productive pluralism" and of establishing a "discursive unity of sociology" (Greshoff 2010, pp. 182–185). As with the positivism dispute, an attempt should be made to objectivize and "scientize" (*verwissenschaftlichen*) the intellectual struggles.

The following theoretical positions were represented: Habermas presented his theory of communicative action, Luhmann the functionalist systems theory, Joachim Matthes (1930–2009) advocated an interactionist phenomenological theory, Karl-Dieter Opp (*1937) represented the theoretical-behavioral approach, and Karl Hermann Tjaden stood for a historical-materialist theory. As a preparation, all of them had received a discussion paper on the topic of "evolution/social change." Not everyone felt represented; in particular, a decidedly critical sociology was missing and it was questioned why evolution was discussed instead of revolution (see the critiques in Krysmanski et al. 1975). No women were involved in the debate. For a long time, female sociologists were not actively involved in the *Soziologentage*, not even in the "debate on theory comparison" (*Theorienvergleichsdebatte*). Only after the founding of the section

"Women's Studies in the Social Sciences" in the GSA in 1979, the number of female lecturers at the *Soziologentag* increased. However, overall it can be said that despite the expansion of the personnel in the 1970s, a very strong dominance of male sociologists continued to prevail (Vogel 2006, p. 11).

The aim of the *Soziologentag*—namely to order and systematize the pluralism of theories and to transform it into a productive pluralism based on a sociological division of labor—was not fulfilled. Nevertheless, the debate resulted in the establishment of the GSA section on "Sociological Theory," founded in 1980.

The failure and lack of consequences of the comparison of theories led to a growing mood of crisis in sociology (cf. Leendertz 2010, pp. 52–55). In the USA, Alvin Gouldner had already invoked *The Coming Crisis of Western Sociology* (1970). Similar to Gouldner, sociologists in Germany criticized that sociology did not face the new social challenges and that it contributed to the stabilization of the unjust social order. The criticism was foremost directed at the board of the GSA. The board was said to have fled all too readily from concrete social developments into the abstraction of a comparison of theories in order to avoid a necessary politicization (Krysmanski et al. 1975). Critics challenged, above all, the fact that official sociology had not done enough to oppose the "occupational bans" issued in 1972, which in practice mainly affected people from the left spectrum, most of them from the *Deutsche Kommunistische Partei (DKP)*, founded in 1968 (a reconstitution of the KPD, banned in 1956), and also members of the *Deutsche Friedensgesellschaft* (German Peace Society) and the *Vereinigung der Verfolgten des Naziregimes—Bund der Antifaschistinnen und Antifaschisten* (Association of Persecutees of the Nazi Regime/ Federation of Antifascists).

While left-wing sociologists criticized that sociology did not deal enough with its own society and the obvious social antagonisms (Krysmanski et al. 1975), critical voices were also raised from the right-wing spectrum. The right-wing critics claimed that the crisis of sociology was mainly caused by the Americanization as well as by the critical orientation of the 1968 generation and its "revolutionary theology" (Eisermann 1976). Even Critical Rationalism was "too critical" for these "anti-critics" (Mongardini 1976, p. 59). All in all, there was an ideological split between left-wing and conservative sociologists, which often reached as far as into the sociological institutes, poisoning the social climate there, and in some places continuing up until the 1990s as for example in Bremen.

## Anti-sociology

Well-known and leading sociologists, such as Helmut Schelsky and Friedrich Tenbruck, an expert on Max Weber who taught in Tübingen, saw sociology in such a deep crisis that they openly and clearly distanced themselves from it. They presented themselves as "anti-sociologists" (Schelsky 1981). Paradoxically, they saw the crisis precisely in the "boom" of sociology, in the rise of the social importance of the subject due to the student movement and the left (cf. Rehberg 2010, p. 218). The "boom" was also evident in the media and the educational institutions, which increasingly adopted sociological categories of interpretation. Other academic disciplines, such as history, integrated sociological knowledge too (cf. Weischer 2004, pp. 246–249). A veritable popularization of the sociological vocabulary occurred; a popularization that was received with great skepticism by the "anti-sociologists."

In the book *Die Arbeit tun die anderen. Klassenkampf und Priesterherrschaft der Intellektuellen* ([1975] 1977; the title literally translates as *The Others do the Work. Class Struggle and Hierocracy of the Intellectuals*) Schelsky warned vehemently of the "time-determining effect of all sociology," the "dissolution of the person" that is sometimes only understood in a functional manner as a role resulting from a person's social conditions (Schelsky 1977, p. 359). Moreover, he feared that sociology would increasingly become a kind of "new social religion" and sociologists a "class of salvation-promising producers of meaning" (Schelsky 1977, p. 399). In addition to the critique of sociology, there was also the critique of public intellectuals—an old topos of conservative anti-sociology, which Émile Durkheim had already been exposed to in the Dreyfus Affair. And paradoxically, Schelsky was himself one of the "star-intellectuals" of that time (Schäfer 2015) who himself once had successfully promoted sociology as an academic discipline.

Friedrich Tenbruck, too, feared the sociological "abolition of man as an acting being": According to Tenbruck, sociology increasingly regarded humans either as class subjects or as role bearers only, but would no longer consider their individuality (Tenbruck 1984, p. 49). His criticism was directed against Marxist currents, the Frankfurt School, and role theory, as well as against structural functionalism, the latter being perceived as overly influential. Tenbruck perceived these directions as the mainstream of sociology. His counter-program was a cultural sociology following Max Weber and Georg Simmel, which was intended to distinguish itself also institutionally from the mainstream of the German Sociological Association. However, contrary to what he had expected (in institutional terms), there was no counter-movement to the GSA. Nevertheless, the "Cultural Sociology" section was established and founded *within* the GSA, which, in its understanding of cultural sociology as a *general* sociology, was substantially influenced by Tenbruck (cf. Albrecht and Moebius 2014).

Basically, the anti-sociology of Schelsky and Tenbruck fizzled out relatively soon. From a sociological point of view, Schelsky's and Tenbruck's rejection and criticism was also an attempt to secure their own position and their sociological privilege of interpretation in the sociological field. In essence, therefore, the critique was not so much directed against sociology in general; the critique was rather an expression of a struggle in the sociological field, or to put it in Bourdieu's terms, the critique was primarily directed "against certain competing theoretical concepts" (Rehberg 2010, p. 246). From the perspective of the "anti-sociologists," sociology seemed to be in crisis. Despite different motivations, they shared this critical view of sociology with some of their left-wing colleagues. But such debates were and are relevant to sociology. After all, can these debates and critiques of sociology not be interpreted as processes of self-understanding within sociology as well, which represented a further step in self-reflection and the development of sociology?

## Social Crises

The sociologists debated their subject and observed the disciplinary crises in different ways. By discussing and criticizing their academic discipline, they occasionally lost sight of their real subject: society and its problems. The society of the FRG as a whole went through several crises in the mid-1970s. The political change in 1969 had initially caused a certain euphoria and an optimistic mood:[3] In March 1969, the FRG got a new *Bundespräsident* (Federal President), Gustav Heinemann, who was the first in this office to have campaigned against rearmament and who had shown sympathy for the student movement. He also criticized the confrontation between Marxism and Christianity, propagated by Adenauer. For, according to Heinemann, Jesus did not die in opposition to Marx, but for all of us.

[3] For the here described historical processes I especially refer to Wolfrum (2007a).

In September 1969, a social-liberal government came to power for the first time in the history of the FRG. Willy Brandt of the SPD, who had been in exile and a resistance fighter, became Chancellor. Initially, for many Germans, the political change proved that a strong democratic mindset was taking root. The expansion of the welfare state, legal liberalization, and more opportunities for participation gave hope for a positive change in society. The new Chancellor Brandt was widely associated with the political style and charisma of John F. Kennedy (Wolfrum 2006c, p. 315). In particular, Brandt's genuflection in front of the memorial of the former Warsaw Ghetto (*Kniefall von Warschau*) symbolized the new *Ostpolitik* and a new self-image of the government. A policy of détente and reconciliation with the East was sought. In 1971, Brandt was awarded the Nobel Peace Prize. After the chancellorship of Brandt, the central event of the policy of détente was the signing of the CSCE Charter (Helsinki Accords of the Conference on Security and Co-operation in Europe) in 1975. However, by the end of the 1970s the policy of détente had come to an end. The Soviet Red Army invaded Afghanistan and Ronald Reagan pushed the military armament of the USA. The Cold War reached yet another peak.

With regards to domestic policy, the situation in the FRG was by no means settled. Germany was afflicted by terrorism. During the 1972 Olympic Games in Munich, members of the Israeli team were murdered by Palestinian terrorists. However, it was above all the internal German terrorism of the *Rote Armee Fraktion* (RAF, Red Army Faction or Baader-Meinhof Group), which, alongside the economic crisis, became the greatest challenge for the Federal Republic. The terrorism of the RAF reached back into the 1960s, to the murder of Benno Ohnesorg (cf. Terhoeven 2017), and reached its "peak" in autumn 1977, the so-called Deutscher Herbst ("German Autumn") (Wolfrum 2007a, p. 13). Through numerous murders of high-ranking figures from the judiciary, politics, and business, the RAF sought to obtain the release of its imprisoned founders Andreas Baader, Gudrun Ensslin, and Jan-Carl Raspe. Palestinian terrorists supported this demand by hijacking a plane in October 1977. However, the newly formed police counter-terrorist unit GSG 9 succeeded in freeing the passengers. Subsequently, the RAF prisoners committed suicide. The "German Autumn" was overcome, but society was frightened and "polarized" (Wolfrum 2007a, p. 13). Some even wished to reintroduce the death penalty, while others saw the rule of law in jeopardy because of the numerous internal security measures.

In domestic politics, a turmoil had already taken place in 1974. Brandt resigned as Chancellor. The reason for this was that the Chancellor's personal advisor, Günter Guillaume, was identified as a spy of the German Democratic Republic (GDR). Even though Brandt could not be held responsible for this negligence of the secret services, he assumed political responsibility with his resignation. His successor as Chancellor in 1974 was Helmut Schmidt, who first had to face the struggle against terror.

Another problem that Germany faced in the mid-1970s was the 1973 oil crisis. The global economy fell into a state of emergency. For Germany, too, it became clear: The *Wirtschaftswunder* (economic miracle) had come to its real end. The post-war "boom" was over (Doering-Manteuffel and Raphael 2012). The market of the automotive industry collapsed. However, the textile industry, shipbuilding, and the steel industry were particularly affected (Abelshauser 2011, p. 392). Nevertheless, the crisis also revealed that Germany had developed into an important global player over the previous years and was one of the most powerful industrial nations (Abelshauser 2011, p. 396). In line with the growing international significance, international transfer payments, for example the contribution to the UN or the expenditure on development aid, had increased "in the 1970s from 8 to 20.1 billion DM [German mark; S.M.]" (Abelshauser 2011, p. 397). Expenditure on the further development of the welfare state, such as pension reform, minimum social security benefits, or the expansion of health insurance, also entailed high costs.

The crisis had a particular impact on employment. The unemployment rate rose from 0.7% to 2.5%; one million people were out of work. Measured by current standards, this may seem little, but for the former FRG it was an enormous number. The recruitment of foreign *Gastarbeiter* (guest workers) was stopped. Yet a partial change of mentality also occurred. The exploitation of nature, the waste of resources, and consumption at the expense of the so-called Third World increasingly became a concern. According to Habermas, "late capitalism" entered into a "crisis of legitimization" (1973).

An "ecological awareness" increasingly developed. In 1972, the *Club of Rome*, an association of scientists and industrialists, urged to consider the limits of growth and warned of a further overexploitation of natural resources. In addition to the peace movement and the women's movement, various environmental movements then emerged, in which around two million Germans were involved by the end of the 1970s (Wolfrum 2007a, p. 14). The environmental movements gained in popularity, especially through the increasing criticism of nuclear power plants. A separate anti-nuclear movement emerged, which—particularly as a result of the Three Mile Island accident (1979) and the Chernobyl disaster (1986)—grew in the 1980s and 1990s and contributed to the founding of the political party *Die Grünen* (The Greens). The movement's greatest success was the decision taken in 2000 to phase out nuclear power.

The political and economic crises fueled a feeling of insecurity among Germans. Some had lost their utopias of "1968." Many were seeking new providers of meaning and found them in the emerging esotericism and psycho-boom or in the fitness studios that were appearing everywhere (Wolfrum 2007a, p. 107). Identity search was the big issue. For some, the search began with a romantic transfiguration of the past. This became evident, for example, in fashion, where retro-chic appeared, in architecture with the rebuilding of many medieval town centers, in literature that focused on homeland (*Heimat*) themes, and a growing interest in local history (Wolfrum 2007a, p. 108). The identity of the Germans was also shaken by the Nazi past, as the US-American TV series "Holocaust" revealed in an unvarnished way. The stories portrayed in the series—on the one hand, the terrible fate of the Jewish family Weiß and on the other, the plot from the perspective of a perpetrator—shocked many people. The series made the crimes of the Germans become visible to many and contributed significantly to the development of a culture of remembrance in Germany—but only now, more than 30 years after these crimes had been committed.

## DIFFERENTIATION AND NEW (QUALITATIVE) METHODS IN THE "GREAT AGE" OF EMPIRICAL SOCIAL RESEARCH

In retrospect, the much-lamented crisis of sociology was interpreted as the inability of sociology to deal with the aforementioned social transformation processes and crises. But some sociologists also saw this as a challenge. It eventually led to a stronger focus of sociology in West Germany on specific problems, very concrete questions, and empirical research on industry, labor, education, and urban planning. Empirical social research and so-called special sociologies or hyphen-sociologies, such as industrial sociology , therefore regained importance. By contrast, discussions on the theory of science, such as the Positivism Dispute, receded into the background for sociologists in general (cf. Schmidt 1980, p. 272).

The 1970s led to a further specialization of sociology, which was reflected, among other things, in the founding of new chairs on specific topics and the establishment of new sections in the GSA (for the genesis of the sections see Borggräfe 2018): Newly founded sections of the GSA from the 1970s onwards were concerned with methods (1971), education (1971), family and youth (1971), religion (1971), cities and urbanism (1971), Eastern Europe (1971), social indicators (1972), industry (1972), developing countries (1973), law (1973), medicine (1973), science (1974), language (1977), social problems (1977), social policy (1979), and women's studies (1979). New developments took place at the higher level of the organization too: In 1976, the *Berufsverband deutscher Soziologinnen und Soziologen* (Professional Association of German Sociologists) was founded, which in particular represents sociologists on the free market outside of academia.

As Christoph Weischer (2004) has shown in detail in his comprehensive study on the history of empirical social research in Germany, "three guiding principles" characterized social research in the 1970s: "improvement," "emancipation," and "scientification" (Weischer 2004, pp. 321–338). With reference to the guiding principle of "improvement," social research was seen in the light of its social technological application. This involved planning and evaluating as well as producing social reports with the help of social research and social indicators research. Against the background of this guiding principle, sociologists such as Fritz Scharpf (*1935) and Renate Mayntz contributed significantly to the expansion and reflection of sociological policy advice and policy research. They pleaded for "active political control of social development" (Leendertz 2010, pp. 70–71). The ability to control and plan social processes was also the central concern of the GSA in the mid-1970s and was the key issue at the 1976 *Soziologentag* (cf. Borggräfe 2018, p. 878). Many considered this kind of empirical research a non-ideological science, but failed to reflect upon its inherent ideological character. The guiding principle of "emancipation" (Weischer 2004, pp. 330–336) aimed to initiate critical and emancipatory social processes through social research. Central to this was industrial sociology, which was based on the theory of Marx or Critical Theory, and on concepts for the "humanization of work" (Weischer 2004, p. 331, p. 334). It often applied interpretative or participatory methods. The third guiding principle, "scientification," had been particularly formative for the beginning of empirical social research after 1945 and consisted, in accordance with the perspective of René König, in establishing social research as the foundation of sociology as an academic discipline. Empirical social research became increasingly important in the 1970s and was successfully institutionalized. Training in methods grew immensely. The number of textbooks and courses on methods increased by a factor of 20 (Weischer 2004, pp. 347–355). Standardization, canonization, and specialization took place. Some also described the period up to the end of the 1970s as the "great era of empirical social research" (Weischer 2004, pp. 235–366).

Despite the criticism of empirical social research, as was formulated especially from the perspective of Critical Theory, it was institutionalized and expanded in the study programs at the universities. Above all, empirical social research experienced a "boom" at institutions beyond the universities (Weischer 2004, pp. 250–251). In particular, research related to social democratic reform policy was funded (cf. Kern 1982, p. 243). Thus, social research in this period was more "externally driven" than in the 1950s and 1960s (Weischer 2004, p. 360). The number of empirically oriented papers in journals also increased. Along with the institutional success of empirical social research, expectations and hopes increased that it could be applied directly and beneficially in a socio-technological sense (Weischer 2004, p. 321).

The 1970s saw not only a boom in social research, but also a change in the field of empirical social research: "Qualitative" research methods (cf. Ploder 2018) were established in the field, which—to this day—are fiercely contested by some representatives of quantitative methods (cf. Weischer 2004, pp. 400–431). Quantitative methods had long been regarded as the ideal of the development of methods. Not only were they increasingly applied, but in the course of this they were also increasingly refined. In certain locations, a veritable cult of methods emerged, in which practical application receded into the background in favor of a method-technocratism. By its representatives, quantitative social research was closely and positively associated with progress, modernization, and rationalization. If it was related to theories, then, as Weischer (2004, p. 357) points out, it was initially linked to functionalist approaches, and today especially to concepts of methodological individualism. Current representatives refer to it as an "empirical-analytical sociology."[4] The constant

---

[4] See the website of the so-called *Akademie für Soziologie* (Academy of Sociology), founded in opposition to the GSA in 2017: https://www.academy-sociology.net/the-academy/goals-and-responsibilities/ (November 19, 2019). For further information about the Academy see the last chapter.

refinement and mathematization of methods were considered an advancement and fostered "the (romantic or dogmatic) idea of a *unified science*" (Weischer 2004, p. 357, emphasis in original). Research that was not based on quantitative methods or that was even perhaps more theoretically oriented seemed irrational, pre-modern, and unworthy of being included in a unified science. Under these circumstances, the establishment of qualitative research was difficult and, accordingly, its successful institutionalization took a long time in Germany. It was not until 2003 that a separate section on qualitative social research could be established within the GSA.

According to the detailed analysis by Andrea Ploder (2018, p. 736), the development of qualitative research in post-World War II Germany was significantly influenced by two research traditions from the USA: Right after the war, the main resource was empirical social research in the tradition of Paul F. Lazarsfeld and Robert K. Merton. In the late 1960s and early 1970s, the German reception focused on so-called interpretive approaches in the tradition of the Chicago School, ethnomethodology, and sociolinguistics. Different interpretive approaches were combined with each other and with philosophical German traditions of phenomenology and hermeneutics, and inspired a number of novel traditions of qualitative research. In addition, other qualitative approaches like action research (*Aktionsforschung*), depth hermeneutics, and ethno-psychoanalysis were developed during this time (Ploder 2018, p. 736; for further details on action research see Kern 1982, pp. 246–272).

As Andrea Ploder (2018, pp. 744–745) has pointed out, four centers shaped the emerging field of qualitative research in Germany throughout the 1970s: In Frankfurt am Main, the group around Ulrich Oevermann (*1940) represented objective hermeneutics. Another center was formed in the 1970s by the "Working Group of Bielefeld Sociologists" around Joachim Matthes (1930–2009) and Fritz Schütze (*1944). In 1973, they published under the title "Alltagswissen, Interaktion und gesellschaftliche Wirklichkeit" (literally translated as "Everyday knowledge, interaction and social reality"), a widely read volume with translations of texts by American colleagues in the field of ethnomethodology, ethnotheory, and ethnography of communication (e.g., Herbert Blumer (1900–1987), Aaron

Cicourel (*1928), Harold Garfinkel (1917–2011)). The third center was in Bonn, around Hans-Georg Soeffner (*1939), who later also taught in Konstanz as the successor of Luckmann. The fourth center was in Konstanz around Thomas Luckmann (1927–2016), who returned from the USA, and his phenomenologically oriented sociology of knowledge and sociology of language. Luckmann, a student and colleague of Alfred Schütz, had written the book *The Social Construction of Reality* with Peter L. Berger (1929–2017) in the USA in 1966. The book was published in German in 1969 and became one of the most widely read books in sociology. Many understood it not only as a new perspective for sociology, but also as a simple, easy-to-read introduction to sociology (cf. Tuma and Wilke 2018, p. 602). In Germany, Luckmann thus founded a Konstanz School, which today is dominant in the field of the sociology of knowledge and of qualitative, hermeneutical social research, and which has spread throughout the German-speaking world. In 1977, the exchange between these groups led to a joint section, "Sociology of Language," in the GSA, which was later renamed as "Sociology of Knowledge" section. Today it is the section of the GSA with nearly the most members. Numerous edited volumes and conferences followed, to which, among others, Anselm Strauss, Erving Goffman, and Aaron Cicourel were invited. In 1979, a working group on biographical research was established within the section.

The emerging women's and gender studies, too, contributed significantly to the establishment of qualitative research (cf. Ploder 2018, p. 750). The women's movement as a whole did not only focus on equal rights and participation, but strived for a complete "change of society" (Gerhard 2012, p. 110). Research was similarly oriented. In the 1970s, it was emphasized—prominently by the feminist Maria Mies—that research should be "emancipative," a "view from the bottom," and at the same time political, and it should "give women a voice of their own again" (Paulitz 2019, pp. 384–385).

## The Establishment of Women's Research and Gender Studies

Similar to other countries, in Germany too, research on gender and women's issues developed from the women's movement of the 1960s and 1970s, although there had been research by women and on women as well as on gender relations before that. Until the 1970s, however, most of this research had been conducted by individual female researchers (and sometimes also by male researchers—think, e.g., of Georg Simmel). But they often lacked a fundamental critique of patriarchal domination (cf. Paulitz 2019, pp. 380–382).⁵

Feminist sociological perspectives mainly developed from the women's movement. A central theoretical tool that was now being widely received was Simone de Beauvoir's book *Le deuxième sexe* (1949) (Paulitz 2019, p. 380). The main thesis of this book was: "One is not born, but rather, becomes a woman." De Beauvoir's book became a central theoretical tool for feminist sociology.

From the 1970s onwards, the criticism of the social situation of women became louder and a kind of "thought collective of feminism" emerged (Paulitz 2019, p. 382). The criticism did not only concern the mainstream of society. Also, the experiences of the marginalization of women during "1968" were a driving force (cf. Paulitz 2019, p. 383). In spite of Marxism, enlightenment, and emancipation, women had often been marginalized in this movement, too. The problems women addressed as well as their social preconditions either had been excluded from the discussions or were dismissed as so-called "side contradiction" (Paulitz 2019, p. 383), that is, as problems that would vanish into thin air if socialism were to become established.

The critique of gender discrimination affected most areas of society, including academia. Feminist scholars now demonstrated that science was not as gender-neutral as it claimed to be (cf. Paulitz 2019, p. 384). It was shown, for example, to what extent scientific statements, which at first glance appeared to be gender-neutral, were shaped by a male, "androcentric" gaze and permeated by patriarchal mechanisms of domination (Paulitz 2019, p. 384). They now reinterpreted the relationship between science and emancipative politics in such a way that feminist research was not limited to the established fields and institutions of science. Instead, they argued, science was to be employed and changed in such a way that it would serve the goals of feminist politics, that is, the goal of economic, political, social, and cultural equality. At the same time, research on women's issues also saw itself as an institutionalized form of self-reflection that allowed for the critical evaluation of the political practice of the women's movement (Hark 2005, p. 253).

---

⁵ In the following, I mainly draw on Tanja Paulitz's (2019) historical reconstruction of feminist sociology in Germany and Sabine Hark's (2005) history of feminist discourse.

As Tanja Paulitz (2019, p. 376) has pointed out, "in confrontation with and critical further development of different sociological ways of thinking, different paradigms of sociological engagement with gender were finally formed." Thus, there was not only one or "the" feminist perspective in sociology. Rather different theoretical perspectives on women and gender developed (Paulitz 2019, p. 376).

In the first phase of research on gender and women's issues, it was mainly the social inequality affecting women that was criticized. This research did not yet appear under the name of "gender studies," but was referred to as "research on women's issues" . It focused "on women's perspectives and on women as key actors" (Paulitz 2019, p. 383). Initially research was limited to the structural discrimination of women. It opened up only slowly and became concerned with gender inequality more generally. Helge Pross (1927–1984), for example, a former assistant of Horkheimer and Adorno, who was one of the first female professors in sociology after 1945 (1965, she got a professorship at the University of Gießen, cf. Tegeler 2003, p. 224), showed in her empirical studies that the so-called "women's question" is always also a "men's question" (Tegeler 2003).[6]

As Sabine Hark (2005, p. 209) argues in her history of feminist discourse, the idea of women's studies was "ignited" at West German universities around 1973. Throughout the 1970s and early 1980s, women's studies focused on family, education, (house)work, the division of labor, and female careers.[7] Carol Hagemann-White (*1942), for instance, who became a professor in Osnabrück in 1988, conducted research on violence, housework, education, and socialization (cf. Hagemann-White 1984, 2006). Others, such as Ilona Ostner (* 1947), Elisabeth Beck-Gernsheim (*1946), Gudrun-Axeli Knapp (*1944), or Regina Becker-Schmidt (*1937) studied employment, housework, and social policy (cf. Ostner 2006; Beck-Gernsheim 2006; Knapp 2006; Becker-Schmidt 2006). Also in the 1980s, a debate, in which, among others, Frigga Haug, Habermas, and Gertrud Nunner-Winkler (*1941) were particularly involved, unfolded around Carol Gilligan's (*1936) thesis of a specifically female morality (Gilligan 1982; Habermas 1983; Haug 1984; Nunner-Winkler 1986).

---

[6] For the first generation of women who have achieved a professorship in the social sciences in Germany, see the autobiographical texts in Vogel (2006).
[7] For the following examples I mainly refer to Lucke (2003, p. 2).

Some of these female researchers were related to one of the already mentioned sociological "schools," even if these relations were not uncritical. Ute Gerhard (*1939), known among other things for her research on women, law, and the women's movement, attended lectures by René König (Gerhard 2006, p. 53). Becker-Schmidt was influenced by the early Critical Theory, especially by Adorno. Drawing on these influences and existing theoretical paradigms, they developed a genuinely independent branch of sociological thinking which understands itself not as a mere add-on to general sociology (Becker-Schmidt 1987a). This also applies to sociologists like Irene Dölling (*1942) and Beate Krais (* 1944), who took up Pierre Bourdieu's research on masculine domination (Dölling 2006, p. 120; Dölling and Krais 1997; Krais 2000).

An important step toward the institutionalization of a feminist perspective in sociology was the founding of the section "Women's Studies in the Social Sciences" in the GSA in 1979. The section understood itself as a critical, "semi-autonomous corrective" (Paulitz 2019, p. 386). This means that the section was not concerned with adapting to the institutionalized discipline, but rather with its transformation—it was a matter of "dissident participation" (Hark 2005). In other words, the system was to be transformed from within. This led to both a "*feminist turn* of science" and an "*academic turn* of feminism" (Hark 2005, p. 10; emphasis in original). The institutional success of gender and women's research had to do with a generational change and the fact that, since the 1960s, more and more women had been able to start studying. Between 1970 and 1975, the proportion of female students rose from approximately 8% to 14%; at the level of professors, the number doubled (Hark 2005, pp. 223–224), although their number still remained well below the number of male professors.

The pathways of the institutionalization of academic feminism were often contradictory and complex, but always highly self-reflexive. If it had been the merit of early research on women's issues to have initiated a fundamental change of paradigms and perspectives in the first place, deficits within this discourse were soon addressed. On the one hand, it was criticized that the demands for equality were still oriented toward the male mainstream. On the other hand, older approaches became more and more dominant that insisted on an essential difference between women and men. But even these were increasingly challenged, as the academic focus on the category "woman" neglected the differences between women (e.g., due to sexuality, class, and ethnicity).

The 1980s brought about a crucial change: Instead of the category of "women," the categories of "gender" or "gender relations" increasingly became the primary focus of interest: "Characteristic of the German-speaking discussion is the emergence of relational approaches that moved the category of 'gender relations' into the center of attention and made gender a structural category" (Paulitz 2019, p. 389). This change of perspective, toward a focus on gender as a key social "structural category" (Beer 1984; Becker-Schmidt 1987b), led to an increased "sociologization of the feminist discourse" as well as to a "feminist re-reading and continuation of the sociological tradition" (Paulitz 2019, p. 389).

In the USA, the distinction between sex and gender had been fundamental since the 1970s. This distinction allowed for a differentiation between biological notions of sex and cultural notions of gender. In the 1980s it was considered to be an "intellectual common property of the feminist tradition of thought" (Paulitz 2019, p. 390). As already mentioned, the discussions in Germany dealt with the category "woman" in a similar vein, but initially this was done without the theoretical differentiation between sex and gender. Many discourses revolved more around the equality-difference debate (Gerhard et al. 1990; Maihofer 1997).

Gender was not yet seen as the key concept (cf. Paulitz 2019, p. 392); the central concept was rather the concept of "structure" (Paulitz 2019, p. 395), as especially Ursula Beer has pointed out (Beer 1984; 1990). Following Marxist theory in some point, feminism concentrated on the relations of gendered and capitalist structures, instead of problematizing primarily questions of identity. Gendered and capitalist structures, as pointed out, for example, by Becker-Schmidt (1987a), are "interdependent"; "gender and class-specific inequalities reinforce each other," and therefore women are subject to a "twofold societalization" (Becker-Schmidt 1987a). Social inequality is thus not the result of the supposed nature of women, but of "structural conditions" (Paulitz 2019, p. 393).

This perspective of feminist sociology, as it was developed in the 1980s, was indeed already a central step toward problematizing notions of a "natural" sex, toward "de-naturalization." Nevertheless, the discussions often still remained in a discourse that problematized neither the distinction between sex and gender nor the coupling of the category of gender to certain notions of reproduction, heterosexuality, and binary coding. This only happened in the 1990s with the publication and discussion of Judith Butler's *Gender Trouble* (1990), a book that also changed feminism in Germany considerably (cf. Hark 2005, pp. 269–332). I will come back to this in the last chapter.

## Historical Self-reflections in the Transition from the 1970s to the 1980s

The transition into the 1980s led to an important historical self-reflection of sociology in Germany. Around 1980, two special issues of the *Kölner Zeitschrift für Soziologie und Sozialpsychologie* (KZfSS, Cologne Journal of Sociology and Social Psychology) which dealt with the history of German-speaking sociology were published, which marked important steps in this process: *Soziologie in Deutschland nach 1945* (*Sociology in Germany after 1945*) and *Soziologie in Deutschland und Österreich von 1918–1945* (*Sociology in Germany and Austria from 1918–1945*). This process led to sometimes heated discussions, in which Schelsky (1981) and König (1987) were also involved. The controversy regarding the history of sociology developed particularly between Lepsius and König on the one side and Schelsky on the other. The dispute was about whether sociology in Germany had already come to its end before 1933, as Schelsky (1981, p. 15) claimed, or whether it was, on the contrary, very much alive toward the end of the Weimar Republic, but then brutally brought to a complete stand-still by the Nazi regime, as König (1987, pp. 343–387) and Lepsius (2017d, p. 86) argued. In the end, however, both represented a discontinuity thesis.

In 1981, Wolf Lepenies published four volumes on the history of sociology, which were internationally oriented. Also, Dirk Kaesler (1984) too did research on the very early phase of German sociology. He also has published several volumes on the classics of sociology since the mid-1970s, which are still used in teaching today.[8] These historical studies of sociology at the beginning and during the 1980s were also an expression of the desire to bring order to the increasingly complex sociological field with the help of history, and to help the discipline to develop its own "identity" (Lepenies 1981). After the 1980s, there was a relative silence regarding the history of sociology. As we shall see, the study of the history of sociology gained more attention again only in the 1990s and then again after 2010 in discussions about the role of sociology during National Socialism. However, it was not until 2019 that a section on the history of sociology was established in the GSA.

---

[8] On the question of how some thinker becomes a classic of sociology, see Holzhauser (2021).

## The Theory Boom of the 1980s

In Europe there was a boom in sociological theories in the 1970s, but even more so in the 1980s, which Hans Joas and Wolfgang Knöbl (2009, p. 199) attribute to the fact that the relationship between sociology and philosophy was still closer there than it was in the USA. In Germany it was Jürgen Habermas and Niklas Luhmann who contributed to this "theory boom" in the early 1980s with two major sociological theories, which were already prepared in the 1970s. In 1981 Habermas published his seminal and widely discussed study *Theorie des kommunikativen Handelns* (*The Theory of Communicative Action*). The two volumes of the book were published in the same year in which Habermas resigned from his position as co-director of the Max Planck Institute (MPI) in Starnberg (cf. Müller-Doohm 2014, pp. 272–273; Leendertz 2010, p. 9; Leendertz 2018).[9]

*The Theory of Communicative Action* was both a novel theory of action and a sociological analysis of contemporary society. The theory of action aims at attributing a prominent role to the function of communicative understanding in social action. In contrast to instrumental or strategic action, communicative action is concerned with interaction, dialogue, and the domination-free development of consensus. Habermas' analysis of contemporary society comes down to the claim that the system, especially administration, economy and technology, and the elements of the system such as the monetary economy, bureaucracy, and success-oriented action, increasingly permeate the relationships and structures within the lifeworld. Habermas refers to this as a "colonization of the lifeworld by the system." Hence, Habermas combines crucial elements of systems theory with a theory of the lifeworld which is based on communicative action. Moreover, for Habermas, communicative action and deliberation also function as a normative standard in political and democratic theory.

However, Habermas not only shaped the theoretical debates in the 1980s with *The Theory of Communicative Action*. In addition, his commitment to the "project of modernity" was an important contribution. Habermas tried to defend this "project" against the discourse of postmodernism that emerged in the 1980s. He wrote against so-called critics of

---

[9] The resignation was the culmination of conflicts at the MPI in the wake of the retirement of Carl Friedrich von Weizsäcker (cf. Müller-Doohm 2014, pp. 268–270). The institute in Starnberg was finally dissolved. As its replacement, the Max Planck Institute for the Study of Societies in Cologne was established in 1984 under the management of Renate Mayntz (Leendertz 2010; Leendertz 2018).

reason such as Adorno, Heidegger, and Georges Bataille (1897–1962), but also against postmodernism and the poststructuralists (Habermas 1985) and thus became a central actor in the international debates on modernity and postmodernism (cf. Moebius 2010). According to Habermas, the postmodernist critique of the "grand narratives" of progress, modernization, and rationalization ran the risk of renouncing practical critique of social conditions. Moreover, postmodernism also became entangled in a performative self-contradiction: After all, a radical critique of reason must itself argue rationally. The debates on postmodernism in the German-speaking sociological field continued into the 1990s and 2000s (cf. Neumeister 2000).

Until the 1990s, the controversies about the "project of modernity" dominated the image of Habermas as an intellectual. Habermas increasingly became one of the most important intellectuals in Germany and beyond. This was also apparent in his intellectual involvement in the *Historikerstreit* (historians' dispute) between 1986 and 1989.[10] In the 1980s and 1990s, he increasingly produced publications on the philosophy of law and sociology of law as well as writings oriented toward concrete social processes in the fields of bioethics, religion, and European policy.

A further milestone of sociological theory in West Germany was the systems theory of Niklas Luhmann. At the beginning of the 1980s, Luhmann published papers on *Social Structure and Semantics*, in which he sociologically analyzed the historical change of concepts such as "culture," "state," "individual," and "nature." The highlight, however, was the book *Soziale Systeme (Social Systems)* from 1984. *Soziale Systeme* was the beginning of a series of analyses of individual functional systems, which Luhmann then presented from the end of the 1980s onwards and which, among other issues, dealt with the subsystems of economy, science, law, art, politics, religion, and media. In contrast to Habermas, Luhmann rarely spoke on current political issues. Despite, or perhaps because of, the rejection of politically intended real changes, systems theory initially became one of the most influential theoretical concepts in sociology in the 1990s. The journal *Soziale Systeme*, founded in 1995, also contributed to this

---

[10] The *Historikerstreit* was a public debate on the singularity of the Holocaust provoked by the conservative historian Ernst Nolte (cf. Piper 1987). Nolte saw the Holocaust as a reaction to the mass crimes in the Soviet Union. Habermas criticized the attempts to relativize the Holocaust and the crimes of the Nazi regime by making comparisons between different mass crimes against humanity using theories of totalitarianism.

development. Habermas' theory, on the other hand, was increasingly received in political philosophy rather than in sociology (cf. Müller 2001, p. 44).

Even though with the theories of Habermas and Luhmann independent (West) German "grand theories" were available, West German sociology continued to deal with another major theory in the 1980s: with Parsons' theory synthesis. As elsewhere—consider Edward Shils, Shmuel Eisenstadt, Robert Bellah, and Jeffrey C. Alexander—a "renewal of Parsonianism" took place in West Germany too (Joas/Knöbl 2009, pp. 308–338). Richard Münch was a key player in this renewal. As early as 1976, Münch published two books, *Theorie sozialer Systeme (Social Systems Theory)* and *Legitimität und politische Macht (Legitimacy and Political Power)*, in which Parsons played a prominent role. Several essays followed immediately after Parsons' death in 1979, in which Parsons' work was reconstructed and reinterpreted in the light of Kant and Weber. Münch's *Theorie des Handelns. Zur Rekonstruktion der Beiträge von Talcott Parsons, Emile Durkheim und Max Weber (Action Theory: Towards a Reconstruction of the Contributions of Talcott Parsons, Emile Durkheim and Max Weber)*, written in 1982, aimed at renewing Parsons' voluntarist theory of action. In the sociological field of the 1980s, Münch's book was perceived as a "competing product" to Habermas and as a demarcation to Luhmann. Luhmann did indeed follow Parsons in part. But in Luhmann's theory, the subsystems become independent to such an extent that each follows its own inherent logic, so that the different systems can only "irritate" each other. In contrast, Münch emphasized Parsons' theory of interpenetration, that is, the mutual influence of the subsystems. Furthermore, Münch criticized that in contrast to Parsons, neither Habermas nor Luhmann could explain the emergence of social order. Other books of Münch on the structure and culture of modernity followed. In recent years, Münch's interest has shifted to the theory of Pierre Bourdieu (1930–2002). Currently, Münch's (2009, 2014) critical analyses of the neoliberal reorganization of (higher) education and academia, that is, the economization of education, are of particular importance.

In contrast to the reception of Parsons, other theoretical concepts had a more lasting and vivid effect that is still observable today. This is true, for example, of (post-)structuralism, Michel Foucault (1926–1984), Pierre Bourdieu, the popular and media culture theories of the Birmingham

Centre for Contemporary Cultural Studies (CCCS),[11] as well as symbolic interactionism and American pragmatism, which Hans Joas in particular introduced in Germany and developed further in the 1990s into a theory of the *Kreativität des Handelns* (1992, *The Creativity of Action* 1997).

Already in the 1970s, René König had promoted the reception of the Durkheim School. Alfred Schütz and Norbert Elias were also perceived more widely in the 1980s. When the interest in Marx tended to decline, Elias' theory of the civilizing process (Elias 1977) seemed more "conciliatory" than Marxism, and advanced to a "refuge" and a "medium of survival of historical-materialist critique" (Rehberg 1979, p. 122). The reception of Elias, a student of Alfred Weber and Karl Mannheim, was at the same time an attempt to take up again the characteristic historical sociology of the Weimar period.

This revival of the German tradition of historical sociology, which was also associated with the name Max Weber, could be seen most clearly among the new cultural sociologists. Cultural sociology experienced a "renaissance" (Albrecht and Moebius 2014). This renaissance has to be understood not only against the background the general *cultural turn* in the humanities and social sciences and the massive cultural changes in Western countries since the 1970s, but also in the light of the theory boom. As mentioned, in the mid-1970s, Friedrich Tenbruck had encouraged the revival of a cultural sociology oriented toward Max Weber in order to oppose the dominant tendencies of Marxism and Parsonianism. In the mid-1980s, the section on "Cultural Sociology" was founded in the GSA. Inspired by Tenbruck, in this section, those sociologists found an institutional space who wanted to go beyond Marx, Parsons, Habermas, and Luhmann and to concentrate increasingly on pioneers such as Weber and Simmel, but also on Foucault, Elias, Bourdieu, philosophical anthropology, phenomenology, or historical sociology. The section considered itself to be an alternative to the "Sociological Theory" section of the GSA, which was founded around 1980 and in which the debate on the comparison of theories still continued. In particular, the "Cultural Sociology" section understood itself as an alternative to the dominant concepts of Parsons and sociobiology. With its references to philosophy and to the historical sociology of the 1920s, cultural sociology in Germany has developed a unique profile (cf. Moebius 2019) that goes further than a mere sociology

---

[11] In this context see also the combination of poststructuralism and cultural studies in the postcolonial studies.

of culture and that does not exist in other countries and which also differs from American cultural sociology, which was shaped by Jeffrey C. Alexander (*1947) and draws mainly on Durkheim's later sociology of religion.

It was in the 1980s, too, that the reception of Pierre Bourdieu intensified (cf. Rehbein 2018). Today, alongside Weber and Marx, he is one of the best-known and "most received authors among students of sociology in Germany" (Schneikert et al. 2019). Here, too, one is faced with a "grand theory." However, unlike Habermas or Luhmann, Bourdieu developed his theoretical notions and concepts in close connection with empirical research, using both qualitative and quantitative methods. Furthermore, Bourdieu is one of the few sociologists who have reflected sociologically on the emergence of their respective sociology (Bourdieu 2002). Books by Bourdieu had already appeared in German in the 1970s (e.g. Bourdieu and Passeron 1971). There were also already links to Bourdieu in the sociology of education. However, it was above all his book *La distinction. Critique sociale du jugement* (*Distinction. A Social Critique of the Judgement of Taste*) published in 1979 and translated into German in 1982, that attracted enormous attention and interest. Bourdieu's books were then successively translated into German and his theory has been widely received to this day. The reception of Bourdieu's work in Germany (similar to that in other countries) became more and more differentiated, so that today, in addition to sociological theory, his work has an impact on almost all sociological subfields. Research on social structure analysis, milieus, lifestyles, and inequality research refer to Bourdieu just as studies in the sociology of education, of gender, of culture, of language, and of intellectuals.

Bourdieu's great success was also related to the social problems facing West German society. In contrast to Anthony Giddens (*1938) or Ulrich Beck (1944–2015), for example, who supported the so-called Third Way of Social Democracy of Tony Blair and Gerhard Schröder, Bourdieu's theory provided a fundamental critique of the conditions of contemporary society and saw itself as a committed sociology, which, in view of the major problems such as unemployment, social exclusion, precarization, and economization of the social, in a way suggested itself.

Bourdieu's sociology was part of a larger theoretical movement that could be observed internationally in the 1980s: the overcoming of the micro-macro dualism (see Alexander 1988). In other words, the social was understood and explained neither primarily on the basis of individual actions nor exclusively by structures and systems. Instead, action and structure were seen as being closely intertwined.

Other theories could also be found in the sociological field in West Germany in the 1980s. In close connection to quantitative social research were rational choice theories. Since the end of the 1980s, the individualistic theory program has become more differentiated. Since then it has been possible to distinguish clearly between approaches and actors of rational choice theories and those of "explanatory sociology" (Maurer 2019, p. 300). Here it was Rolf Ziegler (*1936), Karl-Dieter Opp (*1937), Günter Büschges (1926–2017), and later especially Hartmut Esser (*1943), who, from the 1980s onwards, starting from Cologne, developed the "model of sociological explanation." In doing so, they set themselves apart from simple rational choice theories. "Explanatory sociology" was based on a close connection between critical rationalism, rational choice, the analysis of objective structures, Max Weber's theory of action, and the analysis of institutions (Maurer 2017, pp. 15–33). Important impulses came from James Coleman (1926–1995), Raymond Boudon (1934–2013), and Siegwart Lindenberg (*1941). Today there are close connections to network research (Harrison White (*1930), Mike Granovetter (*1943)), neo-institutionalism, actor-centered institutionalism (Renate Mayntz, Fritz Scharpf), analytical sociology, and sociology of social mechanisms (Peter Hedström (*1955), Peter Bearman (*1956)).

As can be seen from the diverse theories, the related theoretical debates, and the institutional differentiation into different sections, a "pluralization of perspectives" (Borggräfe 2018, p. 883) developed in the sociological field in the 1980s, which made the unity of sociology that some had hoped for impossible. On the one hand, this was due to the increasing complexity of society, but on the other hand, it also resulted from internal disciplinary processes, especially the multiplication of positionings in the sociological field. A further indication of the complexity, specialization, and increasing pressure to establish a position of one's own in the field is the growing trend away from overarching, large-scale sociological theories toward rapidly changing analyses of contemporary society that can be observed since the mid-1980s (cf. Osrecki 2018).[12]

---

[12] The genre of the *soziologische Zeitdiagnose* (sociological analysis of contemporary society) was previously present in the German-speaking world, especially in the historical sociology of the interwar period (Alfred Weber, Werner Sombart, Franz Oppenheimer, and Karl

In 1986, Ulrich Beck made a much-noticed beginning to this sociological trend with his book *Risikogesellschaft. Auf dem Weg in eine andere Moderne* (*Risk Society. Towards a New Modernity*, published in English in 1992). The success of the book was greatly facilitated by the fact that it was printed shortly before the nuclear accident in Chernobyl on April 26, 1986. Beck's diagnosis of large-scale technological risks coincided exactly with the critique of technology and skepticism about progress of the environmental and anti-nuclear movements, which were growing in the 1980s. Beck had actually written the book as a diagnosis of the future, but instead it had become a direct analysis of the present. The central argument of *Risk Society* was that modern societies are increasingly faced with self-produced, transnational risks (nuclear power, forest dieback, terrorism, etc.) that potentially affect all population groups. Thus, technical and economic "progress," which was initially interpreted as a gain in power, also has a downside: the production and redistribution of risks. The progressive processes initiated by modern society and their secondary consequences fall back on the society as problems. The uncertainty that this brings about is intensified by processes of individualization that radically change class affiliation, religious and political commitments, work processes, and family relationships. At the end of the book, Beck sketched the first outlines of what was systematically elaborated further in the 1990s as the "theory of reflexive modernization."

## Processes of Differentiation and Pluralization in the Face of Social Change

It was not only the field of sociological theory that was characterized by processes and dynamics of differentiation and pluralization in the 1980s. Rather, the entire sociological field was characterized by this. It was oriented toward increasingly specific fields of social practice and toward new problems (Weischer 2004, p. 376), which were closely related to social change in Germany: Like many other Western countries, Germany, too, was transformed from an industrial society to a post-industrial service society (Schildt 2007, p. 56), sometimes referred to as the "knowledge society" or "information society." This change was driven by technological change and the transformation of media and it was

---

Mannheim) and played a rather marginal role from 1945 to 1986—with the exception of the works of Helmut Schelsky.

intimately linked to processes of globalization that took place in the sphere of economics, politics, and culture.[13] In the USA and in Western Europe, economic neoliberalism triumphed and many areas of society were "economized." This "economization" also affected sociology. In his analysis of the history of empirical social research in Germany, Weischer (2004, p. 371) describes this as a veritable "economization of sociology," which was demonstrated by the fact that economic patterns of interpretation and rational choice theories became increasingly important within the sociological field and a certain fetishism of third-party funding (cf. Münch 2014) also spread there.

The continuing rationalization and technical progress led to major changes in industrial production. New forms of work emerged. Debates about the "end of the division of labor" (Kern and Schumann 1984) and the effects of technical rationalization dominated discussions, for example, in the field of industrial sociology and the sociology of work. In Germany, the economy recovered in the 1980s from the crises of the 1970s. In particular, the traditional industries such as the automotive industry and chemical industry boomed. At the same time, there was rising mass unemployment (cf. Abelshauser 2011, p. 470), which did not disappear as a result of the boom, since the economic profits were often no longer reinvested in industry, but were used as "speculative funds on the financial markets" (Fülberth 2012, p. 72).

In the early 1980s social democracy in Germany fell into a crisis, when in 1982 Helmut Kohl of the CDU became the new Chancellor. The power of the trade unions was diminished (cf. Fülberth 2012, p. 73). Unemployment and poverty grew, intensified by the neoliberal dismantling of the welfare state. These tendencies were intensified after reunification, especially in East Germany. These ongoing developments continue to shape the discourses on precarity and right-wing extremism to this day. Currently, sociologists characterize German society as a "society of decline" (Nachtwey 2016).

The Cold War entered a hot phase in the early 1980s. During Ronald Reagan's first term as president of the USA, a massive rearmament program began. As reaction, the peace movement grew stronger. In the mid-1980s, the Cold War took a radical turn when Reagan and Soviet party leader Mikhail Gorbachev sought to end the arms race.

---

[13] For the historical processes here described see Wolfrum (2007b).

Other new social movements such as the environmental movement also became stronger. The peace and environmental movements gave rise to the Green Party in 1980. The ecological awareness of the Germans grew, fueled by the "forest dieback," the environmental risks of industry, and by the Chernobyl disaster.

In the cultural sphere, besides the discourses on postmodernism in art, literature, architecture, and science, what was then seen as new media and technologies were particularly influential in the 1980s. Since the mid-1980s, numerous private broadcasting stations have been established. In the field of music, punk and pop were dominant in that era.

As a reaction to these processes, sociology also turned to new topics: Industrial society and service society, unemployment, poverty, mass communication, cultural change (postmaterialism, postmodernism), environmental problems, migration, urban life, gender, individualization, life courses, social change, and social milieus were the major topics of sociological research in the 1980s, which also attests to the increasing differentiation of the sociological field—both institutionally and with regard to its subject matter. This differentiation was, then again, the subject of the perception of an "identity crisis" (Beck 1982, p. 6). There were fears that sociology could "dissolve itself" in the course of parceling out specific fields of problems (Beck 1982, p. 7). The atmosphere of crisis was intensified by the fact that the number of sociology students stagnated in the 1980s (Stockmann 2002, p. 239) and the number of sociological staff at the universities decreased (Lamnek 1991, p. 715).

As the discourse on identity and postmodernism made clear, the belief that sociology would facilitate progress and plannability diminished ever more. Doubts regarding the potential of sociology and its practical application arose. These doubts led to numerous debates on the relationship between theory and practice (Neun 2016) and to reflections on the utilization of sociological knowledge (Beck 1974; Beck 1982; Beck and Bonß 1989). These controversies were influenced by American discussions from the 1960s (cf. Neun 2016, p. 335). In retrospect, they appear to be an early step in the direction of current discussions about "public sociology" in Germany.

As far as social research is concerned, the 1980s marked the end of its growth and heyday. Sociology and social research had successfully established and institutionalized themselves in Germany. As contemporaries noted, the social sciences had become a *"normal science"* (Weischer

2004, p. 375). At times, sociology was so successful that sociological knowledge had become common knowledge or was widely received in other academic disciplines. The downside of this, however, was that a broad sociologization and expansion up to the everyday use of sociological terms simultaneously threatened the status of sociology as an independent discipline (cf. Weischer 2004, p. 377; Moebius 2009).

Everything changed after 1989: The collapse of the Eastern Bloc, the fall of the Berlin Wall, and the German reunification led to massive ruptures and great transformations in sociology in both Germanies. In addition, a generational change took place. The sociologists born before 1930 retired. As Lepsius (2017h, p. 367) showed, 25% of the 400 professorial positions had to be filled. This also contributed to the great transformation of sociology in the 1990s.

**Open Access** This chapter is licensed under the terms of the Creative Commons Attribution 4.0 International License (http://creativecommons.org/licenses/by/4.0/), which permits use, sharing, adaptation, distribution and reproduction in any medium or format, as long as you give appropriate credit to the original author(s) and the source, provide a link to the Creative Commons licence and indicate if changes were made.

The images or other third party material in this chapter are included in the chapter's Creative Commons licence, unless indicated otherwise in a credit line to the material. If material is not included in the chapter's Creative Commons licence and your intended use is not permitted by statutory regulation or exceeds the permitted use, you will need to obtain permission directly from the copyright holder.

CHAPTER 5

# Sociology in the German Democratic Republic

The *Deutsche Demokratische Republik* (DDR, German Democratic Republic (GDR)) was founded in 1949—the FRG had already been constituted—after World War II in the zone of Germany occupied by the Soviets. Shortly after the war, the *Kommunistische Partei Deutschlands* (*KPD*, Communist Party of Germany) and the East German branch of the Social Democratic Party (SPD) merged to form one party, the *Sozialistische Einheitspartei Deutschlands* (SED, Socialist Unity Party of Germany, SUPG). While in the beginning it was a rather heterogeneous party, soon it was dominated by those voices that wanted to move the party closer to the Soviet role model of the Communist Party of the Soviet Union (CPSU) (Roesler 2012, p. 25). The rapprochement with the Soviet Union was also an expression of the incipient Cold War. Moscow had initially favored the founding of a neutral Germany (Roesler 2012, pp. 16–17; Staritz 1985, p. 12), but after the conflicts over Berlin in 1948 (catchwords: Soviet blockade, Allied airlift) and the currency reform in the Western zones, it became clear that a unity of Germany was not intended, not even by the West. Consequently, although major interests of the Soviet Union played a role in the development of the GDR, the founding of the GDR on October 7, 1949, was not the result of a long-cherished plan of Moscow; rather, it has to be seen in close relation and as a reaction to the founding of the FRG and the conflicts in the incipient Cold War (Staritz 1985, p. 11; Roesler 2012, p. 28).

The SED was able to expand its power rapidly. From 1950 it was headed by Walter Ulbricht (1893–1973), who became General Secretary of the party that year. The aim of the party was to build up socialism. Marxism-Leninism was to be imposed as the leading worldview. Ideologically it was sought to take action against all possible "capitalist elements." In different ways, this affected art and culture too. For example, 1949 Bertolt Brecht and Helene Weigel founded the Berliner Ensemble, a German theatre company which even had a great impact in the West. It was also well attended by workers. Another, different example of the ideological effect on art was that artists turned away from the abstract art of the West and proclaimed Socialist Realism.

Already four years after the foundation of the GDR, on June 17, 1953, an uprising took place (Roesler 2012, p. 36) which could not be prevented, not even by the propaganda of a "new course" that was to be taken after Stalin's death in 1953. The starting point for the uprising in June 1953 was the economic difficulties of the GDR. Among other things, the GDR leadership had decided to raise worker norms, so that the workers had to work 10% more for the same wage (Wolfrum 2008, p. 14). This led to immense discontent among the workers. At first, construction workers protested and went on strike against the increase of the working standards. The protests soon expanded and eventually became protests against the SED regime in general. There were nationwide strikes and demonstrations. The SED leadership finally called on the Soviet military for help. The uprising was suppressed with military force. June 17, 1953, engraved itself deeply in the collective consciousness of the GDR citizens as well as into that of the GDR leadership. The citizens were then increasingly intimidated and the leadership expanded its apparatus of repression and control. They avoided an all too sharp confrontation with the population and relied on "more subtle mechanisms of surveillance" (Mählert 2009, p. 78).

State repression reached a further peak in 1961, when over three million people had already left the GDR. The FRG became increasingly threatening to the existence of the GDR, as life in the West seemed much more attractive thanks to the *Wirtschaftswunder* (economic miracle) of the 1950s. When in 1960 the economy in the GDR started to slow down and a shortage of supplies led to a crisis, the number of refugees from the GDR to the FRG increased enormously: "At the beginning of 1961, an average of 19,000 people left each month" (Wolfrum 2008, p. 15). The leaders of the SED reacted by building the Berlin Wall, beginning on August 13, 1961.

The years after 1961 were marked by "reforms and modernization" (Malycha 2011, p. 37; see also Sywottek 2003): In 1962, for example, general conscription was introduced, and in 1963 the "New Economic System" was implemented, by means of which it was hoped that the economy would be modernized toward profit orientation. The "planned economy" and the market were to be combined. The reform was associated with a certain opening and led to a general "spirit of optimism" (Roesler 2012, pp. 58–62), also in the arts and literature. Some believed that once it had been proven that the GDR was superior to the capitalist West, the Wall would be unnecessary. Although the growth in productivity was very slow, the supply with consumer goods such as television sets, refrigerators, and washing machines increased. The demand for consumer goods such as cars was intense, so that there were waiting periods of several years. Television in particular, however, would prove to be a boomerang (Lehmann 2019). Many people in the GDR had secret access to Western TV channels. Now the citizens could directly compare the developments in the GDR with those in the West, or at least with what the culture industry there conveyed as Western reality. Over time, this led to frustration and a subtle renunciation of the socialist project.

Within the political elite, a conservative circle formed that strongly opposed the reform and the "ideological blurring" (Roesler 2012, p. 65), among them the later Secretary General Erich Honecker (1912–1994). Ulbricht made concessions to the conservatives in the areas of culture and youth, but not in the area of economics, where the reform programs should continue to be maintained. There were also reforms of the universities, which in fact brought less of an opening but, rather, more centralization. As we shall see, sociology was also centralized through a Scientific Council for Sociological Research.

The academic personnel also changed in the years after 1945, and the proportion of professors who had a family background in the educated middle classes decreased significantly over the years. People from other classes were now also able to enter the educational sector. For a certain time, students were selected according to social and political criteria, children of workers and farmers were advantaged in the admissions to universities.

The natural sciences, in particular, were funded and closely linked to the economy. This was related to the ideology of the "scientific and technological revolution" propagated by the SED, which came about as a result of the rapid developments in science and technology (Malycha

2011, p. 41). One of these developments could be seen in the field of space research: Yuri Gagarin's 1961 space flight had caused euphoria in the entire Eastern Bloc and fueled technological visions of the future. Science was regarded as an important productive force and it "should deliver technical innovations for the modernization of the economy" (Malycha 2011, p. 41). However, science could not deliver as quickly as had been hoped for and research was far more expensive than politicians thought. Already in the early 1970s "resources for science were increasingly being cut and invested in social policy" instead (Malycha 2011, p. 42).

When Soviet tanks put down the "Prague Spring" at the end of 1968, a lot of people in the GDR lost hope that socialism could be reformed. While the reform of the economy had initially had a positive effect on living standards, in the end the reform did not produce the desired results. At the end of the 1960s economic problems arose that were also related to those in the Soviet Union (Malycha 2011, p. 47). This led to an economic crisis in the GDR and to "reform fatigue and resignation" (Roesler 2012, p. 69) among the population. The Politburo of the Central Committee became increasingly critical of Ulbricht's plans for modernization. The course of Ulbricht's rapprochement with the social-liberal coalition of Chancellor Willy Brandt in West Germany was also heavily criticized by conservative circles (Malycha 2011, p. 48). Finally, on May 3, 1971, Ulbricht was overthrown by Erich Honecker and his circle of reform critics.

In 1971, the SED decided on the "unity of economic and social policy." This led to numerous subsidies, increases in salaries, and the financing of social projects, while at the same time reducing investment in research. At the beginning of the 1970s, the GDR experienced a brief economic upswing that it owed to those measures that had been taken by Ulbricht (Roesler 2012, p. 75). Therefore, the years 1970–1975 have often been described as the best in the GDR. Various modernization measures as well as the admission to the UN took place during these years (Wolfrum 2008, p. 16).

However, similar to the FRG, the oil crisis in the mid-1970s plunged the GDR, too, into a crisis. Debt continued to rise, but initially very few people were aware of this (Roesler 2012, p. 84). Repression also increased. The Ministry of State Security (*Ministerium für Staatssicherheit*, commonly known as *Stasi*), the secret police and intelligence agency of the GDR, established in 1950, was massively expanded in the 1970s (Roesler 2012, p. 80). Discontent among the population grew as it became increasingly obvious that the promises and expectations raised by Honecker would not be fulfilled (Wolfrum 2008, p. 75). In the 1980s opposition groups emerged, especially environmental, church and peace groups. However, these were not fundamentally opposed to a socialist system; rather, they hoped for a different kind of socialism (Roesler 2012, p. 94). Mikhail Gorbachev further nurtured hopes for such a change.

When the border between Hungary and Austria was torn down in May 1989, a wave of emigration began. In Prague, citizens of the GDR occupied the embassy of the FRG. In autumn 1989 there were mass protests. The GDR was in a deep crisis. Even the GDR leadership noticed this. In October, Erich Honecker finally had to resign. The secretary of the Central Committee, Günter Schabowski, presented new travel regulations at a press conference on November 9, 1989, including visa-free travel to the FRG, and in a moment of obvious overstrain and insecurity at the press conference he declared that these were effective immediately. In a moment, thousands headed for the border crossings and finally arrived in West Berlin. The Wall fell. One year later, the GDR no longer existed. In 1990 it became (via "Beitritt") part of the Federal Republic of Germany.

## "Sociology—is that really necessary? We have excellent statistics, excellent statistics!"

At a meeting of the Politburo in 1964, Erich Honecker, who was then still Walter Ulbricht's deputy, questioned: "Sociology—is that really necessary? Yet, we have an excellent statistics, excellent statistics!" (quoted from Sparschuh and Koch 1997, p. 88). Despite this skepticism, sociology was able to establish itself in the GDR and was even officially institutionalized in the same year, 1964. How did this come about?

The development of sociological research in the GDR is embedded in the larger process of social reorganization in the Soviet-occupied zone after 1945. The ideological class struggle was not limited to the political field; in fact, it affected academia too. The universities were undergoing a massive transformation. Besides the early denazification measures, efforts were made to make universities accessible for all social classes. A central concern was the distancing from "bourgeois" Western conceptions of science, which reached as far as into the development of theories, methods, and research strategies (Peter 2018, p. 388). Therefore, it was difficult to tie in with the thinking of early proponents of sociology. The ideological guideline was Marxism-Leninism.

As Frank Ettrich, sociologist from the GDR and now professor in Erfurt, has pointed out, sociology in the GDR can be divided into three phases (Ettrich 1997, pp. 272–292; Sparschuh and Koch 1997, p. 106): The first phase is characterized by the fact that the remnants of "bourgeois" sociology gradually disappeared. In the second phase, sociology re-institutionalized itself in the system of Marxist-Leninist social sciences and a "Marxist-Leninist sociology" emerged. In the third phase, Marxist-Leninist sociology became *normal science* (Kuhn) and empirical research dominated. Only in the 1980s did a "quest for new approaches" and "a new reflection on the sociological heritage" begin (Steiner 1997, p. 225).

## Separation from "Bourgeois" Sociology

In the first phase of sociology in the Soviet-occupied zone there were certain continuities with Weimar sociology (see Chap. 2). Scholars from the Weimar Republic, such as Theodor Litt or Hans Freyer, who was engaged with the Nazis, were still teaching in Leipzig. But they left the GDR fairly quickly. Richard Thurnwald and Alfred Vierkandt, among others, taught at the Humboldt University in Berlin. Thurnwald quickly moved to the West, to the Free University of Berlin, and Vierkandt retired. Also at Humboldt University were Alfred Meusel (1896–1960), a former disciple of Tönnies, and Jürgen Kuczynski (1904–1997), who both had returned from exile. Others, who had come to the GDR on purpose and in hope of a new society, such as Heinz Maus, turned away with disappointment from the GDR after a few years (Peter 2018, p. 389). However, a look at the course lists at that time reveals that after 1945 all universities offered a large number of sociological courses (Steiner 1988, p. 79). These covered topics ranging from the sociology of law to the position of women in society. Sociological essays were published as well. And sociology was also taught in other disciplines (Meyer 1992, p. 263).

After the founding of the state in 1949, however, a stronger separation from Western sociology, which was described as "bourgeois" (Thomas 1990, p. 2), began, which was often equated with a critique of sociology as a whole (Steiner 1988, p. 87). The Frankfurt School, too, was criticized for offering a "bourgeois critique" and therefore for being "theoretically misoriented" (Dieter Ulle quoted by Rust 1973, p. 149). But since sociology itself did not propose any alternative, such as an independent Marxist sociology, and a university reform in 1952 made Marxist-Leninist studies compulsory for all, sociology came to its "institutional end" (Ettrich

1997, p. 275). Instead, political economy, materialistic philosophy, and Marxism-Leninism, as a kind of "science of society" (as, e.g., in the form of "scientific communism"), were now dominating the interpretation and explanation of social processes (Meyer 1992, p. 264).

## The Institutionalization of Marxist-Leninist Sociology

In the mid-1950s, the first impulses for a "new development in sociology" emerged from philosophy and political economy (Sparschuh and Koch 1997, p. 60). The reform policies of Nikita Khrushchev (1894–1971), his critique of Stalin, and the "vision of a scientific and technological revolution" fostered these new developments (Meyer 1992, p. 265). When at the end of the 1950s "a new type of social thinking" appeared in the Eastern Bloc (Meyer 1994, p. 36, English in original), the academic system also began to open up for new disciplines and a slow process of differentiation of academic disciplines began. "[A]lso the idea of instigating empirically oriented social research arose" and social research was equated with sociology (Meyer 1994, p. 36, English in original). Through this differentiation, the individual disciplines, such as sociology, "were relieved of the demands of Marxist-Leninist philosophy to such an extent that they could now establish themselves as separate empirical disciplines, albeit with the condition that they be founded as Marxist-Leninist disciplines" (Ettrich 1997, p. 276).

Sociology was able to evolve as a distinct discipline, but it was not fully independent, because it still stood under "the curatorship of Marxist-Leninist ideology" (Peter 2018, p. 389). Furthermore, it was to serve only the implementation and consolidation of the socialist state. The Marxist-Leninist sociology that emerged from this was basically structured in such a way that it incorporated the empirical methods of "bourgeois" sociology, applied the results to social technology and technocratic reforms, and finally expressed all this in terms of Marxism-Leninism (Ettrich 1997, p. 277). From now on, Marxist-Leninist scientists of society (*Gesellschaftswissenschaftler\*innen*) and Marxist-Leninist sociologists, the latter being reproached for the adoption of "bourgeois" sociology, stood in opposition to each other (Meyer 1992, p. 264). Sociology could only defend itself by emphasizing the need for empirical social research (Kaube 1998, p. 275) and by offering itself as a "service discipline for social progress"

(Kaube 1998, p. 276), an argument that Marxist-Leninist social scientists had difficulty arguing against, since Marx and Engels had already pointed out the usefulness of empirical research (Meyer 1992, pp. 264–265). In the course of the attempts to implement the "scientific-technical revolution" by means of empirical social research, with which sociology tried to establish itself, there were certainly "parallels" to sociology in West Germany (see Chap. 3), which at that time also saw itself as an important means of social technology, prognosis, and "planning knowledge" (Kaube 1998, p. 274). However, while sociology in West Germany soon turned back to the formation of theories, this could not be done to the same extent in the GDR (Kaube 1998, p. 277), because sociology in the GDR had to limit itself to empirical research—theory already existed in the sense of historical materialism.

The new beginning of sociology in the GDR was particularly visible at the universities of Leipzig, Berlin, Rostock, Merseburg, and Halle (Meyer 1992, pp. 268–269; Pasternack 2013). Scholars of the founding generation of GDR sociology mostly came from the fields of economics and philosophy, among them Robert Schulz (1914–2000) (Leipzig) and Herbert Franz Wolf (1927–1993) (Leipzig), Kurt Braunreuther (1913–1975) (Berlin), Hermann Scheler (1911–1972) (Berlin), and Jürgen Kuczynski (Berlin).

Robert Schulz, for example, taught sociology from 1954 onwards and dealt with the history of sociology as well as with French and US-American sociology. In 1956, together with Hermann Scheler, Schulz headed a delegation to the ISA World Congress in Amsterdam (Sparschuh and Koch 1997, p. 42), where he also met René König, who supported the GDR sociologists and tried to integrate them into the international community. Schulz set up a sociological research group and pursued industrial sociology. Industrial sociology was initially one of the preferred topics of sociology in the GDR (Meyer 1992, pp. 269–270), since industry was considered to be of particular relevance not only for economic development, but also for ideological reasons, as the "basic type of the new social relations of the leading class of workers" was to be found there (Meyer 1992, p. 269). In addition, since the end of the 1950s there had also been research in the field of sociology of youth in Leipzig, which was intensified in 1966 with the founding of the *Zentralinstitut für Jugendforschung* (ZIJ) (Central Institute for Youth Research).

From 1956 onwards, Kurt Braunreuther also dealt with sociology in his seminars on the history of economics. He founded a working group on the "critique of bourgeois sociology," from which the Research Association for Sociology and Society (*Forschungsgemeinschaft für Soziologie und Gesellschaft*) emerged in 1961 (Meyer 1994, p. 36, English in original). In this research association Helmut Steiner, Georg Aßmann, Manfred Lötsch, Siegfried Ransch, and others discussed West German sociology. Günther Rudolph (1929–2017), who was studying the work of Tönnies, also belonged to the circle around Braunreuther. The discussion of leading Western German sociologists resulted in rather voluminous dissertations: Herbert Wolf wrote (1963) about the *Formale Soziologie* by Leopold von Wiese, Georg Aßmann (1965) about Schelsky as an apologist of West German imperialism, Günther Rudolph about Tönnies (1966), and since 1962 Braunreuther and Steiner focused on fascist tendencies in several sociological works (Freyer, Ipsen, Höhn, Pfeffer, Schelsky, Müller).

In 1961, the same year the Berlin Wall was built, the *Sektion Soziologie der Vereinigung der philosophischen Institutionen der DDR* (Section for Sociology of the Association of the Philosophical Institutions of the GDR) was founded, which became the national representation of the GDR sociologies in the ISA starting from 1963 (Ettrich 1997, p. 277).[1] The chairman was Hermann Scheler. In 1958, he published the book *Probleme des historischen Materialismus und der marxistischen Sozialforschung* (*Problems of Historical Materialism and Marxist Social Research*), which is seen by some as "the first sociological document of the GDR" (Sparschuh and Koch 1997, p. 67).

Sociology experienced an important boost in 1963. The political background of this boost was "the turn towards a technocratic socialism" (Thomas 1990, p. 3). It was hoped that sociology would provide support for the political leadership of the party and the state. At the VI Party Congress of the SED, it was therefore stated in the party program that sociological research should be intensified. In addition, efforts were made to centralize sociology. Against the background of this political decision, sociology was finally officially institutionalized in 1964. A department was established at the Institute for Economic Sciences at the German Academy of Sciences in Berlin, with Helmut Steiner, Manfred Thiel, Rainer Schubert, Manfred Lötsch, and Hansgünter Meyer, working on industry, organization, labor, and social structure (Meyer 1994, pp. 36–37). Braunreuther became a member of the Scientific Council for Sociological

---

[1] On the process of institutionalization see the overview in Sparschuh and Koch (1997, pp. 273–287).

Research in the German Democratic Republic, founded in 1964. The founding of this Council was based on a decision of the Politburo of the Central Committee (CC) of the SED. The chairman of the Council from 1968–1971 was Erich Hahn (*1930), and from 1972–1989 it was Rudi Weidig (1931–2012) (Weidig 1997, Sparschuh and Koch 1997, p. 53, footnote 34). The Scientific Council was located at the Department for Sociological Research at the *Institut für Gesellschaftswissenschaften* (IfG) (Institute for Social Sciences) at the SED CC (Weidig 1997, p. 61).[2] The scholars were ambivalent about the Council. They perceived it "as a disciplining body on the one hand, and as a protective shield for the discipline against political intervention on the other" (Sparschuh and Koch 1997, p. 93).

The SED now increasingly demanded and supported sociological research, hoping that it would be of use for the political leadership and for political planning. Unlike in the West, however, the institutionalization that now took place did not mean an increase in autonomy. Rather, as Frank Ettrich emphasizes, the institutionalization of sociology served the purpose of instrumentalizing sociology for the requirements of preserving the system. Sociology was now "within the party, officially the 'science of the management and development of society'" (Ettrich 1997, p. 278). Two complementary positions could be observed in the sociological field. One was oriented more toward the technocratic guidelines of the SED for the "objectivization of social planning," the other followed the guiding idea and research of the "socialist human community" and sought to prove that the "scientific-technical revolution would lead to the socialist human community" (Ettrich 1997, pp. 281–282).

Despite or perhaps because of the control and orientation toward the party, there was an "upswing in sociology" (Sparschuh and Koch 1997, p. 71). This initially concerned empirical research. But also studying: Since the mid-1960s, students of an economics or philosophy major could choose sociology as a minor. However, there was no full-fledged sociology program until 1975 (Meyer 1994, p. 38; Kaube 1998, p. 268). By 1989 there were 600 graduates with a sociology diploma (Meyer 1994, p. 38). There was also a small "boom" in institutionalization in the form of congresses: From 1969 onwards, the Scientific Council organized congresses; altogether they organized five major congresses, one about every five

---

[2] In the mid-1970s, the Institute for Social Sciences at the SED CC became the Academy for the Social Sciences at the SED CC.

years. However, other important elements of successful institutionalization were missing: The establishment of a separate association or journal was not permitted. This was justified by the fact that sociologists could publish in the *Deutsche Zeitschrift für Philosophie* or in one of the journals of the economists (Sparschuh and Koch 1997, p. 88). However, research results could also be published in the periodical of the Scientific Council *Information on Sociological Research in the German Democratic Republic* (Thomas 1990, p. 5). In addition, there was a publication series titled "Sociology" of the party publisher Dietz. It was not until the 5th Congress in 1990 that an independent *Gesellschaft für Soziologie der DDR* (GfS) (Society for Sociology of the GDR) was established and the *Berlin Journal of Sociology* (*Berliner Journal für Soziologie*), edited by Manfred Lötsch (1936–1993), Artur Meier (*1932), Hansgünter Meyer (1929–2015), Peter Voigt (1939–2014), and Herbert F. Wolf, was published, with Frank Ettrich (*1958) as editor-in-chief (Meyer 1994, p. 39). These processes took place immediately after the collapse of the GDR.

## Marxist-Leninist Sociology on Its Way to a Normal Science?

Many sociologists perceived the period up to the transfer of power from Ulbricht to Honecker in 1971 as the "productive phase" of sociology in the GDR (Sparschuh and Koch 1997, p. 108). An indication of the gradual consolidation and canonization was the publication of the *Wörterbuch der marxistisch-leninistischen Soziologie* (*Dictionary of Marxist-Leninist Sociology*) in 1969 and the textbook *Grundlagen der marxistisch-leninistischen Soziologie* (*Principles of Marxist-Leninist Sociology*) in 1977, but this canonization was at the same time also perceived as "normalization" (Sparschuh and Koch 1997, pp. 108–109). The hope was that empirical social research could be conducted under the theoretical framework of historical materialism. However, as Thomas (1990, p. 20) has pointed out, social research was also increasingly subject to "control measures," such as bans on publications or interventions in the design of empirical research.

While the main focus of sociology in the GDR until the end of the 1960s was on industrial sociology, the sociology of labor, sociology of organizations, sociology of agriculture, sociology of culture, sociology of education and youth, as well as the development of personality (Ludz

1972a, 1972b; Wittich and Taubert 1970), it continued to differentiate itself in the following years (Hamm 1989, p. 142). In addition, there were social policy research, demography, sociology of science, of medicine, of religion, of development, sociolinguistics, research on mass communication, urban sociology, and sociology of sports (Meyer 1992, pp. 268–269; 1994, pp. 40–46; Kaube 1998, pp. 286–290).

As of the 1970s, analyses of social structure and social change became central topics (Thomas 1990, p. 7). It had become apparent that the social reality of the "socialist human community" was more complex and differentiated than expected and that social policy measures had to be tailored to the specific situation. For this reason, research on social structure was closely related to the party's efforts to achieve a "unity of economic and social policy" and an "alignment of other classes and strata with the working class" (Ettrich 1997, p. 287). Sociology was to accompany and legitimize the policies of the SED. This led to a "re-actualization of the class theorem" (Peter 2018, p. 400), to an increased revaluation of the working class and to the view that there were also differentiations within the working class. In accordance with the focus on social and political planning, the second Sociological Congress in 1974 was devoted to the "Contribution of Marxist-Leninist sociology to the management and planning of social processes in the shaping of the developed socialist society."

Although sociology was actually supposed to serve the legitimation of the state, it simultaneously unfolded, "even in its crudest empirical form, a force that was delegitimizing ideological normativity" (Ettrich 1997, p. 289). For example, sociological research revealed that it was not the working class but the class of white-collar workers that was growing, and that not a proletarian but, rather, a petty-bourgeois white-collar worker habitus prevailed. Nevertheless, the phase of the 1970s was marked by system adjustment and self-censorship. This often led to results that conformed to the system and to highly speculative forecasts. For example, indications were seen that the two classes of "workers and peasants" and the class of scientific-technical intelligentsia would merge (Peter 2018, pp. 400–401). This idea of levelling correlated with the assumption that society is a coherent, uniform organism—that the "socialist society was a [...] uniform entity" (Kaube 1998, pp. 263–264). As Jürgen Kaube has pointed out, sociologists in the GDR saw themselves as a functional component of this "organic solidarity" (Durkheim), as "part of a society based on the division of labor" (Kaube 1998, p. 263).

Often the sociologists focused on the possibilities of political application of their results in order to justify their research (Thomas 1990, p. 9). "Since the methods and techniques of empirical research were adapted to the state's monopoly of political planning, they could thus only sporadically contribute to findings in which a critical processing of social processes and relationships manifested itself" (Peter 2018, p. 398). If the results did not fit into the political concept, they were kept secret; the researchers were disciplined or dismissed (Meyer 1992, p. 271). For example, in 1978 the Institute for Opinion Research at the SED CC was closed down. Honecker justified this by arguing that the surveys should not fall into the hands of the "class enemy"—"the reasoning allows the conclusion that the results of the survey research had turned out to be less favorable for the politics of the SED than the General Secretary had expected" (Thomas 1990, p. 19).

In 1980, the "concept of the socialist way of life" moved into the center of sociological attention (Thomas 1990, p. 18). It was intended as an alternative approach to "the research on the 'standard of living', 'quality of life' or 'lifestyle' that began in the FRG in the 1960s" (Kaube 1998, p. 289). The third Sociological Congress was dedicated to the topic "Social structure and way of life in shaping the developed socialist society." Sociologists tried to develop social indicators and to make them useful for the planning of society. In particular, the Institute for Sociology and Social Policy, founded in 1978 at the Academy of the Sciences and headed by Gunnar Winkler (1931–2019), was leading in this field (Thomas 1990, p. 18; Kaube 1998, pp. 267–268).

At the beginning of the 1980s, it was especially Manfred Lötsch, Rudi Weidig, Frank Adler, Albrecht Kretzschmar, and Ingrid Lötsch who criticized the theorem of the convergence of classes and the notion of social homogeneity (Thomas 1990, p. 21; Peter 2018, pp. 401–402). According to them, the social processes of differentiation that were also noticeable in the GDR as well as the inequalities between the working class and the class of the scientific-technical intelligentsia were not to be denied but to be used productively. On the basis of a study of engineers in the GDR, as a group belonging to the class of scientific-technical intelligentsia, it could be shown that this group could only play a central role in the process of modernization if its specific social position and status characteristics were acknowledged. The analyses of Lötsch et al. (1988) gave rise to debates. These analyses were agreed upon by most sociologists but not used for political practice (Thomas 1990, p. 21). Innovation by sociologists was neither expected nor desired; critical findings were kept secret. The state was satisfied—if at all—if sociologists stuck to their role of "sociotechnological assistants" (Thomas 1990, p. 21).

The change in the 1980s toward more critical tones was, among other things, the result of a change of generations (Sparschuh and Koch 1997, p. 112; Kaube 1998, p. 292), of increasing professionalization, and of the general transformation in the Eastern Bloc (perestroika and glasnost) (Sparschuh and Koch 1997, p. 106). In 1988, at the joint *Soziologentag* of the Swiss, Austrian, and German Sociological Associations in Zurich, further official exchanges with the West took place when "the first official delegation of East German sociologists" took part (Meyer 1994, p. 34, English in original). The 1980s saw a further relative expansion and pluralization of the fields of research. In addition to social structure, demography, change in values, sociology of work, youth, family, and urban sociology, there was now an increasing amount of research on crime, war and peace, family, leisure, the environment, and on the role of women in society (Meyer 1994, pp. 40–46).

However, women's studies had a particularly difficult position because, according to the ideology under socialism, there was no discrimination against women. The reality was of course different (Adler and Kretzschmar 1993; Kaminsky 2020). Even male colleagues in sociology sometimes polemically distanced themselves from feminist positions. Although there had previously been research on the position of women, the inequalities between men and women were always regarded as a so-called "side contradiction" which would dissolve automatically once the social antagonisms between the classes had disappeared; or, women's studies were "ridiculed as a hobby" (Dölling 1993). In contrast to sociology in West Germany, where gender was considered a central category of social structure by then, the "women's question" was subordinated to the "social question." "The possibility that gender relations could be an independent social structural category that did not merge with the relations of production, let alone be the determining structural element of modern societies in general, was persistently denied, not even admitted as a debatable research question" (Peter 2018, p. 405). This only changed in the 1980s with researchers such as Hildegard Maria Nickel (*1948) or Irene Dölling who were also important for the reception of Bourdieu in the unified Germany. Influenced by Bourdieu, by Symbolic Interactionism, Structuralism, and Feminist Marxism, Dölling and other female researchers in the GDR were interested in the "cultural constructions of femininity and masculinity, their concrete manifestations, for example in literature or the visual arts, and their role in establishing and stabilizing relationships of power and domination" (Dölling 1993, p. 400; 2006).

## THE CHARACTERISTICS AND ROLE OF SOCIOLOGY IN THE GDR

What were the characteristics of sociology in the GDR? Sociologists from the GDR characterized them in "terms of sources" as "German three times over": firstly, through its relation to Karl Marx and the classical German philosophy incorporated in his work, "secondly through its dependence on the classical bases of German sociology, and finally through its incessant efforts to attain the professional format of West German sociological practice" (Meyer 1994, p. 34, English in original). Frank Ettrich (1997, p. 272) considers the following to be the peculiar characteristic of sociology in the GDR: It wanted to follow the "universalistic rules of science" and, at the same time, the "particularistic demands of the political system." According to Kaube, another "dilemma of sociology in the GDR" was that sociology saw its function in the orientation toward social problems, but politics had little interest in "taking on this service function" (Kaube 1998, pp. 276–277).

As for the specific role that sociology played in the GDR, referring to Lothar Peter (2018, pp. 413–415), the following points can be made: Firstly, sociology played "no orienting intellectual role" in the transformation processes around 1989. It was predominantly conformist with the system and, if at all, it tended to make cautious proposals for reform. It was therefore far from being a kind of critical discipline. This was not only due to pressure from the state, but also to a dogmatic interpretation and application of the work of Marx and Engels. Secondly, in its "fixation on social laws and regularities," sociology could not turn its attention to those social processes, events, and structural changes that did not follow regularities. Even if one can find parts of such thinking in Marxism, at the same time this contradicted that part in Marx and Engels that assumes a historicity of everything that has to do with society. Thirdly, despite all that, sociological approaches developed which had a "relatively independent profile." By this, Lothar Peter refers in particular to those analyses that turned to empirical reality. These approaches tried, so to speak, to dissolve the connection between the base and the superstructure "from below" (Peter 2018, p. 415). Although extremely productive, however, even these approaches did not succeed in "breaking through the established paradigm of Marxism-Leninism and in developing a qualitatively new, independent form of critical sociological analysis" (Peter 2018, p. 415). Fourthly, GDR sociology was always under the "guardianship of economics and philosophy," and fifthly, it largely detached itself from the international discourse. Sociology in the GDR was limited exclusively to "the presence of its own state" (Kaube 1998, p. 283).

It was only during the final years of the GDR that one could observe hopeful signs of an opening and renewal. In 1990, at the 5th Congress of GDR Sociology, the *Gesellschaft für Soziologie* was founded (Schäfers 2016) in the hope that GDR sociology would become an equal partner of West German sociology (Lepsius 2017h, p. 334). It would also have been interesting to see what view of West Germany GDR sociology would have developed. But by then it was already too late. After the reunification at the beginning of the 1990s, sociology in the GDR was "completely wound up" (Kaube 1998, p. 297) and the elaboration of an independent Marxist or critical sociology was thus denied. Many researchers were dismissed; sociology was reorganized from the West. A considerable number of sociologists from West Germany have been offered positions at universities in the East. They have thus benefited from the "winding-up" of the universities in the East and assumed the power of definition of "good" sociology.

In addition, as Jürgen Kaube (1998, p. 271) points out, in contrast to sociology in West Germany, there was no real formation of different, opposing "schools" in the GDR sociology. If one follows Kaube (1998, p. 271), however, it is precisely the internal controversies, conflicts, and competitive situations that not only produce new knowledge and innovations, but also give academic disciplines their structure (cf. Kneer and Moebius 2010). This is another reason why a "unified science", as some sociologists are now demanding in Germany, is not desirable. Sociology in the GDR understood itself, analogous to the ideology of its social model, as a conflict-free entity. GDR sociology "externalized" conflict and competition; there was competition only in the "external relationship of the social sciences to the 'bourgeois class'," but this external competition was not sufficient, because it "did not have a structure-building effect internally" (Kaube 1998, p. 271).

**Open Access**  This chapter is licensed under the terms of the Creative Commons Attribution 4.0 International License (http://creativecommons.org/licenses/by/4.0/), which permits use, sharing, adaptation, distribution and reproduction in any medium or format, as long as you give appropriate credit to the original author(s) and the source, provide a link to the Creative Commons licence and indicate if changes were made.

The images or other third party material in this chapter are included in the chapter's Creative Commons licence, unless indicated otherwise in a credit line to the material. If material is not included in the chapter's Creative Commons licence and your intended use is not permitted by statutory regulation or exceeds the permitted use, you will need to obtain permission directly from the copyright holder.

CHAPTER 6

# Sociology in Germany After 1990

After Hungary had opened its borders to Austria in May 1989, numerous citizens of the GDR were able to travel to the FRG via Austria. This increased the pressure on the GDR leadership. They could not expect any help from Mikhail Gorbachev. Rather, Gorbachev's reform politics of "glasnost" and "perestroika" encouraged the opposition groups. Many of these groups had supported the peace movement in the GDR in the 1980s and had already formed networks. However, it had become clear that the protesters did not aim for the end of the GDR, but for "a different GDR" (Conze 2009, pp. 689, 694).[1] In September 1989, the *Neue Forum* (New Forum) had been founded, as well as the group *Demokratie Jetzt* (Democracy Now); this was followed by the foundation of the *Sozialdemokratische Partei in der DDR* (Social Democratic Party in the GDR). It was not only the emigrants who advanced the transformation process of the GDR; the SED regime (*Sozialistischen Einheitspartei Deutschlands*) was, to a large extent, brought down by the aforementioned political groups, that is, by people who were still remaining in the GDR. The growing commitment of the people eventually became evident in the ever-growing "Monday demonstrations" in Leipzig.

The images of the demonstrations in Leipzig, especially the "Monday demonstration" of October 9, 1989, which was attended by 70,000

[1] In the following brief summary of the historical developments, I refer mainly to Conze (2009) and Görtemaker (2004, 2009).

people, suggested that profound social and political changes were taking place within the society of the GDR. The GDR was in a deep crisis; by that time even the GDR leadership realized this. It was losing more and more control. In October, finally, the General Secretary Erich Honecker had to resign. The power of the state party, the SED, decayed ever more.

A central date was November 9, 1989. As already mentioned in Chap. 5, at a press conference the secretary of the Central Committee Günter Schabowski presented new travel regulations and declared the possibilities for traveling abroad to be "effective immediately". As a result, thousands headed for the border crossings and finally to West Berlin. The Wall fell.

In the beginning, confederative relations between the GDR and the FRG were still being considered (and many of the civil rights activists had been hoping for these relations); however, the situation changed due to economic and political developments. While in 1989 the GDR's productivity lagged 45% behind that of West Germany (Heske 2005, p. 76), the GDR was now increasingly in danger of an economic collapse. Former trading partners of the "Eastern Bloc" were themselves in crisis and GDR products were increasingly in competition with West German consumer goods. Numerous citizens left the GDR and sought their fortune in the West. Politically, the GDR government lacked popular support. This dynamic led to the reunification of Germany becoming more realistic than a two-state solution or confederation.

Expectations were high. With the fall of the Berlin Wall, the social problems of the Federal Republic, which became increasingly apparent in the 1980s, faded into the background for a short time. For a few months there was a mood of "collective effervescence" (Durkheim). This situation of transformation in part corresponded to a "liminal phase" (van Gennep), which, according to Victor Turner (1969), is characterized by a great sense of community ("communitas"). Everything seemed possible, although it was not yet certain that the protests of autumn 1989 would result in German reunification—it was a highly contingent situation.

After a few weeks, however, the initial enthusiasm gave way to disillusionment, not because of the collapse of the GDR, but because of the ways and effects of the process of transformation. At first, the protest groups that had contributed a great deal to the fall of the Berlin Wall were disappointed. In the process of transformation, they lost their leading political role. Moreover, they had not hoped for a takeover of the GDR by the FRG, but for a transformation of the GDR. However, the political weight of the FRG and of Chancellor Helmut Kohl was too great. Kohl pushed for a quick reunification. In March 1990, elections were held in the GDR. The winning parties were not only those that wanted to join the FRG quickly, but also those that had the decisive support of the established West German parties. On August 23, 1990, the new government of the GDR decided on the GDR's accession to the FRG as of October 3, 1990. On this date, Germany was officially reunified. Some historians, however, describe it as more of an "expansion of West Germany," because it was "not a reunification of two equal states" (Ther 2019, p. 77).

The costs of the reunification "exceeded the forecasts considerably" (Görtemaker 2004, p. 768). As economists had predicted, purchasing power flowed out of the former GDR economy. Income disparities within the eastern parts of Germany grew ever wider. Although there were some beneficiaries of the reunification, there were a great many people who were now economically worse off. After 1990, social differences increased to a level that had been unknown in the GDR. The West German private sector contributed to the "economic decline" of the East. They refrained from investing. Capital flows from the West were almost non-existent. Therefore, more public resources were channeled to the East (Görtemaker 2004, p. 769). Privatization and deindustrialization processes took place, which benefited companies in West Germany. A central player in this radical privatization process was the "Treuhand agency," established to privatize the East German *Volkseigene Betriebe* (publicly owned enterprises). After the companies were privatized, only every fourth job remained (Böick 2018), and many felt that they had lost out in the transformation. This further fueled the discontent and disappointment of many East German citizens about the process of reunification.

These social changes were embedded in wider processes of global transformation. However, the process of winding-up the GDR proceeded at such a rapid pace that many people were no longer able to process them in their subjective experiences; nor were the political, cultural, and economic institutions able to do so. This led to experiences of anomie. The ways of life changed radically and very quickly. This can be seen from the rental costs. They rose to 20 times the levels of the GDR era, while incomes only doubled. All this led to a "fragmented development" (Land 2003) and to many social problems and frustrations among people socialized in the GDR.

Not only economically, but also with respect to the political, legal, educational and scientific institutions, East Germany was adapted to Western conditions. A unilateral transfer of elites and culture from West to East could be observed (Conze 2009, p. 780), which many people socialized in East Germany experienced as degradation and devaluation. The transformation processes were often perceived as a real "culture shock" (Wagner 1996). The unilateral transfer could also be observed with regard to the academic system (Kocka 1998, p. 7). The opportunities for a general restructuring were squandered. As far as sociology is concerned, there was a complete "unwinding of the structures of sociological research in the GDR" (Kaube 1998, p. 297; see also Schäfers 1993, p. 831).

One thing is certain: The reorganization of sociology and "the new appointments were carried out under West German rule" (Lepsius 2017g, p. 275). The commissions that decided on the future of sociology in East Germany were composed of sociologists from West Germany. They did not have much insight into sociology in the GDR. Some did not even consider the research of their colleagues from the GDR to be sociology, but considered it to be socialism. Although this might not have been intended, at the end of the transformation process sociologists from West Germany dominated the newly established institutes in the East. Apart from a few exceptions, there were hardly any GDR sociologists remaining (Lepsius 2017h [1993], p. 362). "Within three years, about 40 new professorships were established, a unique growth considering the 350 professorships in West Germany. After a phase in which the expansion of personnel in West Germany stagnated from about 1980 onwards, for many [sociologists] new career opportunities arose" (Lepsius 2017g, p. 275). But even 20 years after the fall of the Berlin Wall, in 2009, just fewer than 4% of the sociology professors were from the former GDR (Mau and Huschka 2010).

But back to 1990: Sociology in the GDR had attempted to reorganize and renew itself. As mentioned in Chap. 5, in February 1990, the 5th Congress of GDR sociology took place. Subsequently, a *Gesellschaft für Soziologie* (GfS, Society for Sociology) was founded (Schäfers 2016). At this time, it was clear that the GDR would be annexed to the FRG, but the conditions under which this would be done were not yet known (Meyer 1992, p. 5). There were hopes that GDR sociology would become an "equal partner" of West German sociology (Lepsius 2017h [1993], p. 334). In 1991, the GfS still organized a *Soziologentag* in Leipzig. It was a last, but futile attempt to promote East German sociology. The GfS disbanded in 1992. However, it still managed to found a sociological journal which is still one of the most renowned sociological journals in Germany, the *Berliner Journal für Soziologie* (*Berlin Journal of Sociology*) (Ettrich 2018).

Within three years, sociology in East Germany was re-established. It was recommended that the newly established professorships and institutes be structured in such a way that the fields of "theory, macrosociology, microsociology and methods" would be covered, preferably with one or two additional professorships for one of the special sociologies (Lepsius 2017g, p. 276, 2017h [1993], pp. 340–341). The first appointments to the professorships were made in 1992. Non-university research institutions that had employed the majority of sociologists were disbanded or reorganized (Lepsius 2017h [1993], pp. 336–337). The process of structuring sociology in East Germany was not without problems. For example, unequal gender relations established themselves here as well. "Of the 38 professors of sociology appointed in the new federal states until the end of 1993 [...] only 4 were women [...]" (Nickel 2006, p. 266).

## Reflections on Transformations in the Social Sciences

Nobody thought that the GDR would collapse. In a project that I am conducting together with my colleagues Karl-Siegbert Rehberg (*1943) and Joachim Fischer (*1951) from Dresden, we interview older sociologists from German-speaking countries. At the end of the interview, we ask the following question: Which social processes were surprising for you despite your sociological expertise? The answer from respondents such as Thomas Luckmann, Peter L. Berger, Renate Mayntz and Ulrich Beck was unanimous: The most surprising event was the collapse of the GDR and of the Eastern Bloc. Sociology was completely unprepared for this (e.g., see Beck 1991).[2]

The social dynamics of the reunification were the driving force for new initiatives in the field of the social sciences (Krause and Ostner 2010; Schäfers 1996). The surprise and failure of sociology to foresee the collapse of the Eastern Bloc led to increased reflection and analysis. Sociological research on transformations began relatively soon after the reunification (Hauser 2010). This trend was promoted by the establishment of a *Kommission für die Erforschung des sozialen und politischen Wandels in den neuen Bundesländern* (KSPW, Commission for the Study of Social and Political Change in the New Federal States). This

---

[2] Among the few exceptions who boast of having foreseen the collapse is Randall Collins (1995).

commission was to reorganize the East German research system. The establishment of a priority program of the *Deutschen Forschungsgemeinschaft* (DFG, German Research Foundation) titled "Social and Political Change in the Course of the Integration of the GDR Society" (Esser 2000, pp. 7–8) was central to this process. Numerous research projects on social change were conducted in this context. Other institutions such as the *Wissenschaftszentrum Berlin* (Berlin Social Science Center), the *Max-Planck-Institut für Bildungsforschung* (Max Planck Institute for Human Development), the *Zentrum für Umfragen, Methoden und Analysen* (ZUMA, Center for Surveys, Methods and Analyses) in Mannheim and the *Demoskopische Institut* (Demoscopic Institute) in Allensbach also contributed to the fact that empirical social research was intensified in an "incomparable manner" (Rehberg 2000, p. 14).

Everyone, including researchers from the East, had to venture into uncharted territory. It can be critically remarked that this was also a kind of "appropriation by research" (Rehberg 2000, p. 15). An equally extensive research program and transfer of financial and infrastructural means would also have been good for the old federal states, because there was still enough research to be done there (Rehberg 2000, p. 15).

Different perspectives and approaches could be observed in the sociological research of transformations (see, for the following summary, Joas and Kohli 1993a). The spectrum ranged from modernization theory (represented for example by Wolfgang Zapf (1937–2018)),[3] systems theory (Detlef Pollack (*1955)), sociology of institutions (Wolfgang Schluchter), sociology of law (Bernhard Schäfers (*1939)), sociology of gender (Hildegard Nickel), sociology of social movements (Dieter Rucht (*1946)) to rational choice (Karl-Dieter Opp). For some, such as Detlef Pollack (1990), a sociologist of religion originally from East Germany, the collapse of the GDR was the result of a contradiction. According to him, the contradiction was that the GDR was on the one hand a modern, functionally differentiated industrial society, but on the other hand politically and ideologically undifferentiated and run by one party. Others like Wolfgang Zapf (1991, pp. 23–24) saw the theory of modernization confirmed. Since the GDR had lagged far behind in modernization, in Zapf's eyes it was inevitable that it would collapse. Even Jürgen Habermas (1990), who was usually not a supporter of the theory of modernization, called this "a

---

[3] Here I only mention a few names representing these approaches; of course, there were further individuals contributing to them.

catching-up revolution" (*nachholende Revolution*), with which the East was now normatively annexed to the Western democracies. For a short time, this view of the theory of modernization prevailed and experienced a brief comeback (not only in sociology, but in the public at large), after it had previously been abandoned in the course of the discourses on postmodernism. Francis Fukuyama's thesis of the "end of history" (Fukuyama 1992) became famous in this context.

There were also criticisms of these explanations for the collapse of the GDR. It was criticized that some theoretical concepts were not even considered in the analysis. According to Thomas Bulmahn (1996), there was initially a lack of concepts dealing with social inequalities and the German social structure. Gender relations were also ignored in research on the transformations (Nickel 2006, p. 271). Similarly, there were hardly any analyses of the effects of international processes. There was also a lack of "comparative analyses" comparing the transformation in Germany with other processes in Eastern and Central Europe (Bulmahn 1996, p. 25). These concepts, too, would have contributed toward an further explanation. But they were lost due to the hegemony of modernization theory and rational choice approaches. However, novel perspectives emerged as well. For instance, following the boom in the sociology of emotions that began in 1980 the effects of the "*Wende*" (a different term for the reunification) on the control of affects, the management of emotions, and the specific feeling cultures of East Germans (Neckel 1991) were analyzed. Other studies looked into the nostalgia for the time in the GDR the so-called Ostalgie (a word that blends "*Osten*", which is the German term for "eastern", and "nostalgia") (Neller 2006; Frevert 2020, pp. 285–288).

Because foreign policy factors, the regime's lack of resistance, and also the factor of historical contingency were neglected, the explanations often resembled teleological stories of progress, sacralized the people, or lapsed into a heroic narrative, according to which only the people of the GDR had brought about reunification, in a "revolution." In order to give more weight to foreign policy factors and the regime, Hans Joas and Martin Kohli (1993b, p. 9) more precisely referred to the transformation as a "collapse of the GDR" and not a "revolution" (Joas and Kohli 1993b, p. 9).

When it became obvious that theories of modernization and rational choice theories could not adequately explain the processes of upheaval and the crisis phenomena, the specific power relations, the historically contingent developments, the often one-sided cultural transfers, and the experience of disintegration associated with these processes, the attractiveness of alternative theories of social change increased. The focus of interest was not limited to the transformation of the GDR, but also included the larger processes of transition in Eastern Europe, transformations of the welfare states, and the process of European unification. In Germany, it was especially the "theory of reflexive modernization" of Ulrich Beck that was widely discussed in the course of the 1990s (Beck et al. 1994). The thesis was as follows: The processes of technological progress initiated by modern society and their secondary consequences fall back on society in a "reflexive" manner. The resulting uncertainty is further intensified by "thrusts of individualization" that radically change class affiliation, religious denominations, political divisions, work processes, and family relationships. The prevailing sociological picture of industrial society, Beck claimed, must therefore be redrawn. This means that modernity itself reacts with modernization mechanisms to the secondary consequences it brings about. In this context, "reflexive" means less the increase in conscious knowledge about the side effects and problems of modernization processes than ignorance of them, which is why Beck does not intend "reflexive" to be understood in the sense of conscious, intentional reflection (Beck et al. 1994, pp. 5–6), but rather in the sense of reflexive behavior, that is, the reactive attempts to control "latent side effects" (Beck et al. 1994, p. 5). Beck examined not only processes in Germany, but also called for greater consideration of global processes (Beck 1997). In his view, sociology was still focused far too much on nation states. According to Beck (2007), a sociology of the present, however, had to detach itself from national analyses and pursue a so-called methodological cosmopolitism, that is, to examine societies as globally interdependent entities.

Beck's theory of reflexive modernization and globalization was not the only theory postulating a new kind of modernity. In addition to this, very popular among sociologist at that time was Shmuel Eisenstadt's theory of multiple modernities, postcolonial studies, and Zygmunt Bauman's theory of postmodernism. However, with the turning away from the grand theories of Habermas and Luhmann, two major trends could be observed: a trend toward "special sociologies" or "hyphen-sociologies" (*"Bindestrichsoziologien"*), and a trend toward "diagnoses of contemporary society" (*"Zeitdiagnosen"*). In the GSA there are now 36 sections (research networks) for fields ranging from sociology of age and aging to sociology of law. Looking at the topics covered in leading sociological journals in Germany, the sociology of culture[4] and the sociology of knowledge have experienced a boom, followed by the sociology of work, economy, and politics. As a result of this differentiation and specialization process, nowadays the so-called hyphen-sociologies often have their own journals. As the foundation of the Section for Qualitative Research shows, these differentiation processes were often the result of struggles within the sociological field. The section for Qualitative Research could not to be established until 2003, because there was strong resistance against it from the more quantitatively dominated GSA-section on "Methods of Empirical Social Research" (Ploder 2018, p. 751).

The topics of the booming diagnoses of contemporary society range from "risk society" (Beck 1986) to "experience society" (Schulze 1995), "knowledge society" (Stehr 1994), "fear society" (Bude 2014), "multi-option society" (Gross 1994), or "society of decline" (Nachtwey 2016)—to name but a few. Since the 1990s, these often one-sided diagnoses have been increasingly frequent and were presented in shorter intervals, fueled by demands for public sociology and promoted by a corresponding literature market that has made profitable use of these diagnoses. For politics, however, all the explanations of sociology have remained relatively inconsequential—with the exception of Ulrich Beck's "risk society", as we will see.

The boom and the rapid change in sociological diagnoses correlated with the social experiences of fragmentation, flexibilization, discontinuity, and disintegration. While the theories of Luhmann, Habermas, and Bourdieu were still characterized by the fact that they regarded society as a relatively stable system whose elements are not randomly associated, this now changed. As in other countries, in French sociology, for example (cf. Moebius and Peter 2004), in the 1990s, concepts such as social system, social field, or social totality were increasingly replaced by categories that focused on sub-aspects of what in the traditional concept of society was only relevant as a part of the whole. Now society was *merely* seen as a

---

[4] It should be noted that the sociology of culture or cultural sociology in Germany, both in terms of its tradition (Lichtblau 1996) and in the course of its revitalization by Friedrich Tenbruck, encompasses more than the analysis of culture in the narrower sense (music, literature, art, and theater), but also education, values, lifestyles, and so on, and above all theory (Moebius 2019; see also Chap. 4). At times, the section cultural sociology understood itself as the "true" theory section.

"knowledge society," "experience society," or "information society."[5] Thus, these diagnoses often suggested that society is not a systematically structured, holistic entity. Sociological diagnoses replaced the theory of society. In contrast to previous theories, these diagnoses were characterized by the fact that they often made a very radical distinction between a before and after of the state of society and only emphasized individual aspects of society (cf. Osrecki 2011).

## WHY DO WE NEED SOCIOLOGY TODAY?

The pluralization into many special sociologies ("hyphen-sociologies") was also a central aspect in a revived self-critical debate about the purpose of sociology. In the mid-1990s a series of articles appeared in the renowned weekly newspaper *DIE ZEIT* under the title *Der Streit um die Soziologie* ("The Dispute over Sociology"), which dealt with the role of sociology in society (see the articles in Fritz-Vannahme 1996). "Is there anything that sociology can contribute to contemporary German society?" "Why do politicians and the public today turn more to geneticists and brain researchers than to sociologists when seeking advice?" Questions like these were raised in the articles. Once again, sociology was perceived as being in crisis. The critical argument was that society had already disintegrated to such an extent that, in fact, it no longer existed: instead of society there were only individuals. This was reminiscent of the famous quote by Margaret Thatcher: "There is no such thing as society. There are individual men and women and there are families." In the debate in *DIE ZEIT*, the falling apart of sociology was diagnosed, too. Sociologists such as Dirk Kaesler, Ralf Dahrendorf, Hans-Peter Müller (*1951), Peter Wagner (*1956), Gerhard Schulze (*1944), and Renate Mayntz reacted to the criticism, and Pierre Bourdieu also wrote an article. In response to the critique of sociology, some of the sociologists demanded a return to a greater social engagement of sociology. Sociology was said to be both a means of improving society and a troublemaker, drawing attention to social problems and revealing hidden power relations. Moreover, some authors argued, it was perhaps not sociology that was in crisis, but the general idea of science in society, which increasingly relied only on mathematicized scientific products. Many people would wish that sociology

---

[5] In a certain manner, the concept of "world society" by Rudolf Stichweh (2000) is one exception here.

would provide invariant insights, but as society is dynamic, this maybe is impossible. "The scientific paradigm is indestructible; one finds this attitude even in academic sociology itself. One reduces 'variance,' plays around with systems of equations, falsifies, correlates, quantifies, and is not bothered by the fact that the social dynamics repeatedly cause the laboriously erected models to collapse. The longing for mathematically supported analyzability is stronger than common sense" (Schulze 1996, pp. 54–55).

## The Gender Turn in Feminist Sociology

With regard to the sociology of gender in Germany, it is noteworthy that, with the exception of Marxism, early Critical Theory, and the theory of reflexive modernization, it was hardly influenced by the grand theories from Germany. There are, for example, only very few who pursue a sociology of gender with systems theory or explanatory sociology. There isn't even a sociology of gender that is based on Habermas, as Nancy Fraser's (*1947) theory is. Instead, the sociology of gender was often inspired by Bourdieu, Foucault, Harold Garfinkel, or, since the 1990s, Judith Butler.

Around 1990, there were major transformations and debates in feminist sociology (see in detail Hark 2005, pp. 269–332; Paulitz 2019, pp. 395–406). Feminist sociology experienced a deconstructivist turn, caused by the publication of Judith Butler's *Gender Trouble* (1990). Because of the German translation of the title as *Das Unbehagen der Geschlechter* (1991, literally translates back to English as "The Uneasiness of Gender"), many thought the book was a critique of feminism and not, as Butler emphasized, a contribution to feminist theory (Hark 2005, p. 269). The debate within feminist sociology revolved around the "relationship between the nature and culture of gender" (Paulitz 2019, p. 395), because Butler, following Michel Foucault, made the argument that every description of nature is culturally mediated—there can be no "pure," precultural description of sex and gender. Many accused Butler of neglecting the body and materiality. Even when Butler reacted with *Bodies That Matter* (1997) and indeed attributed a major role to materiality, this elaboration of her approach was mostly lost in the tangle of voices. She was also accused of destroying the politics of feminism by dissolving the category of "woman." The political discourse that prevailed in Germany when Butler's books were published was totally different from the one in the United States. As Tanja Paulitz (2019, p. 402) points out, while in the

United States there were already "critical discussions of identity politics" and of questions of racism and the exclusion of black and lesbian women, in Germany such discussions were more likely to be held in left-wing autonomist circles outside the universities. This also changed with Butler.

Despite the initially critical, often even hateful attitudes against Butler, feminist sociology changed lastingly as a result of the reception of her work. To this day, Butler remains an important point of reference in feminist and sociological debates in Germany (cf. Villa Brasvlasky 2020). Foucault, whom Butler referred to in her argumentation, has now been received even more in sociology. Butler was therefore not only important for feminist sociology, but also for the field of sociological theory: she was regarded not only as a feminist but also as a poststructuralist theorist and contributed to the boom of poststructuralism (Moebius and Reckwitz 2008). This boom of poststructuralism in Germany was also related to a new generation entering the sociological field. This new generation no longer followed Habermas in his exaggerated criticism of French intellectuals (Habermas 1985), but wanted to reconcile the two camps that stood in opposition to each other in Germany; these were the camps of Critical Theory and poststructuralism. In the 1990s, there was a younger generation of sociologists who increasingly studied Foucault, Jacques Derrida (1930–2004), and Butler, and this to contribute to a critical sociology. In sociology, these developments also resulted in the establishment of a "poststructuralist social science" (Stäheli 2000; Moebius 2003; Moebius and Reckwitz 2008).

The debate over Butler brought about many changes in feminist sociology. The term "women's studies" was increasingly being dropped as new terminological notions such as "gender studies" or "sociology of gender" (Paulitz 2019, pp. 398–406) arose. Feminist sociology was increasingly able to show that all areas of society are always gendered. Furthermore, the focus was no longer only on women, with research on masculinities being increasingly carried out. Gender was no longer primarily understood as a structural category, but as a "process category" (Paulitz 2019, p. 396). There was the general question about how gender is produced and reproduced. To what extent have our ideas about the nature of sex always been cultural ideas? How can we talk about nature if speaking is always already an effect of a cultural discourse? And how do the ideas of sex and gender relate to our ideas of (hetero-)sexuality? Based on questions like these, the inclusion of the category of sexuality in the analysis of gender relations was also central. However, the shift from the category of "woman" to the general category of "gender" was not without criticism, because of the fear that the still existing "masculine domination" (Bourdieu 1998) over women would be lost of sight (cf. Fleig 2014).

In the feminist field, differentiations and splits into different camps, different positions ranging from essentialism to constructivism, increased. The constructivist reading was further enhanced by the fact that, almost parallel to Butler's books, Candace West and Don H. Zimmerman's (1987) approach of "doing gender" was promulgated in Germany by the feminist researchers Regine Gildemeister (*1949) and Angelika Wetterer (*1949) (Gildemeister and Wetterer 1992; see also Paulitz 2019, pp. 400–401).[6] With their contribution they also called attention to the delayed reception of the earlier writings of Carol Hagemann-White, who had attempted to bring the "doing gender" approach into the German discussion already in the mid-1980s (Hagemann-White 1984). This approach was, among others, inspired by microsociological studies of Harold Garfinkel and Erving Goffman. Garfinkel's ethnomethodological approach was applied to questions of gender already in 1978 in an influential study published by the American sociologists Suzanne J. Kessler (*1946) and Wendy McKenna (*1945) (Kessler and McKenna 1978). This study, then, played a crucial role for the adaption of the microsociological idea of "doing gender" in Germany.

According to Tanja Paulitz, who is currently analyzing the history of feminist sociology in Germany in more detail, the debate on Butler "favored" the reception of the constructivist "doing gender" approach (Paulitz 2019, p. 401). The concept of "doing gender" tried to establish itself in the field of feminist sociology as a counter position to Butler. Butler's approach was accused of being "non-sociological," whereas it was claimed that the approach of "doing gender" was (Paulitz 2019, pp. 403–404). The accusation of not being sociological and of being out of touch with reality was in turn used by other positions in the field of feminist sociology against the approach of "doing gender" (Paulitz 2019, pp. 405–406).

However, the struggle for interpretive power eventually led to a "victory" of "doing gender" *and* Butler. Further differentiations took place, which also had an institutional impact (Paulitz 2019, pp. 407–411), for example, in the establishment of study programs in gender studies. While

---

[6] I would like to thank Tanja Paulitz for helpful remarks on the "doing gender" approach and for comments on this section on the gender turn in general.

gender studies and gay/lesbian studies had previously been rather separate, due to the reception of Butler's theory they were now often combined as queer studies. The relations between feminist sociology, gender studies, and queer studies are, however, diverse. Sometimes there are close relations between the approaches, sometimes they engage in "boundary work" (Gieryn). In contrast to gender studies, however, queer studies has so far not been able to institutionalize itself at universities in the form of chairs in Germany.

The current trend, however, is toward analyses of intersectionality, that is, on analyses of the intersection especially of gender, class, "race", and sexuality (Paulitz 2019, p. 410). Intersectionality, a concept that has been discussed for some time already in other countries, is considered the new paradigm in feminist theory in Germany.

Gender studies have successfully established themselves in the academic field. However, for some years now they have been confronted with fierce attacks (Paulitz 2019, pp. 410–411). In particular, the right-wing populist movements, currently observable in Europe and the USA, have intensified the attacks on gender and queer studies. The attacks are not only directed against gender studies alone, though. They concern feminism and the demands for sexual self-determination in general. Instead of looking for the causes of the processes of social disorientation, the fears of social relegation, and the cultural insecurities associated with the economic and political actors and structures, these are again projected onto women, strangers, and minorities. Anti-intellectualism, anti-feminism, and sexism have become socially acceptable again in Germany, as in many other countries.

## The Reception of New Theories of Capitalism

In the 1990s, one of the most pressing social problems of the Federal Republic of Germany was high unemployment. At the beginning of 1994, almost four million people were unemployed, and the unemployment rate was around 10%.[7] Unemployment was caused not only by the process of reunification, but also by economic globalization (Görtemaker 2009, pp. 101–105). When the Kohl government was re-elected by a narrow

---

[7] See the Statistics of the Federal Employment Agency https://statistik.arbeitsagentur.de/DE/Navigation/Statistiken/Fachstatistiken/Arbeitsuche-Arbeitslosigkeit-Unterbeschaeftigung/Produkte/Zeitreihen-Arbeitslose-Arbeitsuchende-Arbeitslosenquoten/Zeitreihen-Arbeitslose-Arbeitsuchende-Arbeitslosenquoten-Nav.html (accessed April 30, 2020).

majority in 1994, it attempted to solve these problems with neo-liberal measures such as "reducing continuation of payments in the case of sick leave, lifting protection against dismissal for companies with no more than ten employees and raising the retirement age, or cutting unemployment benefits" (Görtemaker 2009, p. 104). In East Germany there were processes of anomie and disintegration. The social inequalities aggravated the general discontent. Hopes that living conditions in East Germany would improve immediately were betrayed. The "flourishing landscapes" in the East, promised by Helmut Kohl, failed to appear.

As a result of this, a growing interest in theories of capitalism developed in Germany. These theories were not so much systematic economic analyses but focussed on cultural processes. Examples of these newer approaches included works such as Richard Sennett's *The Corrosion of Character* (1998) or Luc Boltanski (*1940) and Ève Chiapello's (*1965) *Le Nouvel Esprit du Capitalisme* (1999; *The New Spirit of Capitalism*). This cultural perspective on anomie and cultural disorientation was also related to the fact that capitalism now had a different effect than previously. As Lothar Peter (2009) has pointed out, theories of capitalism before the 1990s, as, for example, Marcuse's *One-Dimensional Man* (1964), emphasized the socially integrative function in the apparatus of power. Although it led to alienation and disillusionment, capitalism was thought to have a socially inclusive effect. In contrast, after 1990 new mechanisms of capitalism were identified that had exactly the opposite effect. Instead of over-integration into capitalist society, it was now argued, the current dynamics of capitalism lead to new social divisions, structural unemployment, and experiences of disintegration. The concept of class society therefore reappeared in sociological debates. Likewise, the analysis of elites became increasingly important (Hartmann 1996, 2002; Krais and Hartmann 2001). The concept of a classless or socially leveled society was no longer discussed.

## KEY SOCIAL PROBLEMS IN THE EARLY 1990S: UNEMPLOYMENT, POVERTY, RIGHT-WING EXTREMISM, AND RACISM

The concept of "poverty" also returned to the public and sociological debate (Schildt and Siegfried 2009, pp. 481–482; Honneth 1994). The special issue 32 of the *Cologne Journal of Sociology and Social Psychology* (KZfSS) may be regarded as an indication and reaction: In 1992, it was devoted to "Poverty in the modern welfare state." "Poverty despite prosperity" (Bohle 1997), that was the finding. Poverty was understood in terms of deprivation and as "a blatant lack of means to participate in 'normal' social life" (Bohle 1997, p. 129). Especially at the end of the 1990s, research on precarity and social exclusion increased. Exclusion is still a topic that is relevant today, particularly with regard to the ongoing social problems in East Germany, which are a breeding ground for right-wing populism (Bude and Willisch 2007).

However, the trend of social erosion and exclusion affected not only Germany. It was not only a consequence of the reunification, but was generally observable in capitalist societies. In European societies, the "endangerment of the social in highly developed capitalism" (Kronauer 2010) was often already virulent before the fall of the Iron Curtain. What was new, however, was the prominence of the terms "exclusion" and "precarity" for the sociological description of these processes.[8] In Germany, in particular those analyses that had been initiated in France since the mid-1990s, for example, Robert Castel's (1933–2013) *Les métamorphoses de la question sociale* (Castel 1999; cf. Castel and Dörre 2009), were considered and further developed.

Particular structural problems in East Germany were poverty and unemployment. For the majority of East Germans, soon after the euphoria over the reunification, feelings of heteronomy, rootlessness, disillusionment, and "cultural devaluation" (Conze 2009, p. 748) began to spread. In the face of a society perceived as "cold," many longed for a "warm" community. In many cases this longing gave rise to backward-looking projections that emphasized the communal character of living together in the GDR. Added to this were fears of strangers. The aggressions were mainly directed against asylum seekers, foreigners, strangers, disabled people, leftists, minorities in general, and also against politicians. At the beginning of the 1990s, extremely violent racist attacks by neo-Nazis on asylum seekers began in the East, often fueled and supported by several thousand sympathizers—sometimes even catered by mobile snack stalls (Prenzel 2017).

Right-wing extremist violence and its approval by the population increased drastically since 1991 (Herbert 2014, pp. 1173–1178). The

---

[8] In this context, a narrow definition of exclusion in accordance with systems theory was explicitly opposed. In systems theory, exclusion merely means falling out of functional systems and is not associated with social inequality.

introduction of new, neo-liberal labor and social policy measures further stoked fears of social relegation. This fear led to a search for security, which was expressed partly in renationalisation tendencies and xenophobia. Debates about identity and the dominant culture arose. The fears were structural. This was shown very clearly, for example, in the studies carried out by Wilhelm Heitmeyer (*1945), which were published every year with the title *Deutsche Zustände* ("*German Conditions*").[9] According to Heitmeyer and his team, one of the most significant disintegration experiences seven years after the "Wende" was the "increasingly deepening splitting apart of two German societies". Despite the so-called "elevator effect", a term introduced by Ulrich Beck (1986, pp. 121–160) to describe the increase in material prosperity, there was an empirically measurable "intensification of social inequality," the "exclusion of social groups and milieus from access to material and cultural goods," cutbacks in institutions of the welfare state and infrastructure, discrimination of minorities, "fragmentation of life contexts," and the "dissolution of the basic consensus on values and norms" (Heitmeyer 1997, pp. 10–11).

## THE RED-GREEN GOVERNMENT AND THE POLITICAL CHALLENGES AROUND 2000

High unemployment was one of the main reasons for the change of government in 1998 and the end of the "Kohl era." After 16 years, voters not only considered the government of Chancellor Kohl to be worn out, they also no longer trusted that he could resolve the high national debt and unemployment. The chancellor who succeeded Kohl in 1998 was Gerhard Schröder from the Social Democratic Party (SPD). He formed a coalition with the Green Party (see in detail Wolfrum 2013). This was possible, on the one hand, because the Greens enjoyed great popular support for their environmental policy and, on the other hand, because their profile increasingly tended toward economic liberalism. The majority of the Greens now stood "for a policy of flexibilization and deregulation as well as a reorganization of social security systems" (Conze 2009, p. 802). This coincided with Schröder's ideas, which were based on Anthony Giddens' (*1938) and Ulrich Beck's idea of the so-called Third Way (Wolfrum 2013, pp. 138–162).

---

[9] These investigations are based on analytical concepts of the classical theories of anomie of Émile Durkheim and Robert K. Merton (Heitmeyer 1997, p. 13).

In addition to high unemployment, the dismantling of social security systems, and an ecological tax reform, the domestic agenda of the red-green coalition included the phasing out of nuclear power and the reform of citizenship laws (see Herbert 2014, p. 1221; Görtemaker 2009, p. 112). In terms of foreign policy, the "Kosovo conflict" posed the greatest challenge to the coalition. There was no uniform approach by the UN. NATO "agreed to threaten to launch air strikes against Serbia" (Görtemaker 2009, p. 116). The participation of Germany was increasingly demanded. The new government, including the formerly pacifist Greens, finally agreed to the demands for participation in the NATO mission. A refusal by the Greens would have made the continuation of their coalition with the SPD unlikely; the only party in the Bundestag that voted against a participation was the *Partei des Demokratischen Sozialismus* (PDS, Party of Democratic Socialism, today: *Die Linke*, literally The Left). "It was the first combat mission of German armed forces since World War II—ordered, ironically, by a red-green coalition government, and without a clear UN mandate." (Görtemaker 2009, p. 118)

The attacks by radical Islamist terrorists on September 11, 2001, on the World Trade Center in New York and the Pentagon in Washington, marked another crucial historical turning point. It seemed that the geopolitical conflicts were now again being fueled far more by religious and cultural differences than had been the case during the Cold War. As a result, the perception of the political role of religion increased in many areas of society; in the social sciences in Germany, too, there was a renaissance of the sociology of religion (cf. Pollack 2015, p. 435).

In the 2002 elections to the German *Bundestag*, the red-green government was again victorious. It was a narrow victory. Chancellor Schröder was able to convince the voters of his merits, because he took a clear stance against German participation in the war in Iraq and because he was able to present himself well publicly and perform better in the media than his opponents (Wolfrum 2013, pp. 410–497). All this took place in an ongoing global process accelerated by the digitalization of communication, which was described as the new post-industrial economic form of digital financial-market capitalism, the New Economy (Conze 2009, p. 823). Since 2003, the neo-liberal reforms of labor market policy, that the red-green government implemented, the "Agenda 2010" and the so-called Hartz concept,[10] became effective. Over four million people were

---

[10] The new labor market reforms of the red-green government, that were implemented since 2003, were called "Hartz" concepts after their "inventor," the Volkswagen manager Peter Hartz.

unemployed around 2003. The aim of the reforms was to reduce unemployment till 2005 by two million (Wolfrum 2013, p. 528). The so-called Agenda 2010, which chancellor Schröder presented in 2003, was also in line with the general trend of the New Economy. The "Agenda 2010" meant, among other things, that after one year unemployed people would receive as little money as those living on social welfare (*Sozialhilfe*), but only on the condition that they were willing to accept any job (Fülberth 2012, p. 104).[11] The results of this change, however, were further processes of disintegration; in particular, stigmatization and prejudice against the long-term unemployed increased, also the proportion of poor people has risen, while at the same time the concentration of capital grew (Hartmann 2010, pp. 272–273). Sociologists even spoke of a "class struggle from above" in which the elites "deliberately" promoted "social disintegration" (Hartmann 2010, 2013). Relaxations in the protection against dismissal and many other measures such as the cuts in social security and unemployment benefits led to large protests, among others by trade unions as well as by the globalization-critical movement Attac (Wolfrum 2013, pp. 528–583).

How are the reforms and deregulation of the labor market to be assessed? Depending on the ideological orientation, this is of course judged differently. Economic sociologists at any rate spoke of a "successful failure" (Dörre 2010). From this perspective, the successes invoked by the proponents of the reforms are more likely to be the result of statistical adjustments and of the "expansion of insecure employment conditions" (Dörre 2010, p. 297).

The processes of the New Economy also had an impact on sociology in Germany: Research on the new dynamics of capitalism (Beckert 2016) and economic individualization emerged, which, for example, led to new concepts in the sociology of work, in economic sociology, and in the sociology of culture. The term "Entrepreneurial Self" (Bröckling 2016 [2007]) was now frequently referred to. According to the diagnosis, everyone was now increasingly responsible for her or his own fortune and had to manage her/his life like a project or enterprise (Dörre 2010, p. 295). In contrast to the United States, this was rather unusual for the

---

[11] Before the "Agenda 2010", unemployment benefit and social welfare were more separated; depending on age, one could receive unemployment benefit for up to three years. Now, in the year 2020, the standard rate of unemployment benefit ("Arbeitslosengeld II") is 432 euros per month for a single person.

people in Germany and was not anchored in the German mentality. For those who were the beneficiaries of the new economic and social structures, individualization often meant an expressive individualism and an increasing self-fulfillment. Those who were not up to these new processes were considered as losers and were now held personally responsible for their failure (Ehrenberg 1998). What was new was that those affected internalized this individualizing perspective and did not blame the state for their structural disadvantage, but themselves (Bröckling et al. 2000; Bröckling 2016 [2007]).

In the mid-2000s, the education system and education policy also moved back into the focus of political attention. In 1999, the so-called Bologna Process was started, an attempt to unify and facilitate the comparability of higher education standards in Europe. However, as in other countries, the universities in Germany were not well prepared for this; there was a lack of personnel and school-like teaching, application-oriented training increased, and teaching of fundamentals and individual academic freedom declined (Schultheis et al. 2008; Lenzen 2014). Instead of standardization, each university now sought to distinguish itself in the competition for students with its own profile, wherever possible. Ultimately, however, these reforms led to a provincialization rather than to a nationwide or European integration of higher education (Nida-Rümelin 2010, p. 135). As a result, a distinctive feature of higher education in Germany, the Humboldt style university, where one could conduct research free from market constraints, was in even more danger than it already was before.[12]

Similar to the labor market reforms, attempts were now made to orient all educational institutions toward *employability* (Sambale et al. 2008; Münch 2014). Science and education were now increasingly viewed from the perspective of their immediate usability (Münch 2009) and the universities were transformed into "enterprises" or "entrepreneurial universities" (Münch 2014, p. 246).[13] The reform of the universities led in Germany,

---

[12] See, for example, the discussions and articles by Ulrich Beck, Judith Butler, Dirk Baecker (*1955), Simon Critchley (*1960), Anselm Haverkamp (*1943), Julian Nida-Rümelin (*1954), Alex Demirović (*1952), and others in Horst et al. (2010), also Schultheis et al. (2008), Lenzen (2014).

[13] This applied not only to universities, but also to schools. The PISA tests ("Programme for International Student Assessment"), comparative achievement tests that revealed the emerging preference for rankings, also contributed to this. Richard Münch (2009, p. 39) points out that education today is reduced to human capital that is primarily oriented on

among others things, to new salary structures, to the introduction of junior professorships, to the limitation of temporary positions to 12 years,[14] and to the so-called Excellence Initiative, a competition between universities aimed at providing a few "top" universities with particularly good financial resources and funding. Although the structural conditions were completely different from those in the United States, the Ivy League universities served as the dominant role model (Münch 2007).

Just a few words about junior professorships: In order to get a professorship at a university in Germany, academics still usually have to write a habilitation thesis (in sociology usually a "second book" written after the doctoral thesis, more recently, it can also be a cumulative habilitation thesis consisting of already published journal articles and a framing introduction) and go through an appointment procedure.[15] This consists of a lecture, discussion, and an internal interview with an appointment committee (*Berufungskommission*). Since 2002, it has been possible to obtain the qualification for a professorship through a junior professorship instead of the habilitation thesis. The junior professorship is limited to six years. When the junior professorships were set up, it was originally planned that all of them would have a tenure track option and, following an evaluation, would lead to a regular professorship. In reality, however, this option is only available for a few of the positions. With the introduction of the junior professorship, there are now three different types of professorships and payments: chair professorships (salary scale W3), professorships (W2),[16] and junior professorships (W1). The payment varies slightly depending on the federal state. Before the W-salary scale there was the C-salary scale, which was a little higher.[17]

---

"usable competences". In comparison with other countries, the PISA tests revealed educational deficits and unequally distributed opportunities in Germany. The resulting "PISA shock" triggered a dynamic of reform measures.

[14] This law is called "Wissenschaftszeitvertragsgesetz" (Fixed-term employment contracts for researchers). After the 12 years, the university must either take over the employees indefinitely or dismiss them. In most cases, the universities decide to dismiss, so that many postdocs have to leave academia.

[15] A detailed description of the German academic career structure can be found on the following website: https://www.eui.eu/ProgrammesAndFellowships/AcademicCareers Observatory/AcademicCareersbyCountry/Germany (accessed October 7, 2020).

[16] There are no chairs at the universities of applied sciences (*Fachhochschulen*), the professorships there have the salary scale W2.

[17] A W1 gross salary is on average about 4800 Euro, a W2 6300 Euro, and W3 7300 Euro. Since the professors are usually civil servants, they pay less tax. Thus, for example, a W3 net

## Sociology and National Socialism: New Debates and New Research

The 1990s and 2000s were also a time of intense public debate about the Nazi past. This could also be observed in sociology. Two phases can be distinguished, one in the 1990s and one after 2010.[18] Since the late 1980s, more detailed research on sociology under National Socialism has been conducted in West Germany. Otthein Rammstedt (1986) examined the constitution of a genuine "German sociology" under National Socialism (referring in particular to Hans Freyer, Andreas Walther, Gunther Ipsen, Max Hildebert Boehm, Max Rumpf, Werner Sombart, Othmar Spann, and others). In addition to Rammstedt's book, it was in particular the work of Carsten Klingemann (1986, 1992, 1996, 2009) that revealed in great detail the entanglements of sociology with the Nazi regime. Klingemann's book *Soziologie im Dritten Reich* (1996, *Sociology in the Third Reich*) led to numerous controversies. Some criticized that empirical social research, but not sociology as an academic discipline, persisted during the Nazi regime. Others saw sociologists like Leopold von Wiese wrongly condemned by Klingemann (see for the discussions van Dyk and Schauer 2015, pp. 165–166). And still others were critical of Klingemann's and Rammstedt's theses, which claimed that after 1945 there was much continuity of sociology with the Third Reich. As Klingemann showed, there was no absolute new beginning of sociology in Germany after 1945, as had been claimed, for instance, by Leopold von Wiese. Instead, there were numerous continuities. The merit of Klingemann's and Rammstedt's studies was that they provided new analyses of the role of sociology and social research in the Nazi era, which finally dispelled the myth that there had been no sociology and social research during that time.

The *Hamburger Institut für Sozialforschung* (Hamburg Institute for Social Research), founded in 1984 by Jan Philipp Reemtsma (*1952), sparked off a major debate. In an exhibition in 1995, the Institute showed the war crimes of the German *Wehrmacht* between 1941 and 1944. The public was polarized, neo-Nazis marched through the streets, riots broke out, the *Bundestag* debated very emotionally. Yet the core thesis of the

---

salary is about 5700 Euros per month, a W2 5200 Euro and W1 4400, calculated with two children and being married (see the calculator on: https://oeffentlicher-dienst.info/beamte/bund, accessed April 30, 2020).

[18] As mentioned in Chap. 2, earlier analyses were provided by Svend Riemer (1932), Heinz Maus (1959), and Ralf Dahrendorf (1965).

exhibition was well documented; a specially founded commission of historians also confirmed the thesis: The *Wehrmacht*, that is, the regular German army, and not only the *SS*, had been actively involved in the war of extermination at the Eastern Front and in the mass murder of Jews, Romani, and other civilians as well as of prisoners of war.

After 2010, the sociological field underwent another phase of historical reappraisal, as evidenced, for example, by the volume *Soziologie und Nationalsozialismus* (2014, *Sociology and National Socialism*) edited by Michaela Christ and Maja Suderland. For too long, sociology had hardly ever dealt with the Nazi regime, leaving this to historians. Especially in Germany, more would have been expected from sociologists on this point. The question arose why National Socialism was "neglected" as an "object of sociology" (van Dyk and Schauer 2015, p. 168). Some answers to this question have been given: After the war one wanted to look ahead and quickly forget the past, like, as we have seen in Chap. 3, Leopold von Wiese for example.

## CURRENT TRENDS AND DEBATES

Sociology holds a solid position in the academic field in Germany. It is represented by two professional organizations, the GSA and the *Berufsverband deutscher Soziologinnen und Soziologen* (Professional Association of German Sociologists), as well as by numerous journals, and is firmly established at most universities (Meja et al. 1987, p. 2). Looking at the number of students, there was a phase of expansion until the mid-1970s, a phase of stagnation in the 1980s, and again an expansion in the 1990s (Stockmann 2002, p. 239). While the number of first-year students in sociology was 2500 in 1988, the number rose again in the 1990s and even doubled in 1999 to over 5000 (Meyer 2002, p. 110). The proportion of women also increased, with an increase of over 60% for the same period. If students taking sociology as a minor are also included, the total number of students also almost doubled from 10,000 in 1988 to 19,000 in 1999 (Meyer 2002, p. 110), which can among others be explained by the growing interest in sociology following the German reunification (Meyer 2002, p. 61). In the 1990s, sociology was one of the most popular subjects (Meyer 2002, p. 62); however when compared to other subjects, it took longer for graduates to get a job (Meyer 2002, pp. 88–109). But these difficulties have decreased. Particularly in the private sector, graduates get jobs (Meyer 2002, p. 111; Behrendt et al. 2002,

p. 191).[19] Overall, the jobs range from more sociology-related such as empirical social research and opinion research to political consulting, education, journalism, social work, healthcare, human resources, administration, and so on (cf. Breger and Böhmer 2007). But here, sociologists are in increasing competition especially with other social scientists like economists, political scientists, and lawyers.

Sociology as academic discipline is still facing another problem: As in other disciplines, many students inscribe themselves in sociology, but a considerable number, almost a quarter, drop out at some point. In addition, there have been large cutbacks in personnel and resources. With the "Aufbau Ost" there was a brief growth, but since the mid-1990s there has been a decline in the number of professorships. This has led to a poor student-to-staff ratio, with an average of 70 students per professor (Stockmann 2002, p. 244). Financial resources have flowed particularly into the life sciences or computer science, which have a strong position in the academic field and also enjoy a better image in society because they appear more useful and "more profitable" (Meyer 2002, pp. 111–112).

Sociology in Germany is also in active exchange with sociological actors from other countries, participating in both the ESA (European Sociological Association) and the ISA (International Sociological Association); some sociologists are also involved in the ASA (American Sociological Association). It is therefore only natural that it is influenced by international trends and participates in them. This applies, for example, to current discussions about public sociology or the sociology of emotions, but also, in the theoretical field, to discussions about networks or the limits of the social. In the theoretical field of sociology in Germany there is a wide variety of approaches, ranging from rational choice, neo-institutionalism, systems theory, Critical Theory, social philosophy, social criticism,

---

[19] As Kreckel (2013, pp. 217–220) shows, the number of students of social science disciplines grew until 2003, but then declined slightly. At the same time, there was a trend in the professorships in the opposite direction. These became fewer. Instead, fixed-term positions below the professorial level were expanded. According to the statistics of the Federal Statistical Office, there were 19,566 sociology students in the winter semester 2018/2019, 63% of these were female. Since 2002, the total number of students in Germany has been around two million, while the number of sociology students has been around 1%. Source: Statistisches Bundesamt (Destatis), Fachserie 11, Reihe 4.1. https://www.statistischebibliothek.de/mir/receive/DEHeft_mods_00110047 (Access: May 10, 2020).

neo-pragmatism, ethnomethodology, feminist sociology, philosophical anthropology, theory of reflexive modernization, historical sociology, theory of practice to poststructuralist concepts such as governmentality studies.

However, grand theories made in Germany—as were developed in the 1980s—are now hardly to be found (Lepenies 1997, pp. 61, 93). Important exceptions, which are also known internationally, are the theory of reflexive modernization of Ulrich Beck and the neo-pragmatism of Hans Joas, who is today, one of the internationally most renowned living sociologist from Germany. Indeed, theories are still a central element of sociology in Germany today and are still held in high esteem in accordance with the German sociological tradition. The aforementioned trend toward *Zeitdiagnosen* (diagnoses of contemporary society) continues (cf. Osrecki 2018). These interpretations, diagnoses, and forms of problematization of the present are even more prevalent than in the past. It is true that this type of sociological diagnosis and public sociology also existed in Germany in the past; consider for example books by Hans Freyer (1955, 1965), Helmut Schelsky (1957, 1965, pp. 391–480, 1977 [1975]), or Ulrich Beck (1986) (cf. Lichtblau 2017 [1991]; Kruse 1994). But at present, the sociological interpretations offered on the book market change every few months at an ever-faster pace. This may perhaps be related to the perception that society itself is accelerating more and more (Rosa 2013)—although that too is just one interpretation among many. It was only yesterday that we lived in a "risk society" (Beck 1986), now we are living in the "society of acceleration" (Rosa 2013). Whereas yesterday it was the "postmodern multi-option society" (Gross 1994) and the "experience society" (Schulze 1995), now it is the "society of decline" (Nachtwey 2016), the "society of fear" (Bude 2014), or the "society of singularities" (Reckwitz 2017) in which we find ourselves. One of the few scholars who are currently working toward a new general theory of society again is Uwe Schimank (*1955) from Bremen, who in recent publications attempts to describe society as a systematic social context (Schimank 2013, 2015).

The trend toward diagnoses of contemporary society is accompanied by a "return of the author" (Lepenies 1997, pp. 94–100). The focus on single persons or individuals that can be observed everywhere today, especially in politics or economic theory—an expression of individualization—is also evident in the current market of sociological commodities.[20] Individual star authors and their diagnoses of contemporary society—also as a consequence of the "Matthew Effect" (Merton 1968)—are gaining more and more attention than constant theoretical patterns and concepts, who develop a systematic theory of society or the social as a whole, like the theory of Bourdieu did it for example.

Because of the boom of "studies," nowadays there are frequently situations of competition among these new interdisciplinary alliances. For instance, science studies, queer studies, or visual studies break down the boundaries of the sociological field and develop more interdisciplinary perspectives—in more or less productive ways. In addition, there are generation-specific trends and field dynamics: While in my student days, the time around 2000, poststructuralism (Stäheli 2000; Moebius 2003) was the most popular theoretical approach for younger scholars, nowadays the theories of Gilles Deleuze (1925–1995), Bruno Latour (*1947), or Donna Haraway (*1944) are preferred (cf. Fischer and Moebius 2014).

In recent decades, sociology in Germany has come ever closer to the globally prevailing understanding of sociology as an empirically operating social science and has also contributed to this global mainstream of sociology. This means that a distinctive German sociology can be observed less and less. Still, one can perhaps identify some specific characteristics of German sociology, which, of course, may also be found in one form or another or with other accentuations in other countries.[21] These are related to its tradition, to the specific social processes in Germany, and to related inner-academic developments. To me, the characteristics of sociology in Germany seem to be, firstly, its affinity for theory, or rather, the great significance of historically and philosophically informed theory (see also Meja et al. 1987, p. 3). The theoretical landscape is quite diverse (Fischer and Moebius 2019) and "cannot be reduced to two ideological axes (conservative and critical traditions)" (Müller 1989, p. 321; see also Meja et al. 1987).

Secondly, as far as empirical social research is concerned, there is also a connection to philosophy. The focus in Germany is more often on the philosophical reflection on empirical research, that is, on methodology,

---

[20] According to Wolf Lepenies (1997, pp. 94–100), in the United States and France the author's return expresses itself through autobiographies, in which he sees rather positive signs of knowledge transfer and considers them currently to be the "best textbooks" (Lepenies 1997, p. 94).

[21] On the question of national traditions in the social sciences see Heilbron (2008, 2015, pp. 218–223).

than it is, for example, in the United States, where more emphasis is placed on research practice. At the same time, a greater abstinence from participation in the direct political realm can be observed in Germany due to the value judgment debates and the implementation of the understanding of sociology of the Cologne School, while in the United States, for example, there is greater emphasis on the direct political relevance of research (cf. Bethmann and Niermann 2015).[22]

Thirdly, to this day, German sociology still lacks self-confidence with respect to US-American sociology, because the latter is perceived by many as more practical and "closer to reality." Fourthly, Volker Meja, Dieter Misgeld, and Nico Stehr (1987, p. 4) consider a fundamentally critical, intellectual attitude to be characteristic of sociology in Germany. This attitude can be found among conservatives and left-wingers as well as in the field of philosophy of science, and it indicates a strong impact on the intellectual and medial public:

> This attitude has remained unchanged from Max Weber to the conservatives Arnold Gehlen, Helmut Schelsky, and Friedrich Tenbruck, from the politically engaged liberal Ralf Dahrendorf to the left-wing intellectuals of the Frankfurt School. It also characterizes the philosophers of social science associated with 'critical rationalism' (Hans Albert, Ernst Topitsch) who have translated 'critical rationalism' into a form of '*Ideologiekritik*', for which there is no parallel among members of Karl Popper's followers in other countries. The widespread participation of sociologists in public debates and disputes, which continues to this very day, indicates not only a particular and widely shared self-conception of sociologists as sociologists but also a receptivity to and an audience for sociological ideas and sociologically informed opinion which is considerably broader than in many English-speaking countries. (Meja et al. 1987, pp. 4–5; English in original)

This view contradicts the frequent lament encountered today that sociology is no longer present in the mass media. And indeed, recent quantitative analyses (Korte 2019) show that these complaints are not justified and that sociology is very present in the media. Sociology is visible in the feuilleton of the newspapers, but on television the interpretations offered by economists prevail. Moreover, sociology continues to have little influence on policy making, where political science and economics are preferably consulted.

---

[22] I would like to thank Andrea Ploder for her remarks on the differences between Germany and the United States in the field of empirical social research.

Fifthly, in German sociology "self-critical crisis debates" (Meja et al. 1987, p. 3, English in original) and controversies (Kneer and Moebius 2010) repeatedly occurred, which led to veritable splits between the different ideological camps and—as I will explain—these controversies still persist today. Some controversies developed between theories, others between theory and empirical sociology, between methodological approaches, and others even called into question the *raison d'être* of sociology as a whole. Besides substantial disagreements—such as that concerning *Werturteilsfreiheit* (freedom from value judgments), the relationship between theory and practice, or the deconstruction of sex/gender, which were primarily methodological or epistemological issues—in the end these debates were also always struggles over power and interests within the sociological field.

One example of a conflict that has recently troubled and churned up the sociological field in Germany is the conflict between the GSA and a group of sociologists who have formed an *Akademie für Soziologie* (Academy of Sociology, hereafter "Academy").[23] According to its own statements, the objective of this Academy is to promote empirical-analytical sociology and quantitative social research. The conflict is particularly exacerbated by the fact that the representatives of the Academy claim that only they would pursue "truly" scientific, rational, and evidence-based sociology. A veritable "craving for rationality" dominates the statements of the members of the Academy, similar to what Friedrich Tenbruck (1979, p. 106, fn. 30) had already identified in the sociological reception of positivism and analytical philosophy of science half a century earlier. The Academy openly advocates a claim to the sole and "true" representation of sociology, which is perhaps not surprising in the struggle for increasingly scarce resources. With this claim, the Academy attempts to determine the generally defining value of the sociological field, which, from their point of view, lies in empirical-analytical sociology. Basically, this is a new version of the old dispute between nomothetic and ideographic conceptions of

---

[23] For further information on the Academy see their website https://akademie-soziologie.de/akademie/. On the conflict, see the websites http://blog.soziologie.de/2017/11/was-fuer-eine-wissenschaft-soll-die-soziologie-sein/ and http://blog.soziologie.de/2017/11/mit-einem-auge-ist-man-halb-blind-von-einheit-und-uneinigkeit-der-soziologie/ and https://wiso.uni-koeln.de/de/forschung/forschung-im-fokus/soziologischer-aschermittwoch/ (all accessed November 20, 2019), Hirschauer (2021), and the articles by Hartmut Esser, Stefan Hirschauer, and Jörg Strübing in *Zeitschrift für Theoretische Soziologie* Vol. 7 (1) and 7 (2)/2018 and Vol. 1/2019.

science, but intellectually it falls far behind corresponding discussions by Max Weber (whom the Academy readily refers to, though for strategic reasons), who did not exclusively advocated either one or the other conception of science.

In addition, however, the founding of the Academy and its separation from the large remainder of sociologists organized in the GSA was also influenced by current power relations in the entire academic field and the reputational gains possible there. The members of the Academy, with their quantitative and analytical orientation, with their "mathematization" of sociology, are closer to the dominant positions in the general academic field, the disciplines of the natural sciences and mathematized economics, and can therefore hope for greater overall reputational gains. Perhaps they also hope for a similar effect that mathematization had for economics: As David M. Kreps (*1950) showed, mathematization led to an inner coherence of economics, not only by excluding other paradigms, such as historical or institutional analysis, but also by establishing a kind of "monolingualism" that was spread by the formulaic language and that connected otherwise heterogeneous parts with each other (Kreps 1997, p. 62).

Already in the 1970s, René König cautioned that his students—similar to Goethe's *The Sorcerer's Apprentice*—considered the techniques of empirical methods and their refinement to be increasingly more important than the problems of the social world they wanted to investigate with them. Often, modeling and mathematization—as is the case with economics—does not promote a sense of the problems of society, but rather a sense of the problems in applying the techniques of modeling. The real problems are being sidelined in favor of the problems of modeling (Barber 1997, p. 96).[24] David M. Kreps (1997) has given a formidable description

---

[24] William Barber (1925–2016) cites the essay by David Colander and Arjo Klamer, "The Making of an Economist," in *Journal of Economic Perspectives* I (2) (Fall 1987): 95–111, which was "sponsored by the American Economic Association, that reported results of surveys of graduate students at six of the nation's leading doctoral programs. One of its central findings was that 'graduates are well-trained in problem-solving, but it is technical problem-solving which has more to do with formal modeling techniques than with real world problems. To do the problems, little real world knowledge of institutions is needed, and in many cases such knowledge would actually be a hindrance since the simplifying assumptions would be harder to accept.' In addition, the survey data indicated that substantial majorities of the survey population perceived two skills as 'very important' to professional success: 'being

of this change in economics in the United States, which can now be increasingly observed among some sociologists in Germany as well, emphasizing both the loss of a sense of reality and the gain in power that mathematization brought with it: "The use of a powerful and somewhat obscure tool confers power on the user. As economists became convinced of the value of mathematical rigor, the reward system (based on peer review) reinforced this tendency" (Kreps 1997, p. 83, English in original).

The founding of the Academy of Sociology is also a reaction to the pluralization of sociological perspectives. The multiparadigmaticity that can be observed today is the result of both the complexity and the normatively infused, antagonistic constitution of the object "society"—a pluralization that once again makes sociology appear in crisis in the eyes of members of the Academy. This mood of crisis nourishes romantic and dogmatic hopes for unification, unified science, standardization, and a clearly defined identity of the discipline. The Academy's secession from the German Sociological Association is the expression of this longing for a "unified science." However, obviously not all researchers are allowed to participate in determining the path and direction of unifying, some are even denied the status of scientist. The members of the Academy reveal a belief in a homogeneous unified science, but this belief seems unrealistic and in reality also *unsociological*. After all, is it not the case that because of our object "society" (or the social), which is normatively permeated, there can only be pluralization in the sociological field, and no unity, because there are heterogeneous positions of interest that are reflected in the sociological field? We sociologists are ourselves part of society, not free-floating above it—we are embedded in society politically, economically, culturally, and familially. In accordance with the different spheres of value, relevances of meaning, and antagonistic spheres of interest of our object "society" and our constitutive and habitual integration in it, our respective sociological viewpoints cannot be homogeneous but can only remain diverse and divergent. The current debate would therefore benefit from more self-reflection. What is needed are more sociological analyses of the

---

smart in the sense of being good at problem solving' and 'excellence in mathematics.' Some 68 percent of the respondents reported a belief that 'having a thorough knowledge of the economy' was 'unimportant'" (Barber 1997, p. 96, English in original). I became aware of the studies of Kreps and Barber by reading Lepenies (1997, pp. 74–92).

opposing positions, like, for example, Schmitz et al. (2019) did it, that contextualize the different positions within the sociological field of power and that understand the emergence of these positions against the background of the history of the discipline. This is a sociological insight that can at least provide a sense of orientation. Thus, current developments prove once more that the historiography of the history of sociology has, in general, a self-reflexive, orienting, critical, and enlightening function for sociology, and this book should be understood in this sense.

**Open Access**  This chapter is licensed under the terms of the Creative Commons Attribution 4.0 International License (http://creativecommons.org/licenses/by/4.0/), which permits use, sharing, adaptation, distribution and reproduction in any medium or format, as long as you give appropriate credit to the original author(s) and the source, provide a link to the Creative Commons licence and indicate if changes were made.

The images or other third party material in this chapter are included in the chapter's Creative Commons licence, unless indicated otherwise in a credit line to the material. If material is not included in the chapter's Creative Commons licence and your intended use is not permitted by statutory regulation or exceeds the permitted use, you will need to obtain permission directly from the copyright holder.

# Bibliography

Abelshauser, Werner (2011) *Deutsche Wirtschaftsgeschichte. Von 1945 bis zur Gegenwart*, 2nd ed. (München: Beck).
Abendroth, Wolfgang (ed.) (1967) *Faschismus und Kapitalismus. Theorien über die sozialen Ursprünge und die Funktion des Faschismus* (Frankfurt/M.: EVA).
Abendroth, Wolfgang (1968) 'Demokratisch-liberale oder revolutionär-sozialistische Kritik?' in ibid. et al. (eds) *Die Linke antwortet Jürgen Habermas* (Frankfurt/M.: EVA), pp. 131–142.
Acham, Karl (1998) 'Historische Umbrüche in dem halben Jahrhundert seit dem Ersten Weltkrieg' in ibid. et al. (eds) *Erkenntnisgewinne, Erkenntnisverluste. Kontinuitäten und Diskontinuitäten in den Wirtschafts-, Rechts- und Sozialwissenschaften zwischen den 20er und 50er Jahren* (Stuttgart: Steiner), pp. 535–566.
Acham, Karl (2013) 'Diltheys Bedeutung für die Soziologie' in Gunter Scholz (ed.) *Diltheys Werk und die Wissenschaften: Neue Aspekte* (Göttingen: Vandenhoeck & Ruprecht), pp. 149–173.
Adamski, Jens (2009) *Ärzte des sozialen Lebens. Die Sozialforschungsstelle Dortmund 1946–1969* (Essen: Klartext).
Adler, Frank & Albrecht Kretzschmar (1993) 'Ungleichheitsstrukturen in der ehemaligen DDR' in Rainer Geißler (ed.) *Sozialer Umbruch in Ostdeutschland* (Opladen: Leske & Budrich), pp. 98–118.
Adorno, Theodor W. (1969 [1968]) 'Einleitungsvortrag zum 16. Deutschen Soziologentag' in ibid. (ed.) *Spätkapitalismus oder Industriegesellschaft? Verhandlungen des 16. Deutschen Soziologentages* (Stuttgart: Enke), pp. 12–26.
Albert, Gert (2010) 'Der Werturteilsstreit' in Georg Kneer & Stephan Moebius (eds) *Soziologische Kontroversen. Beiträge zu einer anderen Wissenschaft vom Sozialen* (Berlin: Suhrkamp), pp. 14–45.

Albrecht, Clemens (1999) 'Vom Konsens der 50er zur Lagerbildung der 60er Jahre: Horkheimers Institutspolitik' in ibid. et al. (eds) *Die intellektuelle Gründung der Bundesrepublik. Eine Wirkungsgeschichte der Frankfurter Schule* (Frankfurt/M./New York: Campus), pp. 132–168.

Albrecht, Clemens (2013) 'Nachwort' in René König, *Soziologie als Krisenwissenschaft. Durkheim und das Paradigma der französischen Gesellschaft, Schriften Vol. 8*, ed. and with an afterword of Clemens Albrecht (Wiesbaden: VS), pp. 387–413.

Albrecht, Clemens & Stephan Moebius (2014) 'Die Rückkehr der Kultur in die Soziologie. Zur Gründungsgeschichte einer Sektion' in ibid. (eds) *Kultur-Soziologie. Klassische Texte der neueren deutschen Kultursoziologie* (Wiesbaden: VS), pp. 9–22.

Albrecht, Clemens et al. (1999) *Die intellektuelle Gründung der Bundesrepublik. Eine Wirkungsgeschichte der Frankfurter Schule* (Frankfurt/M./New York: Campus).

Alemann, Heine von (1981) 'Leopold von Wiese und das Forschungsinstitut für Sozialwissenschaften in Köln 1919 bis 1934' in Wolf Lepenies (ed.) *Geschichte der Soziologie, Vol. 2* (Frankfurt/M.: Suhrkamp), pp. 349–389.

Alexander, Jeffrey C. (1988) 'The New Theoretical Movement' in Neil J. Smelser (ed) *Handbook of Sociology* (Newbury Park: Sage), pp. 77–101.

Baethge, Martin & Michael Schumann (2018) 'Geschichte des Soziologischen Forschungsinstituts Göttingen' in Stephan Moebius & Andrea Ploder (eds) *Handbuch Geschichte der deutschsprachigen Soziologie, Vol. 1* (Wiesbaden: VS), pp. 1045–1064.

Baier, Horst (1981) 'Die Gesellschaft – ein langer Schatten des toten Gottes. Friedrich Nietzsche und die Entstehung der Soziologie aus dem Geist der Décadence' in *Nietzsche-Studien* 10–11/1981–1982, pp. 6–33.

Barber, Williams J. (1997) 'Reconfigurations in American Academic Economics: A General Practitioner's Perspective' *Daedalus* 126 (1), pp. 87–103.

Barboza, Amalia (2010) 'Das utopische Bewusstsein in zwei Frankfurter Soziologien' in Felicia Herrschaft & Klaus Lichtblau (eds) *Soziologie in Frankfurt. Eine Zwischenbilanz* (Wiesbaden: VS), pp. 161–178.

Beck, Ulrich (1974) *Objektivität und Normativität. Die Theorie-Praxis-Debatte in der modernen deutschen und amerikanischen Soziologie* (Hamburg: Rowohlt).

Beck, Ulrich (1982) 'Folgeprobleme der Modernisierung und die Stellung der Soziologie in der Praxis' in ibid. (ed.) *Soziologie und Praxis. Erfahrungen, Konflikte, Perspektiven. Sonderband 1 der Sozialen Welt* (Göttingen: Schwartz & Co), pp. 3–23.

Beck, Ulrich (1986) *Risikogesellschaft. Auf dem Weg in eine andere Moderne* (Frankfurt/M.: Suhrkamp).

Beck, Ulrich (1991) 'Opposition in Deutschland' in Bernd Giesen & Claus Leggewie (eds) *Experiment Vereinigung. Ein sozialer Großversuch* (Berlin: Rotbuch), pp. 21–37.

Beck, Ulrich (1997) *Was ist Globalisierung?* (Frankfurt/M.: Suhrkamp).
Beck, Ulrich (2007) 'The Cosmopolitan Condition: Why Methodological Nationalism Fails' *Theory, Culture & Society* 24 (7–8), pp. 286–290.
Beck, Ulrich & Wolfgang Bonß (eds) (1989) *Weder Sozialtechnologie noch Aufklärung? Analysen zur Verwendung sozialwissenschaftlichen Wissens* (Frankfurt/M.: Suhrkamp).
Beck, Ulrich, Anthony Giddens & Scott Lash (1994) *Reflexive Modernization. Politics, Tradition, and Aesthetics in the Modern Social Order* (Stanford: Stanford University Press).
Beck-Gernsheim, Elisabeth (2006) 'Wie ich zur Soziologie kam und wie ich Professorin wurde' in Ulrike Vogel (ed.) *Wege in die Soziologie und die Frauen- und Geschlechterforschung. Autobiographische Notizen der ersten Generation von Professorinnen an der Universität* (Wiesbaden: VS), pp. 214–221.
Becker, Carl Heinrich (1919) *Gedanken zur Hochschulreform* (Leipzig: Quelle & Meyer).
Becker, Michael (2014) 'Politik des Beschweigens: Plädoyer für eine historisch-soziologische Rekonstruktion des Verhältnisses der Soziologie zum Nationalsozialismus' *Soziologie* 43 (3), pp. 251–277.
Becker, Sabina (2018) *Experiment Weimar. Eine Kulturgeschichte Deutschlands 1918–1933* (Darmstadt: WBG).
Becker-Schmidt, Regina (1987a) Die doppelte Vergesellschaftung – die doppelte Unterdrückung: Besonderheiten der Frauenforschung in den Sozialwissenschaften in Lilo Unterkircher & Ina Wagner (eds) *Die andere Hälfte der Gesellschaft. Soziologische Befunde zu geschlechtsspezifischen Formen der Lebensbewältigung. Österreichischer Soziologentag 1985* (Wien: Verl. d. Österr. Gewerkschaftsbundes), pp. 10–25.
Becker-Schmidt, Regina (1987b) 'Frauen und Deklassierung, Geschlecht und Klasse' in Ursula Beer (ed.) *Klasse Geschlecht, Feministische Gesellschaftsanalyse und Wissenschaftskritik* (Bielefeld: AJZ-Verl.), pp. 187–235.
Becker-Schmidt, Regina (2006) 'Anstiftungen zum Feminismus' in Ulrike Vogel (ed.) *Wege in die Soziologie und die Frauen- und Geschlechterforschung. Autobiographische Notizen der ersten Generation von Professorinnen an der Universität* (Wiesbaden: VS), pp. 33–49.
Beckert, Jens (2016) *Imagined Futures. Fictional Expectations and Capitalist Dynamics* (Cambridge, MA: Harvard University Press).
Beer, Ursula (1984) *Theorien geschlechtlicher Arbeitsteilung* (Frankfurt/M.: Campus).
Beer, Ursula (1990) *Geschlecht, Struktur, Geschichte. Soziale Konstituierung des Geschlechterverhältnisses* (Frankfurt/New York: Campus).
Behrendt, Erich et al. (2002) 'Primat der Theorie? Arbeitsmarkt, Qualifikationen und das Image der Soziologie' in Reinhard Stockmann et al. (eds) *Soziologie im Wandel. Universitäre Ausbildung und Arbeitsmarktchancen in Deutschland* (Opladen: Leske & Budrich), pp. 187–197.

Bethmann, Stephanie & Debora Niermann (2015) 'Crossing Boundaries in Qualitative Research – Entwurf einer empirischen Reflexivität der qualitativen Sozialforschung in Deutschland und den USA' *Forum Qualitative Sozialforschung/Forum Qualitative Social Research* 16 (2), Art. 19, https://www.qualitative-research.net/index.php/fqs/article/view/2216 (accessed April 30, 2020).

Beiser, Frederick C. (2015) *The German Historicist Tradition* (Oxford: Oxford University Press).

Bergmann, Waltraut et al. (eds) (1981) *Soziologie im Faschismus 1933–1945: Darstellung und Texte* (Köln: Pahl-Rugenstein).

Bessel, Richard (2009) *Germany 1945. From War to Peace* (London: Pocket Books).

Bickel, Cornelius (1991) *Ferdinand Tönnies. Soziologie als skeptische Aufklärung zwischen Historismus und Rationalismus* (Opladen: Westdeutscher Verlag).

Biess, Frank (2019) *Republik der Angst. Eine andere Geschichte der Bundesrepublik* (Hamburg: Rowohlt).

Blackbourn, David & Geoff Eley (1980) *Mythen deutscher Geschichte. Die gescheiterte bürgerliche Revolution von 1848* (Frankfurt/M.: Ullstein).

Blomert, Reinhard (1999) *Intellektuelle im Aufbruch. Karl Mannheim, Alfred Weber; Norbert Elias und die Heidelberger Sozialwissenschaften in der Zwischenkriegszeit.* (München/Wien: Hanser).

Blomert, Reinhard (2018) 'Geschichte des Leviathan' in Stephan Moebius & Andrea Ploder (eds) *Handbuch Geschichte der deutschsprachigen Soziologie, Vol. 1* (Wiesbaden: VS), pp. 937–943.

Bock, Klaus Dieter (1972) *Strukturgeschichte der Assistentur. Personalgefüge, Wert- und Zielvorstellungen in der deutschen Universität des 19. und 20. Jahrhunderts* (Düsseldorf: Bertelsmann).

Bock, Klaus Dieter (1986) 'Helmut Schelsky: Hochschulreformer 'auf eigene Faust'. Zur Vorgeschichte der Bielefelder Universitätsgründung' in Horst Baier (ed.) *Helmut Schelsky – ein Soziologe in der Bundesrepublik* (Stuttgart: Enke), pp. 167–181.

Böick, Marcus (2018) *Die Treuhand. Idee – Praxis – Erfahrung 1990–1994* (Göttingen: Wallstein).

Bogart, Leo (1991) 'The Pollster & the Nazis' *Commentary. The monthly magazine of opinion*, August 1991, pp. 47–49.

Bohle, Hans Hartwig (1997) 'Armut trotz Wohlstand' in Wilhelm Heitmeyer (ed.) *Was treibt die Gesellschaft auseinander? Bundesrepublik Deutschland: Auf dem Weg von der Konsens- zur Konfliktgesellschaft, Vol. 1* (Frankfurt/M.: Suhrkamp), pp. 118–155.

Boll, Monika (2004) *Nachtprogramm. Intellektuelle Gründungsdebatten in der frühen Bundesrepublik* (Münster: Lit).

Bollenbeck, Georg (1994) *Bildung und Kultur. Glanz und Elend eines deutschen Deutungsmusters* (Frankfurt/M.: Insel).

Boltanski, Luc & Éve Chiapello (1999) *Le nouvel esprit du capitalisme* (Paris: Gallimard).
Bond, Niall (2013) *Understanding Ferdinand Tönnies' "Community and Society". Social Theory and political philosophy between enlighted liberal individualism and transfigured community* (Münster: Lit).
Borggräfe, Henning (2018) 'Die Ausdifferenzierung der westdeutschen Soziologie nach 1945 im Spiegel der Untergruppen, Fachausschüsse und Sektionen der DGS' in Stephan Moebius & Andrea Ploder (eds) *Handbuch Geschichte der deutschsprachigen Soziologie, Vol. 1* (Wiesbaden: VS), pp. 867–886.
Borggräfe, Henning & Sonja Schnitzler (2014) 'Die Deutsche Gesellschaft für Soziologie und der Nationalsozialismus. Verbandsinterne Transformationen nach 1933 und 1945' in Michaela Christ & Maja Suderland (eds) *Soziologie und Nationalsozialismus: Positionen. Debatten. Perspektiven* (Berlin: Suhrkamp), pp. 445–479.
Borowsky, Peter (1998) 'Große Koalition und Außerparlamentarische Opposition' *Informationen zur politischen Bildung. Zeiten des Wandels. Deutschland 1961–1974*, No. 258/1998, pp. 11–22.
Bourdieu, Pierre (1979) *La distinction. Critique sociale du jugement* (Paris: Les Editions de Minuit).
Bourdieu, Pierre (1998) *La domination masculine* (Paris: Seuil).
Bourdieu, Pierre (2002) *Ein soziologischer Selbstversuch* (first published in German, engl. 2008: *Sketch for a Self-Analysis*) (Frankfurt/M.: Suhrkamp).
Bourdieu, Pierre & Jean-Claude Passeron (1971) *Die Illusion der Chancengleichheit* (Stuttgart: Klett).
Breger, Wolfram & Sabrina Böhmer (eds) (2007) *Was werden mit Soziologie. Berufe für Soziologinnen und Soziologen. Das BDS-Berufshandbuch* (Stuttgart: Lucius & Lucius).
Breuer, Stefan (1995) *Anatomie der Konservativen Revolution*, 2nd ed. (Darmstadt: WBG).
Breuer, Stefan (2002) '"Gemeinschaft" in der "deutschen Soziologie"' *Zeitschrift für Soziologie*, 31/5, pp. 354–372.
Bröckling, Ulrich et al. (eds) (2000) *Gouvernementalität der Gegenwart – Studien zur Ökonomisierung des Sozialen* (Frankfurt/M.: Suhrkamp).
Bröckling, Ulrich (2016 [2007]) *The Entrepreneurial Self* (London: Sage).
Bröckling, Ulrich (2014) 'Die Gründung des Freiburger Instituts für Soziologie' in ibid. et al. (eds) *Fünfzig Jahre Institut für Soziologie Freiburg. 1964–2014* (Freiburg: Jos Fritz), pp. 15–37.
Bruch, Rüdiger vom et al. (ed.) (1989) *Kultur und Kulturwissenschaften um 1900. Krise der Moderne und Glaube an die Wissenschaft* (Stuttgart: Steiner).
Brückweh, Kerstin (2019) 'Arbeitssoziologische Wissensproduktion am Soziologischen Forschungsinstitut Göttingen (SOFI) von 1968 bis heute' in Oliver Römer & Ina Alber-Armenat (eds) *Erkundungen im Historischen:*

*Soziologie in Göttingen. Geschichte, Entwicklungen, Perspektiven* (Wiesbaden: VS), pp. 321–350.
Bude, Heinz (1994) '1968 und die Soziologie' *Soziale Welt* 45th Year (2), pp. 242–253.
Bude, Heinz (2002) 'Die Charismatiker des Anfangs. Helmuth Plessner, René König, Theodor W. Adorno und Helmut Schelsky als Gründer einer Soziologie in Deutschland' in Günter Burkart & Jürgen Wolf (eds) *Lebenszeiten. Erkundungen zur Soziologie der Generationen* (Opladen: Leske & Budrich), pp. 407–419.
Bude, Heinz (2014) *Gesellschaft der Angst* (Hamburg: Hamburger Edition).
Bude, Heinz & Friedhelm Neidhardt (1998) 'Die Professionalisierung der deutschen Nachkriegssoziologie' in ibid. (eds) *Soziologie als Beruf. Erinnerungen westdeutscher Hochschulprofessoren der Nachkriegsgeneration, Soziale Welt Sonderband 11* (Baden-Baden: Nomos), pp. 405–418.
Bude, Heinz & Andreas Willisch (2007) *Exklusion. Die Debatte über die 'Überflüssigen'* (Frankfurt/M.: Suhrkamp).
Bulmahn, Thomas (1996) *Vereinigungsbilanzen: Die deutsche Einheit im Spiegel der Sozialwissenschaften, Discussion Paper FS III* (Berlin: Wissenschaftszentrum), pp. 96–403, http://hdl.handle.net/10419/50197 – English: http://hdl.handle.net/10419/50196 (accessed January 14, 2014).
Busch, Alexander (1959) *Die Geschichte des Privatdozenten. Eine soziologische Studie zur großbetrieblichen Entwicklung der deutschen Universitäten* (Stuttgart: Enke).
Cahnman, Werner J. (1968) 'Toennies and Social Change' *Social Forces* 47 (2), pp. 136–144.
Caspari, Volker & Klaus Lichtblau (2014) *Franz Oppenheimer. Ökonom und Soziologe der ersten Stunde* (Frankfurt/M.: Societäts-Verlag).
Castel, Robert (1999) *Les métamorphoses de la question sociale. Une chronique du salariat* (Paris: Fayard).
Castel, Robert & Klaus Dörre (eds) (2009) *Prekarität, Abstieg, Ausgrenzung. Die soziale Frage am Beginn des 21. Jahrhunderts* (Frankfurt/M./New York: Campus.
Christ, Michaela & Maja Suderland (eds) (2014) *Soziologie und Nationalsozialismus. Positionen, Debatten, Perspektiven* (Berlin: Suhrkamp).
Cobet, Christoph (ed.) (1988) *Einführung in Fragen an die Soziologie in Deutschland nach Hitler 1945–1950. Mit einem Beitrag zur Soziologie in Österreich nach 1945* (Frankfurt/M.: Christoph Cobet).
Collins, Randall (1995) 'Prediction in Macrosociology: The Case of the Soviet Collapse' *American Journal of Sociology* 100 (6), pp. 1552–1593.
Conze, Eckart (2009) *Die Suche nach Sicherheit. Eine Geschichte der Bundesrepublik Deutschland von 1949 bis in die Gegenwart* (München: Siedler).

Dahme, Heinz-Jürgen & Otthein Rammstedt (1984) 'Die zeitlose Modernität der soziologischen Klassiker. Überlegungen zur Theoriekonstruktion von Emile Durkheim, Ferdinand Tönnies, Max Weber und besonders Georg Simmel' in ibid. (eds) *Georg Simmel und die Moderne. Neue Interpretationen und Materialien* (Frankfurt/M.: Suhrkamp), pp. 449–478.

Dahrendorf, Ralf (1965) 'Soziologie und Nationalsozialismus' in Andreas Flitner (ed.) *Deutsches Geistesleben und Nationalsozialismus* (Tübingen: Rainer Wunderlich Verlag), pp. 108–124.

Dahrendorf, Ralf (1974 [1959]) 'Aspekte der deutschen Soziologie der Nachkriegszeit' in ibid. *Pfade aus Utopia. Zur Theorie und Methodologie der Soziologie*, 3rd ed. (München: Piper), pp. 103–126.

Dahrendorf, Ralf (2017 [1958]) 'Homo Sociologicus. Ein Versuch zur Geschichte, Bedeutung und Kritik der Kategorie der Sozialen Rolle (Teil I und II)' in Hans-Jürgen Andreß et al. (eds) *Soziologiegeschichte im Spiegel der Kölner Zeitschrift für Soziologie und Sozialpsychologie, Sonderheft der Kölner Zeitschrift für Soziologie und Sozialpsychologie 56/2017* (Wiesbaden: VS), pp. 159–214.

Dahms, Hans-Joachim (1994) *Positivismusstreit. Die Auseinandersetzungen der Frankfurter Schule mit dem logischen Posititvismus, dem amerikanischen Pragmatismus und dem kritischen Rationalismus* (Frankfurt/M.: Suhrkamp).

Dayé, Christian & Stephan Moebius (eds) (2015) *Soziologiegeschichte. Wege und Ziele* (Berlin: Suhrkamp).

Demirović, Alex (1999) *Der nonkonformistische Intellektuelle. Die Entwicklung der Kritischen Theorie zur Frankfurter Schule* (Frankfurt/M.: Suhrkamp).

Demm, Eberhard (1990) *Ein Liberaler in Kaiserreich und Republik. Der politische Weg Alfred Webers bis 1920* (Boppard: Bohldt).

Dölling, Irene (1993) 'Aufschwung nach der Wende – Frauenforschung in der DDR und in den neuen Bundesländern' in Gisela Helwig & Hildegard Maria Nickel (eds) *Frauen in Deutschland 1945–1992* (Berlin: Akademie-Verlag), pp. 397–407.

Dölling, Irene (2006) 'Arbeiten "zwischen den Disziplinen"' in Ulrike Vogel (ed.) *Wege in die Soziologie und die Frauen- und Geschlechterforschung. Autobiographische Notizen der ersten Generation von Professorinnen an der Universität* (Wiesbaden: VS), pp. 116–124.

Dölling, Irene & Beate Krais (eds) (1997) *Ein alltägliches Spiel. Geschlechterkonstruktionen in der sozialen Praxis* (Frankfurt/M.: Suhrkamp).

Doering-Manteuffel, Anselm (2003) 'Westernisierung. Politisch-ideeller und gesellschaftlicher Wandel in der Bundesrepublik bis zum Ende der 60er Jahre' Axel Schildt et al. (eds) *Dynamische Zeiten. Die 60er Jahre in den beiden deutschen Gesellschaften*, 2nd ed. (Hamburg: Christians), pp. 311–341.

Doering-Manteuffel, Anselm & Raphael, Lutz (2012) *Nach dem Boom. Perspektiven auf die Zeitgeschichte seit 1970*, 3rd ed. (Göttingen: Vandenhoeck & Ruprecht).

Dörk, Uwe (2018a) 'Die frühe Deutsche Gesellschaft für Soziologie' in Stephan Moebius & Andrea Ploder (eds) *Handbuch Geschichte der deutschsprachigen Soziologie, Vol. 1* (Wiesbaden: VS), pp. 809–828.

Dörk, Uwe (2018b) 'Die Deutsche Gesellschaft für Soziologie (DGS) in der Zwischenkriegszeit (1918–1933)' in Stephan Moebius & Andrea Ploder (ed.) *Handbuch Geschichte der deutschsprachigen Soziologie, Vol. 1* (Wiesbaden: VS), pp. 829–848.

Dörre, Klaus (2010) 'Hartz-Kapitalismus. Vom erfolgreichen Scheitern der jüngsten Arbeitsmarktreformen' in Wilhelm Heitmeyer (ed.) *Deutsche Zustände. Folge 9* (Berlin: Suhrkamp), pp. 294–305.

Drehsen, Volker & Walter Sparn (eds) (1996) *Vom Weltbildwandel zur Weltanschauungsanalyse. Krisenwahrnehmung und Krisenbewältigung um 1900* (Berlin: Akademie Verlag).

Duller, Matthias, Christian Fleck & Rafael Y. Schögler (2019) 'Germany: After the Mandarins' in Christian Fleck, Matthias Duller & Victor Karàdy (eds) *Shaping Human Science Disciplines. Institutional Developments in Europe and Beyond* (Cham: Palgrave), pp. 69–110.

Dyk, Silke van & Alexandra Schauer (2015) *"…daß die offizielle Soziologie versagt hat". Zur Soziologie im Nationalsozialismus, der Geschichte ihrer Aufarbeitung und der Rolle der DGS*, 2nd ed. (Wiesbaden: VS).

Eckert, Roland (1970) *Kultur, Zivilisation und Gesellschaft. Die Geschichtstheorie Alfred Webers, eine Studie zur Geschichte der deutschen Soziologie* (Tübingen/Basel: Mohr/Kyklos).

Ehrenberg, Alain (1998) *La Fatigue d'être soi – dépression et société* (Paris: Odile Jacob).

Eisermann, Gottfried (ed.) (1976) *Die Krise der Soziologie* (Stuttgart: Enke).

Elias, Norbert (1977 [1939]) *Über den Prozeß der Zivilisation. Soziogenetische und psychogenetische Untersuchungen, Vol. 1* (Frankfurt/M.: Suhrkamp).

Elias, Norbert (1989/1996) *The Germans: Power Struggles and the Development of Habitus in Nineteenth and Twentieth Centuries* (Cambridge: Polity Press).

Elias, Norbert (1990) *Über sich selbst. Biographisches Interview. Notizen zum Lebenslauf* (Frankfurt/M.: Suhrkamp).

Eßbach, Wolfgang (2014) 'Das Besondere der Freiburger Soziologie' in Ulrich Bröckling et al. (eds) *Fünfzig Jahre Institut für Soziologie Freiburg. 1964–2014* (Freiburg: Jos Fritz), pp. 38–64.

Esser, Hartmut (2000) 'Vorwort' in Hartmut Esser (ed) *Der Wandel nach der Wende. Gesellschaft, Wirtschaft, Politik in Ostdeutschland* (Opladen: Westdeutscher Verlag), pp. 7–9.

Ettrich, Frank (1997) 'DDR-Soziologie: Après la lutte' in Hans Bertram (ed.) *Soziologie und Soziologen im Übergang* (Opladen: Leske & Budrich), pp. 263–304.

Ettrich, Frank (2018) 'Geschichte des Berliner Journals für Soziologie' in Stephan Moebius & Andrea Ploder (eds) *Handbuch Geschichte der deutschsprachigen Soziologie, Vol. 1* (Wiesbaden: VS), pp. 989–994.

Felsch, Philipp (2015) *Der lange Sommer der Theorie. Geschichte einer Revolte 1960–1990* (München: Beck).

Fichter, Tilman P. & Siegward Lönnendonker (2018) *Geschichte des SDS. Der sozialistische Studentenbund 1946–1970* (Bielefeld: Aisthesis).

Fischer, Joachim (2008) *Philosophische Anthropologie. Eine Denkrichtung des 20. Jahrhunderts* (Freiburg: Alber).

Fischer, Joachim (2010) 'Die Rollendebatte – Der Streit um den "Homo sociologicus"' in Georg Kneer & Stephan Moebius (eds) *Soziologische Kontroversen. Eine andere Geschichte der Wissenschaft vom Sozialen* (Berlin: Suhrkamp), pp. 79–101.

Fischer, Joachim & Stephan Moebius (eds) (2014) *Kultursoziologie im 21. Jahrhundert* (Wiesbaden: VS).

Fischer, Joachim & Stephan Moebius (eds) (2019) *Soziologische Denkschulen. Zur Archäologie der bunderepublikanischen Soziologie* (Wiesbaden: VS).

Flasch, Kurt (2000) *Die geistige Mobilmachung. Die deutschen Intellektuellen und der Erste Weltkrieg* (Berlin: Fest).

Fleck, Christian (2011) *A Transatlantic History of the Social Sciences: Robber Barons, the Third Reich and the Invention of Empirical Social Research* (London/New York: Bloomsbury).

Fleck, Christian (2015) *Etablierung in der Fremde. Vertriebene Wissenschaftler in den USA nach 1933* (Frankfurt/M./New York: Campus).

Fleig, Anne (eds) (2014) *Die Zukunft von Gender. Begriff und Zeitdiagnose* (Frankfurt/New York: Campus).

Fornefeld, Gabriele, Lücken, Alexander & Klemens Wittebur (1986) 'Die Soziologie an den reichsdeutschen Hochschulen zu Ende der Weimarer Republik' in Sven Papcke (ed.) *Ordnung und Theorie. Beiträge zur Geschichte der Soziologie in Deutschland* (Darmstadt: WBG), pp. 423–441.

Frei, Norbert (ed.) (2007) *Hitlers Eliten nach 1945*, 3rd ed. (München: DTV).

Frei, Norbert (2008) *1968. Jugendrevolte und globaler Protest* (Bonn: BPB).

Frei, Norbert (2012) *Vergangenheitspolitik. Die Anfänge der Bundesrepublik und die NS-Vergangenheit* (München: Beck).

Freund, Gisèle (1977) 'Norbert Elias als Lehrer' in Peter R. Gleichmann, Johan Goudsblom & Hermann Korte (eds) *Human Figurations. Essays for/Aufsätze für Norbert Elias* (Amsterdam: Amsterdams Sociologisch Tijdschrift), pp. 12–16.

Frevert, Ute (2003) 'Umbruch der Geschlechterverhältnisse? Die 60er Jahre als geschlechterpolitischer Experimentierraum' in Axel Schildt et al. (eds) *Dynamische Zeiten. Die 60er Jahre in den beiden deutschen Gesellschaften*, 2nd ed. (Hamburg: Christians), pp. 642–660.

Frevert, Ute (2020) *Mächtige Gefühle. Von A wie Angst bis Z wie Zuneigung. Deutsche Geschichte seit 1900* (Frankfurt/M.: Fischer).
Freyer, Hans (1930) *Soziologie als Wirklichkeitswissenschaft. Logische Grundlegung des Systems der Soziologie* (Leipzig/Berlin: Teubner).
Freyer, Hans (1931) *Revolution von rechts* (Jena: Diederichs).
Freyer, Hans (1955) *Theorie des gegenwärtigen Zeitalters* (Stuttgart: DVA).
Freyer, Hans (1965) *Schwelle der Zeiten. Beiträge zur Soziologie der Kultur* (Stuttgart: DVA).
Friedlander, Judith (2018) *A Light in Dark Times. The New School for Social Research and its University in Exile* (New York: Columbia University Press).
Frisby, David (1995) *Fragments of Modernity. Theories of Modernity in the Work by Simmel, Kracauer and Benjamin* (Cambridge: Polity Press).
Fritz-Vannahme, Joachim (ed.) (1996) *Wozu heute noch Soziologie?* (Opladen: Leske & Budrich).
Fülberth, Georg (2012) *Geschichte der BRD* (Köln: PapyRossa).
Fukuyama, Francis (1992) *The End of History and the Last Man* (New York: Free Press).
Geiger, Theodor (1926) *Die Masse und ihre Aktion. Ein Beitrag zur Soziologie der Revolutionen* (Stuttgart: Enke).
Geiger, Theodor (1931) 'Soziologie' in Alfred Vierkandt (ed.) *Handwörterbuch der Soziologie* (Stuttgart: Enke), pp. 568–578.
Geiger, Theodor (1932) *Die soziale Schichtung des deutschen Volkes. Soziographischer Versuch auf statistischer Grundlage* (Stuttgart: Enke).
Geißler, Rainer & Thomas Meyer (2000) 'Theodor Geiger (1891–1952)' in Dirk Kaesler (ed.) *Klassiker der Soziologie, Vol. 1* (München: Beck), pp. 278–296.
Gerhard, Ute (2006) 'Wie ich Soziologin wurde – eine Rekonstruktion' in Ulrike Vogel (ed.) *Wege in die Soziologie und die Frauen- und Geschlechterforschung. Autobiographische Notizen der ersten Generation von Professorinnen an der Universität* (Wiesbaden: VS), pp. 50–60.
Gerhard, Ute (2012) *Frauenbewegung und Feminismus. Eine Geschichte seit 1789* (München: Beck).
Gerhard, Ute et al. (1990) *Differenz und Gleichheit. Menschenrechte haben (k)ein Geschlecht* (Frankfurt/M.: Helmer).
Gerhardt, Uta (2006) 'Die Wiederanfänge der Soziologie nach 1945 und die Besatzungsherrschaft' in Bettina Franke & Kurt Hammerich (eds) *Soziologie an deutschen Universitäten: Gestern – heute – morgen* (Wiesbaden: VS), pp. 31–114.
Gerth, Nobuko (2000) 'Karl Mannheim and Hans Gerth' in Martin Endreß & Ilja Srubar (eds) *Karl Mannheims Analyse der Moderne. Jahrbuch für Soziologiegeschichte 1996* (Opladen: Leske & Budrich), pp. 127–144.
Giddens, Anthony (1985) 'Reason without Revolution? Habermas's Theorie des kommunikativen Handelns' in Richard J. Bernstein (ed.) *Habermas and Modernity* (Cambridge: Polity Press), pp. 95–121.

Gildemeister, Regine & Angelika Wetterer (1992) 'Wie Geschlechter gemacht werden. Die soziale Konstruktion der Zweigeschlechtlichkeit und ihre Reifizierung in der Frauenforschung' in Gudrun-Axeli Knapp & Angelika Wetterer (eds) *TraditionenBrüche. Entwicklungen feministischer Theorie* (Freiburg: Kore), pp. 201–254.

Gilligan, Carol (1982) *In a Different Voice: Psychological Theory and Women's Development* (Cambridge, MA: Harvard University Press).

Görtemaker, Manfred (2004) *Geschichte der Bundesrepublik Deutschland. Von der Gründung bis zur Gegenwart* (Frankfurt/M.: Fischer).

Görtemaker, Manfred (2009) *Die Berliner Republik. Wiedervereinigung und Neuorientierung* (Berlin: be.bra).

Gorges, Irmela (1980) *Sozialforschung in Deutschland 1872–1914. Gesellschaftliche Einflüsse auf Themen- und Methodenwahl des Vereins für Socialpolitik* (Königstein: Hain).

Gorges, Irmela (1986) *Sozialforschung in der Weimarer Republik 1918–1933* (Frankfurt/M.: Hain).

Gorges, Irmela (2018) 'The History of the Verein für Socialpolitik. An Unintended Contribution to the Pre-History of the Institutionalization of Sociology' in Stephan Moebius & Andrea Ploder (eds) *Handbuch Geschichte der deutschsprachigen Soziologie, Vol. 1* (Wiesbaden: VS), pp. 791–808.

Gouldner, Alvin (1970) *The coming crisis of Western sociology* (New York: Basic Books).

Greshoff, Rainer (2010) 'Die Theorienvergleichsdebatte in der deutschsprachigen Soziologie' in Georg Kneer & Stephan Moebius (eds) *Soziologische Kontroversen. Eine andere Geschichte der Wissenschaft vom Sozialen* (Berlin: Suhrkamp), pp. 182–216.

Greshoff, Rainer, Gesa Lindemann & Uwe Schimank (2007) *Theorienvergleich und Theorienintegration – Disziplingeschichtliche und methodische Überlegungen zur Entwicklung eines paradigmenvermittelnden 'conceptual framework' für die Soziologie*, Arbeitsgruppe Soziologische Theorie (AST)/CvO Universität Oldenburg, Diskussionspapiere 1, http://www.uni-oldenburg.de/fileadmin/user_upload/sowi/ag/ast/download/dp/ast-dp-1-07.pdf (accessed July 2, 2019).

Greven, Michael Th. & Gerd van de Moetter (1981) 'Vita constructa. Ein Versuch, die Wahrnehmung von Heinz Maus mit seinem Werk in Einklang zu bringen' in Heinz Maus *Die Traumhölle des Justemilieu. Erinnerung an die Aufgaben der Kritischen Theorie*, eds of Michael Th. Greven & Gerd van de Moetter (Frankfurt/M.: EVA), pp. 7–41.

Gross, Peter (1994) *Die Multioptionsgesellschaft* (Frankfurt/M.: Suhrkamp).

Grunenberg, Tina (2007) *Die Wundertäter. Netzwerke der deutschen Wirtschaft 1942–1966* (München: Pantheon).

Habermas, Jürgen (1971) 'Theorie der Gesellschaft oder Sozialtechnologie? Eine Auseinandersetzung mit Niklas Luhmann' in ibid. & Niklas Luhmann *Theorie der Gesellschaft oder Sozialtechnologie* (Frankfurt/M.: Suhrkamp), pp. 142–290.

Habermas, Jürgen (1973) *Legitimationsprobleme im Spätkapitalismus* (Frankfurt/M.: Suhrkamp).

Habermas, Jürgen (1981) *Theorie des kommunikativen Handelns*, 2 Vol. (Frankfurt/M.: Suhrkamp).

Habermas, Jürgen (1983) 'Moralbewußtsein und kommunikatives Handeln' in ibid. *Moralbewußtsein und kommunikatives Handeln* (Frankfurt/M.: Suhrkamp), pp. 127–206.

Habermas, Jürgen (1985) *Der philosophische Diskurs der Moderne* (Frankfurt/M.: Suhrkamp).

Habermas, Jürgen (1990) *Die nachholende Revolution. Kleine politische Schriften VII* (Frankfurt/M.: Suhrkamp).

Habermas, Jürgen (2008 [1967]) 'Kongreß "Hochschule und Demokratie"' in ibid (ed.) *Protestbewegung und Hochschulreform* (Frankfurt/M.: Suhrkamp), pp. 137–152.

Hagemann-White, Carol (1984) *Sozialisation: Weiblich – männlich?* (Opladen: Leske & Budrich).

Hagemann-White, Carol (2006) '"Wege und Brücken"' in Ulrike Vogel (ed.) *Wege in die Soziologie und die Frauen- und Geschlechterforschung. Autobiographische Notizen der ersten Generation von Professorinnen an der Universität* (Wiesbaden: VS), pp. 125–137.

Hager, Don J. (1949) 'German Sociology under Hitler, 1933–1941' *Social Forces* 28 (1), pp. 6–19.

Hamm, Sabine (1989) 'Soziologie in der DDR – ein Überblick' *Soziologie. Mitteilungsblatt der Deutschen Gesellschaft für Soziologie* 2, pp. 137–154.

Hartmann, Heinz (2018) 'Die Gründung der Soziologischen Revue' in Stephan Moebius & Andrea Ploder (eds) *Handbuch Geschichte der deutschsprachigen Soziologie, Vol. 1* (Wiesbaden: VS), pp. 975–987.

Hartmann, Michael (1996) *Topmanager – Die Rekrutierung einer Elite* (Frankfurt/New York: Campus).

Hartmann, Michael (2002) *Der Mythos von den Leistungseliten. Spitzenkarrieren und soziale Herkunft in Wirtschaft, Politik, Justiz und Wissenschaft* (Frankfurt/New York: Campus).

Hartmann, Michael (2010) 'Klassenkampf von oben. Die gezielte soziale Desintegration' in Wilhelm Heitmeyer (ed.) *Deutsche Zustände. Folge 9* (Berlin: Suhrkamp), pp. 267–277.

Hartmann, Michael (2013) *Soziale Ungleichheit – kein Thema für die Eliten?* (Frankfurt/New York: Campus).

Hark, Sabine (2005) *Dissidente Partizipation. Eine Diskursgeschichte des Feminismus* (Frankfurt/M.: Suhrkamp).

Haug, Frigga (1984) 'Die Moral ist zweigeschlechtlich wie der Mensch. Zur Theorie weiblicher Vergesellschaftung' in Claudia Optiz (ed.) *Weiblichkeit oder Feminismus? Beiträge zur interdisziplinären Frauentagung Konstanz 1983* (Weingarten: Drumlin), pp. 95–121.

Hauser, Richard (2010) '„Nahblick" und „Weitblick". Erste Schritte zur Erforschung des sozialen und politischen Wandels in den neuen Bundesländern und frühe Prognosen' in Peter Krause & Ilona Ostner (eds) *Leben in Ost- und Westdeutschland. Eine sozialwissenschaftliche Bilanz der deutschen Einheit 1990-2010* (Frankfurt/M./New York: Campus), pp. 57–81.

Heilbron, Johan (2008) 'Qu'est-ce qu'une tradition nationale en sciences sociales?' in *Revue d'histoire de sciences humaines* 2008/1, No. 19, pp. 3–16.

Heilbron, Johan (2015) *French Sociology* (Ithaca/London: Cornell University Press).

Heitmeyer, Wilhelm (1997) 'Einleitung: Auf dem Weg in eine desintegrierte Gesellschaft' in ibid. (ed.) *Was treibt die Gesellschaft auseinander? Bundesrepublik Deutschland: Auf dem Weg von der Konsens- zur Konfliktgesellschaft, Vol. 1* (Frankfurt/M.: Suhrkamp), pp. 9–26.

Henning, Christoph (2006) '"Der übernationale Gedanke der geistigen Einheit". Gottfried Salomon(-Delatour), der vergessene Soziologe der Verständigung' in Amalia Barboza & ibid. (eds) *Deutsch-jüdische Wissenschaftsschicksale* (Bielefeld: transcript), pp. 48–100.

Hennis, Wilhelm (1987) *Max Webers Fragestellung. Studien zur Biographie des Werks* (Tübingen: Mohr Siebeck).

Herbert, Ulrich (2014) *Geschichte Deutschlands im 20. Jahrhundert* (München: Beck).

Herbert, Ulrich (2018) *Das Dritte Reich. Geschichte einer Diktatur* (München: Beck).

Herbert, Ulrich & Karin Hunn (2003) 'Gastarbeiter und Gastarbeiterpolitik in der Bundesrepublik. Vom Beginn der offiziellen Anwerbung bis zum Anwerbestopp (1955–1973)' in Axel Schildt et al. (eds) *Dynamische Zeiten. Die 60er Jahre in den beiden deutschen Gesellschaften*, 2nd ed. (Hamburg: Christians), pp. 273–310.

Hermand, Jost (2010) *Kultur in finsteren Zeiten. Nazifaschismus, Innere Emigration, Exil* (Köln/Weimar/Wien: Böhlau).

Heske, Gerhard (2005) 'Bruttoinlandsprodukt, Verbrauch und Erwerbstätigkeit in Ostdeutschland 1970–2000: neue Ergebnisse einer volkswirtschaftlichen Gesamtrechnung' *Historical Social Research, Supplement 17*, pp. 1–336, https://www.ssoar.info/ssoar/handle/document/28588 (accessed October 1, 2019).

Hirschauer, Stefan (2021) 'Ungehaltene Dialoge. Zur Fortentwicklung soziologischer Intradisziplinarität' *Soziologie. Mitteilungsblatt der Deutschen Gesellschaft für Soziologie* 1, pp. 46–65.

Holzhauser, Nicole (2015) 'Definitorische und methodologische Probleme bei der Analyse der soziologischen Disziplinentwicklung zur Zeit des Nationalsozialismus' *Österreichische Zeitschrift für Soziologie* 40 (2), pp. 129–146.

Holzhauser, Nicole (2021) 'Quantifying the Exclusionary Process of Canonisation, or How to Become a Classic of the Social Sciences' in *International Review of Sociology*. Special Issue. Volume 31, Issue 1.

Holzhauser, Nicole et al. (2019) *Handbuch Geschichte der deutschsprachigen Soziologie, Vol. 3: Zeittafel* (Wiesbaden: VS).

Honigsheim, Paul (1959) 'Die Gründung der Deutschen Gesellschaft für Soziologie' *Kölner Zeitschrift für Soziologie und Sozialpsychologie* 11, pp. 3–10.

Honegger, Claudia (1993) 'Jüdinnen in der frühen deutschsprachigen Soziologie' in Mechthild Jansen & Ingeborg Nordmann (eds) *Lektüren und Brüche. Jüdische Frauen in Kultur, Politik und Wissenschaft* (Wiesbaden: Hessische Landeszentrale für politische Bildung), pp. 178–195.

Honneth, Axel (1994) *Desintegration. Bruchstücke einer soziologischen Zeitdiagnose* (Frankfurt/M.: Fischer).

Horst, Johanna-Charlotte et al. (eds) (2010) *Unbedingte Universität. Was passiert? Stellungnahmen zur Lage der Universität* (Zürich: diaphanes).

Horster, Detlef (2005) *Niklas Luhmann*. 2nd ed. (München: Beck).

Ilieva, Radostina (2010) 'Soziologie und Lebensstil des Mannheim-Kreises in Frankfurt' in Felicia Herrschaft & Klaus Lichtblau (eds) *Soziologie in Frankfurt. Eine Zwischenbilanz* (Wiesbaden: VS), pp. 123–140.

Jaeggi, Urs et al. (eds) (1983) *Geist und Katastrophe: Studien zur Soziologie im Nationalsozialismus* (Berlin: Wissenschaftlicher Autoren-Verlag).

Jarausch, Konrad H. (1984) *Deutsche Studenten. 1800–1970* (Frankfurt/M.: Suhrkamp).

Jay, Martin (1981 [1973]) *Dialektische Phantasie. Die Geschichte der Frankfurter Schule und des Instituts für Sozialforschung 1923–1950* (Frankfurt/M.: Fischer).

Joas, Hans (2005) 'A Pragmatist form Germany' in Alan Sica & Stephen Turner (eds) *The Disobedient Generation* (Chicago/London: University of Chicago Press), pp. 156–175.

Joas, Hans & Martin Kohli (eds) (1993a) *Der Zusammenbruch der DDR. Soziologische Analysen* (Frankfurt/M.: Suhrkamp).

Joas, Hans & Martin Kohli (1993b) 'Der Zusammenbruch der DDR: Fragen und Thesen' in ibid. (eds) *Der Zusammenbruch der DDR. Soziologische Analysen* (Frankfurt/M.: Suhrkamp), pp. 7–28.

Joas, Hans & Wolfgang Knöbl (2009) *Social Theory: Twenty Introductory Lectures* (Cambridge: Cambridge University Press).

Joas, Hans & Wolfgang Knöbl (2012) *War in Social Thought. Hobbes to the Present* (Princeton: Princeton University Press).

Kaminsky, Anna (2020) *Frauen in der DDR* (Berlin: Links).

Kaesler, Dirk (1981) 'Der Streit um die Bestimmung der Soziologie auf den Deutschen Soziologentagen 1910–1930' in M. Rainer Lepsius (ed.) *Soziologie in Deutschland und Österreich 1918–1945, Sonderheft 23 der Kölner Zeitschrift für Soziologie und Sozialpsychologie* (Opladen: Westdeutscher Verlag), pp. 199–244.

Kaesler, Dirk (1984) *Die frühe deutsche Soziologie und ihre Entstehungsmilieus. Eine wissenschaftssoziologische Untersuchung* (Opladen: Westdeutscher Verlag).

Kaesler, Dirk (2008) 'Die Soziologie auf der Suche nach akademischer Respektabilität – Eine wissenschaftssoziologische Einordnung der Jenaer Debatten von 1922' in Silke van Dyk & Stephan Lessenich (eds) *Jena und die deutsche Soziologie. Der Soziologentag 1922 und das Soziologentreffen 1934 in der Retrospektive* (Frankfurt/M./New York: Campus), pp. 81–97.

Kaesler, Dirk (2014) *Max Weber. Eine Biographie* (München: Beck).

Kaesler, Dirk & Thomas Steiner (1992) 'Academic Discussion or Political Guidance? Social-scientific analyses of fascism and National Socialism in Germany before 1933' in Stephen P. Turner & Dirk Kaesler (eds) *Sociology responds to Fascism* (London/New York: Routledge), pp. 88–126.

Kändler, Ulrike (2016) *Entdeckung des Urbanen. Die Sozialforschungsstelle Dortmund und die soziologische Stadtforschung in Deutschland, 1930 bis 1960* (Bielefeld: transcript).

Kaube, Jürgen (1998) 'Soziologie', in Jürgen Kocka & Renate Mayntz (eds) *Wissenschaft und Wiedervereinigung. Disziplinen im Umbruch* (Berlin: Akademie-Verlag), pp. 255–301.

Kaube, Jürgen (2014) *Max Weber. Ein Leben zwischen den Epochen* (Berlin: Rowohlt).

Kenkmann, Alfons (2003) 'Von der bundesdeutschen "Bildungsmisere" zur Bildungsreform in den 60er Jahren' in Axel Schildt et al. (eds) *Dynamische Zeiten. Die 60er Jahre in den beiden deutschen Gesellschaften*, 2nd ed. (Hamburg: Christians), pp. 402–423.

Kessler, Suzanne J & Wendy McKenna (1978) *Gender. An Ethnomethodological Approach* (New York: John Wiley & Sons).

Kettler, David & Meja, Volker (1993) 'Their 'Own Peculiar Way': Karl Mannheim and the Rise of Women' in *International Sociology* 8/1, pp. 5–55.

Kettler, David & Volker Meja (1994) '"That typically German Kind of Sociology Which Verges towards Philosophy": The Dispute about Ideology and Utopia in the United States' *Sociological Theory* 12 (3), pp. 279–303.

Kettler, David, Loader, Colin & Volker Meja (2008) *Karl Mannheim and the Legacy of Max Weber. Retrieving a Research Programme* (Aldershot/Burlington: Ashgate).

Kern, Horst (1982) *Empirische Sozialforschung. Ursprünge, Ansätze, Entwicklungslinien* (München: Beck).

Kern, Horst & Michael Schumann (1984) *Das Ende der Arbeitsteilung. Rationalisierung in der industriellen Produktion* (München: Beck).

Klautke, Egbert (2016) *Völkerpsychologie in Germany, 1851–1955* (New York/Oxford: Berghahn).

Klingemann, Carsten (1981) 'Heimatsoziologie oder Ordnungsinstrument: Fachgeschichtliche Aspekte der Soziologie in Deutschland zwischen 1933 und 1945' *Kölner Zeitschrift für Soziologie und Sozialpsychologie* Sonderheft 23, pp. 273–307.

Klingemann, Carsten (1986) 'Vergangenheitsbewältigung oder Geschichtsschreibung? Unerwünschte Traditionsbestände deutscher Soziologie zwischen 1933 und 1945' in Sven Papcke (ed.) *Ordnung und Theorie: Beiträge zur Geschichte der Soziologie in Deutschland* (Darmstadt: Wissenschaftliche Buchgesellschaft), pp. 223–279.

Klingemann, Carsten (1988) 'Kölner Soziologie während des Nationalsozialismus' in Wolfgang Blaschke et al. (eds) *Nachhilfe zur Erinnerung. 600 Jahre Universität zu Köln* (Köln: Pahl-Rugenstein), pp. 76–97.

Klingemann, Carsten (1990) 'Das "Institut für Sozial- und Staatswissenschaften" an der Universität Heidelberg zum Ende der Weimarer Republik und während des Nationalsozialismus' in Heinz-Jürgen Dahme, Carsten Klingemann, Michael Neumann, Karl-Siegbert Rehberg & Ilja Srubar (eds) *Jahrbuch für Soziologiegeschichte 1990* (Opladen: Leske & Budrich), pp. 79–120.

Klingemann, Carsten (1992) 'Social-scientific Experts – no Ideologues. Sociology and social research in the Third Reich' in Stephen P. Turner & Dirk Kaesler (eds) *Sociology responds to Fascism* (London/New York: Routledge), pp. 127–154.

Klingemann, Carsten (1996) *Soziologie im Dritten Reich* (Baden-Baden: Nomos).

Klingemann, Carsten (2008) 'Soziologie' in Jürgen Elvert & Jürgen Nielsen-Sikora (eds) *Kulturwissenschaften und Nationalsozialismus* (Stuttgart: Steiner), pp. 390–444.

Klingemann, Carsten (2009) *Soziologie und Politik. Sozialwissenschaftliches Expertenwissen im Dritten Reich und in der frühen westdeutschen Nachkriegszeit* (Wiesbaden: VS).

Knapp, Gudrun-Axeli (2006) 'Geradlinige Umwege' in Ulrike Vogel (ed.) *Wege in die Soziologie und die Frauen- und Geschlechterforschung. Autobiographische Notizen der ersten Generation von Professorinnen an der Universität* (Wiesbaden: VS), pp. 178–189.

Knebelspieß, Stefanie & Moebius, Stephan (2019) 'Programm, personelle und organisatorische Entwicklung des Forschungsinstituts für Sozialwissenschaften von 1918/1919 bis zum heutigen Institut für Soziologie und Sozialpsychologie (ISS)' *Kölner Zeitschrift für Soziologie und Sozialpsychologie* 71/4, pp. 515–552.

Kneer, Georg & Stephan Moebius (eds) (2010) *Soziologische Kontroversen. Eine andere Geschichte der Wissenschaft vom Sozialen* (Berlin: Suhrkamp).

Knie, Andreas & Dagmar Simon (2018) 'Geschichte der Soziologie am Wissenschaftszentrum Berlins' in Stephan Moebius & Andrea Ploder (eds) *Handbuch Geschichte der deutschsprachigen Soziologie, Vol. 1* (Wiesbaden: VS), pp. 1065–1075.

Knorr-Cetina, Karin (2005) 'Culture of Life' in Alan Sica & Stephen Turner (eds) *The Disobedient Generation* (Chicago/London: University of Chicago Press), pp. 176–195.

Kocka, Jürgen (1982) 'Der "deutsche Sonderweg" in der Diskussion' *German Studies Review* 5 (3), pp. 365–379.

Kocka, Jürgen (1998) 'Einleitung' in Jürgen Kocka & Renate Mayntz (eds) *Wissenschaft und Wiedervereinigung. Disziplinen im Umbruch* (Berlin: Akademie-Verlag), pp. 7–19.

Köhnke, Klaus Christian (1988) 'Wissenschaft und Politik in den Sozialwissenschaftlichen Studentenvereinigungen der 1890er Jahre' in Otthein Rammstedt (ed.) *Simmel und die frühen Soziologen. Nähe und Distanz zu Durkheim, Tönnies und Max Weber* (Frankfurt/M.: Suhrkamp), pp. 308–341.

Köhnke, Klaus Christian (1996) *Der junge Simmel in Theoriebeziehungen und sozialen Bewegungen* (Frankfurt/M.: Suhrkamp).

König, René (1967) 'Einleitung' in ibid. (ed.) *Soziologie. Fischer-Lexikon*, revised and extended new edition (Frankfurt/M.: Fischer), pp. 8–14.

König, René (1987) *Soziologie in Deutschland. Begründer/Verfechter/Verächter* (München/Wien: Hanser).

König, René (2002 [1961/1962]) 'Freiheit und Selbstentfremdung in soziologischer Sicht' in Hansjürgen Daheim & Dieter Fröhlich (eds) *Arbeit und Beruf in der modernen Gesellschaft, Schriften Vol. 16* (Wiesbaden: Springer VS), pp. 7–26.

König, René et al. (1952) *Das Interview. Formen, Technik, Auswertung. Praktische Sozialforschung I* (Köln/Berlin: Kiepenheuer & Witsch).

König, René et al. (1956) *Beobachtung und Experiment ind er Sozialforshcung. Praktische Sozialforschung II* (Köln: Verlag für Politik und Wirtschaft).

Korte, Jasper W. (2019) 'Soziologie in der Presse' *Soziologie. Forum der Deutschen Gesellschaft für Soziologie* 3/2019, pp. 273–292.

Krais, Beate (2000) *Wissenschaftskultur und Geschlechterforschung. Über die verborgenen Mechanismen männlicher Dominanz in der akademischen Welt* (Frankfurt/New York: Campus).

Krais, Beate & Michael Hartmann (eds) (2001) *An der Spitze. Deutsche Eliten im sozialen Wandel* (Konstanz: UVK).

Krause, Peter & Ilona Ostner (eds) (2010) *Leben in Ost- und Westdeutschland. Eine sozialwissenschaftliche Bilanz der deutschen Einheit 1990–2010* (Frankfurt/New York: Campus).

Kreckel, Reinhard (2013) 'Der vierte Anlauf: Neuaufbau nach 1990 – Institut für Soziologie' in Peer Pasternack/Reinhold Sackmann (eds) *Vier Anläufe: Soziologie an der Universität Halle-Wittenberg* (Halle: mdv), pp. 211–223.

Kreps, David M. (1997) 'Economics: The Current Position' *Daedalus* 126 (1), pp. 59–85.

Krohn, Claus-Dieter (1987) *Wissenschaft im Exil. Deutsche Sozial- und Wirtschaftswissenschaftler in den USA und die New School for Social Research* (Frankfurt/M./New York: Campus).
Krohn, Claus-Dieter (1995) 'Zur intellektuellen Biographie Emil Lederers' in Emil Lederer (1995 [1940]) Der Massenstaat. Gefahren der klassenlosen Gesellschaft (Graz: Nausner & Nausner), pp. 9–40.
Kronauer, Martin (2010) *Exklusion. Die Gefährdung des Sozialen im hoch entwickelten Kapitalismus*, 2nd ed. (Frankfurt/M./New York: Campus).
Kropp, Kristoffer (2015) *A Historical Account of Danish Sociology: A Troubled History* (Basingstoke: Palgrave).
Kruse, Volker (1994) *Historisch-soziologische Zeitdiagnosen in Westdeutschland nach 1945. Eduard Heimann, Alfred von Martin, Hans Freyer* (Frankfurt/M.: Suhrkamp).
Kruse, Volker (1998) *Analysen zur deutschen historischen Soziologie* (Münster: LIT).
Kruse, Volker & Thomas Strulik (eds) (2019) *"Hochschul-Experimentierplatz Bielefeld" – 50 Jahre Fakultät für Soziologie* (Bielefeld: transcript).
Krysmanski, Hans Jürgen et al. (eds) (1975) *Die Krise in der Soziologie. Ein kritischer Reader zum 17. Deutschen Soziologentag* (Köln: Pahl-Rugenstein).
Lamnek, Siegfried (1991) 'Gesellschaftliche Interessen und Ausbildung' in Harald Kerber & Arnold Schmieder (eds) *Soziologie. Arbeitsfelder, Theorien, Ausbildung. Ein Grundkurs* (Reinbek: RORORO), pp. 704–719.
Land, Rainer (2003) 'Ostdeutschland – fragmentierte Entwicklung' *Berliner Debatte Initial* 14 (6), pp. 76–95.
Landshut, Siegfried (1929/1969) *Kritik der Soziologie und andere Schriften zur Politik*, Neuwied: Luchterhand.
Larsson, Anna & Sanja Magdalenič (2015) *Sociology in Sweden. A History*, Basingstoke: Palgrave.
Lederer, Emil (2014 [1915]) 'Zur Soziologie des Weltkriegs' in ibid. *Schriften zur Wissenschaftslehre und Kultursoziologie* (Wiesbaden: VS), pp. 101–130.
Leendertz, Ariane (2010) *Die pragmatische Wende. Die Max-Planck-Gesellschaft und die Sozialwissenschaften 1975–1985* (Göttingen: Vandenhoeck & Ruprecht).
Leendertz, Ariane (2018) 'Geschichte des Max-Planck-Instituts zur Erforschung der Lebensbedingungen der wissenschaftlich-technischen Welt in Starnberg (MPIL) und des Max-Planck-Instituts für Gesellschaftsforschung in Köln' in Stephan Moebius & Andrea Ploder (eds) *Handbuch Geschichte der deutschsprachigen Soziologie, Vol. 1* (Wiesbaden: VS), pp. 1077–1089.
Lehmann, Maren (2019) 'Von Defizitlisten und Wunschzetteln unter blauem Himmel. Buchforum zu "Lütten Klein" von Steffen Mau' *Soziopolis*, https://www.soziopolis.de/luetten-klein-leben-in-der-ostdeutschen-transformationsgesellschaft-3.html (accessed August 14, 2019).
Lenzen, Dieter (2014) *Bildung statt Bologna!* (Berlin: Ullstein).
Lepenies, Wolf (1981) 'Einleitung. Studien zur kognitiven, sozialen und historischen Identität der Soziologie' in ibid. (ed.) *Geschichte der Soziologie. Studien*

*zur kognitiven, sozialen und historischen Identität einer Disziplin, Vol. 1* (Frankfurt/M.: Suhrkamp), pp. I–XXXV.

Lepenies, Wolf (1997) *Benimm und Erkenntnis – Über die notwendige Rückkehr der Werte in die Wissenschaften. Die Sozialwissenschaften nach dem Ende der Geschichte. Zwei Vorträge* (Frankfurt/M.: Suhrkamp).

Lepsius, M. Rainer (2008) 'Blicke zurück und nach vorn. M. Rainer Lepsius im Gespräch mit Adalbert Hepp und Martina Löw' in Adalbert Hepp & Martina Löw M Rainer Lepsius. Soziologie als Profession (Frankfurt/New York: Campus, pp. 11–75.

Lepsius, M. Rainer (2011) 'Max Weber und die Gründung der Deutschen Gesellschaft für Soziologie' *Soziologie. Forum der Deutschen Gesellschaft für Soziologie* 40 (1), pp. 7–19.

Lepsius, M. Rainer (2017a [1981]) 'Die Soziologie der Zwischenkriegszeit: Entwicklungstendenzen und Beurteilungskriterien' in ibid. *Soziologie und Soziologen. Aufsätze zur Institutionalisierung der Soziologie in Deutschland* (Tübingen: Mohr Siebeck), pp. 3–20.

Lepsius, M. Rainer (2017b [1981]) 'Die sozialwissenschaftliche Emigration und ihre Folgen' in ibid. *Soziologie und Soziologen. Aufsätze zur Institutionalisierung der Soziologie in Deutschland* (Tübingen: Mohr Siebeck), pp. 21–65.

Lepsius, M. Rainer (2017c [1978]) 'Neubegründung' in ibid. *Soziologie und Soziologen. Aufsätze zur Institutionalisierung der Soziologie in Deutschland* (Tübingen: Mohr Siebeck), pp. 79–84.

Lepsius, M. Rainer (2017d [1979]) 'Die Entwicklung der Soziologie nach dem Zweiten Weltkrieg 1945–1967' in ibid. *Soziologie und Soziologen. Aufsätze zur Institutionalisierung der Soziologie in Deutschland* (Tübingen: Mohr Siebeck), pp. 85–136.

Lepsius, M. Rainer (2017e [1972]) 'Die personelle Lage an den Hochschulen in der Bundesrepublik Deutschland' in ibid. *Soziologie und Soziologen. Aufsätze zur Institutionalisierung der Soziologie in Deutschland* (Tübingen: Mohr Siebeck), pp. 185–203.

Lepsius, M. Rainer (2017f [1974]) 'Ansprache zur Eröffnung des 17. Deutschen Soziologentages: Zwischenbilanz der Soziologie' in ibid. *Soziologie und Soziologen. Aufsätze zur Institutionalisierung der Soziologie in Deutschland* (Tübingen: Mohr Siebeck), pp. 209–223.

Lepsius, M. Rainer (2017g) 'Zur Soziologie in der DDR und zum Aufbau der Soziologie in den neuen Bundesländern' in ibid. *Soziologie und Soziologen. Aufsätze zur Institutionalisierung der Soziologie in Deutschland* (Tübingen: Mohr Siebeck), pp. 275–277.

Lepsius, M. Rainer (2017h [1993]) 'Zum Aufbau der Soziologie in Ostdeutschland' in ibid. *Soziologie und Soziologen. Aufsätze zur Institutionalisierung der Soziologie in Deutschland* (Tübingen: Mohr Siebeck), pp. 331–367.

Lichtblau, Klaus (1996) *Kulturkrise und Soziologie um die Jahrhundertwende. Zur Genealogie der Kultursoziologie in Deutschland* (Frankfurt/M.: Suhrkamp).

Lichtblau, Klaus (2001) 'Soziologie und Anti-Soziologie um 1900. Wilhelm Dilthey, Georg Simmel und Max Weber' in Peter-Ulrich Merz-Benz & Gerhard Wagner (eds) *Soziologie und Anti-Soziologie. Ein Diskurs und seine Rekonstruktion* (Konstanz: UVK), pp. 17–35.

Lichtblau, Klaus (2017 [1991]) 'Soziologie und Zeitdiagnose. Oder: Die Moderne im Selbstbezug' in ibid. (2017) *Zwischen Klassik und Moderne. Die Modernität der klassischen deutschen Soziologie* (Wiesbaden: VS), pp. 57–79.

Lichtblau, Klaus (2018) 'Anfänge der Soziologie in Deutschland (1871–1918)' in Stephan Moebius & Andrea Ploder (eds) *Handbuch Geschichte der deutschsprachigen Soziologie, Vol. 1* (Wiesbaden: VS), pp. 11–35.

Liebersohn, Harry (1988) *Fate and Utopia in German Sociology, 1870–1923* (Cambridge: MIT).

Liebold, Sebastian (2012) 'Arnold Bergstraesser und Fritz Caspari in Amerika' in Frank Schale et al. (eds) *Intellektuelle Emigration. Zur Aktualität eines historischen Phänomens* (Wiesbaden: VS), pp. 89–110.

Link, Fabian (2015) 'Die multiple Epistemologie der Sozialwissenschaften. Anmerkungen zu einer Sitzung über das 'Verhältnis von Soziologie und empirischer Sozialforschung' am 1. März1957' in Martin Endreß, Klaus Lichtblau & Stephan Moebius (eds) *Zyklos – Jahrbuch für Theorie und Geschichte der Soziologie. Vol 2* (Wiesbaden: VS), pp. 101–130.

Loader, Colin (2012) *Alfred Weber and the Crisis of Culture, 1890–1933* (New York: Palgrave Macmillan).

Lötsch, Manfred et al. (1988) *Ingenieure in der DDR. Soziologische Studien* (Berlin: Dietz).

Lucke, Doris (2003) *Die Kategorie Geschlecht in der Soziologie*, online: https://www.fu-berlin.de/sites/gpo/soz_eth/Geschlecht_als_Kategorie/Die_Kategorie_Geschlecht_in_der_Soziologie/doris_lucke.pdf (accessed October 8, 2020).

Ludz, Peter Christian (ed.) (1972a) *Soziologie und Marxismus in der Deutschen Demokratischen Republik, Vol. 1* (Neuwied/Berlin: Luchterhand).

Ludz, Peter Christian (ed.) (1972b) *Soziologie und Marxismus in der Deutschen Demokratischen Republik, Vol. 2* (Neuwied/Berlin: Luchterhand).

Luhmann, Niklas (1971) 'Systemtheoretische Argumentationen. Eine Entgegnung auf Jürgen Habermas' in Jürgen Habermas & ibid. *Theorie der Gesellschaft oder Sozialtechnologie* (Frankfurt/M.: Suhrkamp), pp. 291–405.

Luhmann, Niklas (1984) *Soziale Systeme. Grundriß einer allgemeinen Theorie* (Frankfurt/M.: Suhrkamp).

Lundgreen, Peter et al. (2008) *Datenhandbuch zur deutschen Bildungsgeschichte. Band VIII: Berufliche Schulen und Hochschulen in der Bundesrepublik Deutschland 1949–2001* (Göttingen: V & R).

Mählert, Ulrich (2009) *Kleine Geschichte der DDR* (München: Beck).

Maihofer, Andrea (1997) 'Gleichheit und/oder Differenz? Zum Verlauf der Debatte' in *Politische Vierteljahresschrift*, 38/Vol. 28, pp. 155–176.

Malycha, Andreas (2011) 'Im Zeichen von Reform und Modernisierung (1961–1971)' *Geschichte der DDR. Informationen zur politischen Bildung* 312 (3), pp. 37–48.

Mannheim, Karl (2013 [1934]) 'German Sociology (1918–1933)' in Karl Mannheim (2013) *Essays on Sociology and Social Psychology. Collected Works of Karl Mannheim* (London/New York: Routledge), pp. 209–228.

Marty, Christian (2020) *Max Weber. Ein Denker der Freiheit*, 2nd edition (Weinheim: Beltz Juventa).

Matthes, Joachim (1978) 'Die Diskussion um den Theorienvergleich in den Sozialwissenschaften seit dem Kasseler Soziologentag 1974' in Karl O. Hondrich & Joachim Matthes (eds) *Theorienvergleich in den Sozialwissenschaften* (Darmstadt/Neuwied: Luchterhand), pp. 7–20.

Mau, Steffen & Denis Huschka (2010) 'Who is Who? Die Sozialstruktur der Soziologie-Professorenschaft in Deutschland' *Kölner Zeitschrift für Soziologie und Sozialpsychologie* 62 (4), pp. 751–766.

Maurer, Andrea (2017) *Erklären in der Soziologie. Geschichte und Anspruch eines Forschungsprogramms* (Wiesbaden: VS).

Maurer, Andrea (2019) 'Erklärende Soziologie. Anliegen, Positionierung, Netzwerke und Rezeption' in Joachim Fischer & Stephan Moebius (eds) *Soziologische Denkschulen in der Bundesrepublik Deutschland* (Wiesbaden: VS), pp. 277–315.

Maus, Heinz (1959) 'Bericht über die Soziologie in Deutschland 1933–1945' *Kölner Zeitschrift für Soziologie und Sozialpsychologie* 11 (1), pp. 72–99.

Meifort, Franziska (2017) *Ralf Dahrendorf. Eine Biographie* (München: Beck).

Meja, Volker & Nico Stehr (eds) (1990) *Knowledge and Politics: The Sociology of Knowledge Dispute* (London/New York: Routledge).

Meja, Volker, Misgeld, Dieter & Stehr, Nico (1987) 'The Social and Intellectual Organization of German Sociology Since 1945' in ibid. et al. (eds) *Modern German Sociology* (New York/Oxford: Columbia University Press), pp. 1–30.

Merton, Robert (1968) 'The Matthew Effect in Science' *Science* 159 (3810), pp. 56–63.

Meyer, Hansgünter (1992) 'Soziologische Forschung in der DDR' *Berliner Journal für Soziologie* 3/4-1992, pp. 263–286.

Meyer, Hansgünter (1994) 'Sociological Research in the GDR (DDR)' in Bernhard Schäfers (ed.) *Sociology in Germany. Development – Institutionalization – Theoretical Disputes. Special Edition of Soziologie. Journal of the Deutsche Gesellschaft für Soziologie* (Opladen: Leske & Budrich), pp. 33–51.

Meyer, Thomas (2001) *Die Soziologie Theodor Geigers. Emanzipation von der Ideologie* (Wiesbaden: Westdeutscher Verlag).

Meyer, Wolfgang (2002) 'Die Entwicklung der Soziologie im Spiegel der amtlichen Statistik' in Reinhard Stockmann et al. (eds) *Soziologie im Wandel. Universitäre Ausbildung und Arbeitsmarktchancen in Deutschland* (Opladen: Leske & Budrich), pp. 45–113.

Mies, Maria (1978) 'Methodische Postulate zur Frauenforschung-dargestellt am Beispiel der Gewalt gegen Frauen' *Beiträge zur feministischen Theorie und Praxis* 1 (1), pp. 41–63.

Mikl-Horke, Gertraude (2001) *Soziologie. Historischer Kontext und soziologische Theorie-Entwürfe* (München/Wien: Oldenbourg).

Moebius, Stephan (2003) *Die soziale Konstituierung des Anderen. Grundrisse einer poststrukturalistischen Sozialwissenschaft nach Lévinas und Derrida* (Frankfurt/New York: Campus).

Moebius, Stephan (2009) 'Kultursoziologie heute: Entwicklungen und Herausforderungen' in *Sozialwissenschaften und Berufspraxis (SuB). Zeitschrift des Berufsverbandes deutscher SoziologInnen*, 32/1, pp. 5–14.

Moebius, Stephan (2010) 'Debatten um Moderne und Postmoderne' in Georg Kneer & ibid. (eds) *Soziologische Kontroversen. Beiträge zu einer anderen Geschichte vom Sozialen* (Frankfurt/M.: Suhrkamp), pp. 254–290.

Moebius, Stephan (2015) *René König und die "Kölner Schule". Eine soziologiegeschichtliche Annäherung* (Wiesbaden: VS).

Moebius, Stephan (2017) 'Die Geschichte der Soziologie im Spiegel der Kölner Zeitschrift für Soziologie und Sozialpsychologie (KZfSS)' *Kölner Zeitschrift für Soziologie und Sozialpsychologie* 69 (Suppl 1): 3, pp. 3–44.

Moebius, Stephan (2018a) 'Schulen, Akteure und regionale Zentren in der frühen Geschichte der bundesrepublikanischen Soziologie' in ibid. & Andrea Ploder (eds) *Handbuch Geschichte der deutschsprachigen Soziologie, Vol. 1* (Wiesbaden: VS), pp. 391–426.

Moebius, Stephan (2018b) 'Kontroversen in der deutschsprachigen Soziologie nach 1945' in ibid. & Andrea Ploder (eds) *Handbuch Geschichte der deutschsprachigen Soziologie, Vol. 1* (Wiesbaden: VS), pp. 365–390.

Moebius, Stephan (2019) 'Kultursoziologie im deutschsprachigen Raum' in ibid., Katharina Scherke & Frithjof Nungesser (eds) *Handbuch Kultursoziologie, Vol. 1: Begriffe – Kontexte – Perspektiven – Autor_innen* (Wiesbaden: VS), pp. 63–80.

Moebius, Stephan (2021) 'Soziologie in der Zwischenkriegszeit in Deutschland' in Karl Acham & ibid. (eds) *Soziologie der Zwischenkriegszeit. Ihre Hauptströmungen und zentralen Themen im deutschen Sprachraum. Vol. 1* (Wiesbaden: VS) (forthcoming).

Moebius, Stephan & Lothar Peter (eds) (2004) *Französische Soziologie der Gegenwart* (Konstanz/Stuttgart: UVK/UTB).

Moebius, Stephan & Andreas Reckwitz (2008) *Poststrukturalistische Sozialwissenschaften* (Frankfurt/M.: Suhrkamp).

Moebius, Stephan & Martin Griesbacher (2019) 'Gab es eine "Kölner Schule" der bundesrepublikanischen Soziologie? Zu René Königs Professionalisierung der Soziologie' *Kölner Zeitschrift für Soziologie und Sozialpsychologie* 71/4, pp. 553–592.

Mommsen, Wolfgang J. (1994) *Bürgerliche Kultur und künstlerische Avantgarde 1870–1918. Kultur und Politik im deutschen Kaiserreich* (Frankfurt/Berlin: Propyläen).

Mommsen, Wolfgang J. (2004 [1959]) *Max Weber und die deutsche Politik 1890–1920.* 3rd ed. (Tübingen: Mohr Siebeck).

Mongardini, Carlo (1976) 'Die gegenwärtige Krise der Soziologie als Folge ihrer ideologischen Durchdringung' in Gottfried Eisermann (ed.) *Die Krise der Soziologie* (Stuttgart: Enke), pp. 59–71.

Moses, Dirk (2007) *German Intellectuals and the Nazi Past* (Cambridge: CUP).

Müller, Hans-Peter (1989) "The "Distinctiveness" of Modern German Sociology: A Contemporary Myth?' *Contemporary Sociology* 18 (3), pp. 319–322.

Müller, Hans-Peter (2001) 'Soziologie in der Eremitage?' in Eva Barlösius et al. (eds) *Gesellschaftsbilder im Umbruch. Soziologische Perspektiven in Deutschland* (Opladen: Leske & Budrich), pp. 37–63.

Müller, Hans-Peter (2020) *Max Weber. Eine Spurensuche* (Berlin: Suhrkamp).

Müller-Doohm, Stefan (2014) *Jürgen Habermas. Eine Biographie* (Berlin: Suhrkamp).

Müller, Tim B. (2010) *Krieger und Gelehrte. Herbert Marcuse und die Denksysteme im Kalten Krieg* (Hamburg: Hamburger Edition).

Muller, Jerry Z. (1987) *The other God that failed. Hans Freyer and the Deradicalization of German Conservatism* (Princeton: Princeton University Press).

Münch, Richard (1982) *Theorie des Handelns. Zur Rekonstruktion der Beiträge von Talcott Parsons, Emile Durkheim und Max Weber* (Frankfurt/M.: Suhrkamp).

Münch, Richard (2007) *Die akademische Elite. Zur sozialen Konstruktion wissenschaftlicher Exzellenz* (Frankfurt/M.: Suhrkamp).

Münch, Richard (2009) *Globale Eliten, lokale Autoritäten- Bildung und Wissenschaft unter dem Regime von PISA, MCKinsey & CO* (Frankfurt/M.: Suhrkamp).

Münch, Richard (2014) *Academic capitalism: Universities in the global struggle for excellence* (London, UK: Routledge).

Nachtwey, Oliver (2016) *Die Abstiegsgesellschaft: Über das Aufbegehren in der regressiven Moderne* (Berlin: Suhrkamp).

Nave-Herz, Rosemarie (2006) 'Biographische Notizen' in Ulrike Vogel (ed.) *Wege in die Soziologie und die Frauen- und Geschlechterforschung. Autobiographische Notizen der ersten Generation von Professorinnen an der Universität* (Wiesbaden: VS), pp. 17–22.

Neckel, Siegfried (1991) *Status und Scham. Zur symbolischen Reproduktion sozialer Ungleichheit* (Frankfurt/M./New York: Campus).
Neef, Katharina (2012) *Die Entstehung der Soziologie aus der Sozialreform. Eine Fachgeschichte* (Frankfurt/M./New York: Campus).
Neller, Kelly (2006) *DDR-Nostalgie. Dimensionen der Orientierungen der Ostdeutschen gegenüber der ehemaligen DDR, ihre Ursachen und politischen Konnotationen* (Wiesbaden: VS).
Neuloh, Otto et al. (1983) *Sozialforschung aus gesellschaftlicher Verantwortung. Entstehungs- und Leistungsgeschichte der Sozialforschungsstelle Dortmund* (Opladen: Westdeutscher Verlag).
Neumann, Franz et al. (2013) *Secret Reports on Nazi Germany: The Frankfurt School Contribution to the War Effort*, ed. by Raffaele Laudani, with a foreword by Raymond Geuss (Princeton: Princeton University Press).
Neumann, Michael & Gerhard Schäfer (1990) '"Blick nach vorn…": Ein Gespräch mit René König' in Heinz-Jürgen Dahme et al. (eds) *Jahrbuch für Soziologiegeschichte 1990* (Opladen: Leske & Budrich), pp. 219–238.
Neumeister, Bernd (2000) *Kampf um die kritische Vernunft. Die westdeutsche Rezeption des Strukturalismus und des postmodernen Denkens* (Konstanz: UVK).
Neun, Oliver (2016) 'Die Verwendungsdebatte innerhalb der deutschen Soziologie: eine vergessene Phase der fachlichen Selbstreflexion' in Helmut Staubmann (ed.) *Soziologie in Österreich – Internationale Verflechtungen* (Innsbruck: iup), pp. 333–353. open access: https://www.uibk.ac.at/iup/buch_pdfs/soziologie-in-oesterreich/10.152033122-56-7.pdf (accessed August 8, 2019).
Neun, Oliver (2018) 'Geschichte des Verhältnisses zwischen Soziologie und Öffentlichkeit in der deutschsprachigen Nachkriegssoziologie' in Stephan Moebius & Andrea Ploder (eds) *Handbuch Geschichte der deutschsprachigen Soziologie, Vol. 1* (Wiesbaden: VS), pp. 503–529.
Nicolaysen, Rainer (1997) *Siegfried Landshut. Die Wiederentdeckung der Politik*, Frankfurt/M.: Jüdischer Verlag Suhrkamp.
Nickel, Hildegard Maria (2006) 'Biographische Notiz' in Ulrike Vogel (ed.) *Wege in die Soziologie und die Frauen- und Geschlechterforschung. Autobiographische Notizen der ersten Generation von Professorinnen an der Universität* (Wiesbaden: VS), pp. 261–273.
Nida-Rümelin, Julian (2010) 'Zur Aktualität der humanistischern Universitätsidee' in Johanna-Charlotte Hort et al. (eds) *Unbedingte Universität. Was passiert? Stellungnahmen zur Lage der Universität* (Zürich: diaphanes), pp. 121–138.
Nipperdey, Thomas (1990) *Deutsche Geschichte 1866–1918. Band I: Arbeitswelt und Bürgergeist* (München: Beck).
Nolte, Paul (2000) *Die Ordnung der deutschen Gesellschaft. Selbstentwurf und Selbstbeschreibung im 20. Jahrhundert* (München: Beck).
Nunner-Winkler, Gertrud (1986) 'Ein Plädoyer für einen eingeschränkten Universalismus' in Wolfgang Edelstein & Gertrud Nummer-Winkler (eds) *Zur Bestimmung der Moral* (Frankfurt/M.: Suhrkamp), pp. 126–144.

Oberschall, Anthony (1997) *Empirische Sozialforschung in Deutschland 1848–1914* (Freiburg/München: Alber).
Oppenheimer, Franz (1922) *System der Soziologie. Erster Band: Allgemeine Soziologie. Erster Halbband: Grundlegung* (Jena: Fischer).
Osrecki, Fran (2011) *Die Diagnosegesellschaft. Zeitdiagnostik zwischen Soziologie und medialer Popularität* (Bielefeld: transcript).
Osrecki, Fran (2018) 'Die Geschichte der Gegenwartsdiagnostik in der deutschsprachigen Soziologie' in Stephan Moebius & Andrea Ploder (eds) *Handbuch Geschichte der deutschsprachigen Soziologie, Vol. 1* (Wiesbaden: VS), pp. 453–475.
Ostner, Ilona (2006) 'Dabei und doch nicht mittendrin – mein Weg in die Wissenschaft' in Ulrike Vogel (ed.) *Wege in die Soziologie und die Frauen- und Geschlechterforschung. Autobiographische Notizen der ersten Generation von Professorinnen an der Universität* (Wiesbaden: VS), pp. 243–249.
Papcke, Sven (1980) 'Die deutsche Soziologie zwischen Totalitarismus und Demokratie' *Politik und Zeitgeschichte/Das Parlament* vom 17. Mai 1980, pp. 3–19.
Papcke, Sven (1985) *Vernunft und Chaos. Essays zur sozialen Ideengeschichte* (Frankfurt/M.: Fischer).
Papcke, Sven (1986) 'Weltferne Wissenschaft. Die deutsche Soziologie der Zwischenkriegszeit vor dem Problem des Faschismus/Nationalsozialismus' in ibid. (ed.) *Ordnung und Theorie. Beiträge zur Geschichte der Soziologie in Deutschland* (Darmstadt: WBG), pp. 168–222.
Partyga, Dominika (2016) 'Simmels's reading of Nietzsche: The promise of "philosophical sociology"', *Journal of Classical Sociology* 16 (4), pp. 414–437.
Pasternack, Peer (2013) '1947–2013: Drei Institutionalisierungen' in ibid. & Reinhold Sackmann (eds) *Vier Anläufe: Soziologie an der Universität Halle-Wittenberg* (Halle: mdv), pp. 85–210.
Paulitz, Tanja (2019) 'Feministische Soziologie, Gender Studies, Frauen-/Geschlechterforschung als Denkkollektiv: Soziologische Denkstile zu Geschlecht als sozialem Verhältnis und als soziale Kategorie' in Joachim Fischer & Stephan Moebius (eds) *Soziologische Denkschulen in der Bundesrepublik Deutschland* (Wiesbaden: VS), pp. 373–411.
Peter, Lothar (2001) 'Warum und wie betreibt man Soziologiegeschichte?' in *Jahrbuch für Soziologiegeschichte 1997/98*, edited by Carsten Klingemann, Michael Neumann, Karl-Siegbert Rehberg, Ilja Srubar & Erhard Stölting (Opladen: Leske & Budrich), pp. 9–64.
Peter, Lothar (2009) 'Kapitalismuskritik in der neueren Soziologie' in Werner Goldschmidt et al. (eds) *Freiheit, Gleichheit, Solidarität. Beiträge zur Dialektik der Demokratie* (Frankfurt/M.: Lang), pp. 39–56.
Peter, Lothar (2015) 'Warum und wie betreibt man Soziologiegeschichte?' in Christian Dayé & Stephan Moebius (eds) *Soziologiegeschichte. Wege und Ziele* (Berlin: Suhrkamp), pp. 112–146 [short and actualized version of Peter 2001].

Peter, Lothar (2018) 'Soziologie in der DDR. Legitimationsbeschaffung oder "machtkritische Subkulktur"?' in Stephan Moebius & Andrea Ploder (eds) *Handbuch Geschichte der deutschsprachigen Soziologie, Vol. 1* (Wiesbaden: VS), pp. 385–419.

Peter, Lothar (2019) *Marx on Campus. A Short History of the Marburg School* (Boston: Brill).

Peukert, Detlev J. K. (1987) *Die Weimarer Republik* (Frankfurt/M.: Suhrkamp).

Picht, Georg (1964) *Die deutsche Bildungskatastrophe: Analyse und Dokumentation* (Olten/Freiburg im Breisgau: Walter).

Piper, Ernst Reinhard (ed.) (1987) *"Historikerstreit". Die Dokumentation der Kontroverse um die Einzigartigkeit der nationalsozialistischen Judenvernichtung* (München/Zürich: Piper).

Plé, Bernhard (1990) *Wissenschaft und säkulare Mission. "Amerikanische Sozialwissenschaft" im politischen Sendungsbewußtsein der USA und im geistigen Aufbau der Bundesrepublik Deutschland* (Stuttgart: Klett Cotta).

Plessner, Helmuth (1959 [1935]) *Die verspätete Nation. Über die politische Verführbarkeit bürgerlichen Geistes* (Stuttgart: Kohlhammer).

Ploder, Andrea (2018) 'Geschichte Qualitativer und Interpretativer Forschung in der deutschsprachigen Soziologie nach 1945' in Stephan Moebius & ibid. (eds) *Handbuch Geschichte der deutschsprachigen Soziologie, Vol. 1* (Wiesbaden: VS), pp. 735–760.

Pollack, Detlef (1990) 'Das Ende einer Organisationsgesellschaft. Systemtheoretische Überlegungen zum gesellschaftlichen Umbruch in der DDR' *Zeitschrift für Soziologie* 19, pp. 292–307.

Pollack, Detlef (2015) 'Religionssoziologie in Deutschland seit 1945. Tendenzen – Kontroversen – Konsequenzen' *Kölner Zeitschrift für Soziologie und Sozialpsychologie* 67, pp. 433–474.

Pollock, Friedrich & IfS (1955) *Gruppenexperiment. Ein Studienbericht, Frankfurter Beiträge zur Soziologie, Vol. 2* (Frankfurt/M.: EVA).

Prenzel, Thomas (2017) 'Vor 25 Jahren: Die rassistisch motivierten Ausschreitungen von Rostock-Lichtenhagen' in Bundeszentrale für politische Bildung, URL: https://www.bpb.de/politik/hintergrund-aktuell/254347/rostock-lichtenhagen#fr-footnode5 (accessed August 10, 2020).

Radkau, Joachim (1998) *Das Zeitalter der Nervosität. Deutschland zwischen Bismarck und Hitler* (München: Hanser).

Rammstedt, Otthein (1986) *Deutsche Soziologie 1933–1945. Die Normalität einer Anpassung* (Frankfurt/M.: Suhrkamp).

Rammstedt, Otthein (1988) 'Die Attitüden der Klassiker als unsere soziologischen Selbstverständlichkeiten. Durkheim, Simmel, Weber und die Konstitution der modernen Soziologie' in ibid. (ed.) *Simmel und die frühen Soziologen. Nähe und Distanz zu Durkheim, Tönnies und Max Weber* (Frankfurt/M.: Suhrkamp), pp. 275–307.

Rammstedt, Otthein (1999) 'In Memoriam: Niklas Luhmann' in Theodor Bardmann & Dirk Baecker (eds) *"Gibt es eigentlich den Berliner Zoo noch?" Erinnerungen an Niklas Luhmann* (Konstanz: UVK), pp. 16–20.

Raphael, Lutz (2003) *Geschichtswissenschaft im Zeitalter der Extreme. Theorien, Methoden, Tendenzen von 1900 bis zur Gegenwart* (München: Beck).

Recker, Marie-Luise (2009) *Geschichte der Bundesrepublik Deutschland* (München: Beck).

Reckwitz, Andreas (2017) *Die Gesellschaft der Singularitäten. Zum Strukturwandel der Moderne* (Berlin: Suhrkamp).

Rehbein, Boike (2018) 'Die Rezeption Bourdieus im deutschsprachigen Raum' in Stephan Moebius & Andrea Ploder (eds) *Handbuch Geschichte der deutschsprachigen Soziologie, Vol. 1* (Wiesbaden: VS), pp. 683–693.

Rehberg, Karl-Siegbert (1979) 'Form und Prozeß. Zu den katalysatorischen Wirkungschancen einer Soziologie aus dem Exil: Norbert Elias' in Peter Gleichmann, Johan Gouldsblom & Hermann Korte (eds) *Materialien zu Norbert Elias' Zivilisationstheorie* (Frankfurt/M.: Suhrkamp), pp. 101–169.

Rehberg, Karl-Siegbert (1981) 'Philosophische Anthropologie und die "Soziologisierung" des Wissens vom Menschen. Einige Zusammenhänge zwischen einer philosophischen Denktradition und der Soziologie in Deutschland' in M. Rainer Lepsius (ed.) *Soziologie in Deutschland und Österreich 1918–1945. Sonderheft 23 der Kölner Zeitschrift für Soziologie und Sozialpsychologie* (Opladen: Westdeutscher Verlag), pp. 160–198.

Rehberg, Karl-Siegbert (1986) 'Deutungswissen der Moderne oder 'administrative Hilfswissenschaft'? Konservative Schwierigkeiten mit der Soziologie' in Sven Papcke (ed.) *Ordnung und Theorie. Beiträge zur Geschichte der Soziologie in Deutschland* (Darmstadt: WBG), pp. 7–47.

Rehberg, Karl-Siegbert (1992) 'Auch keine Stunde Null. Westdeutsche Soziologie nach 1945' in Walter H. Pehle & Peter Sillem (eds) *Wissenschaft im geteilten Deutschland. Restauration oder Neubeginn nach 1945?* (Frankfurt/M.: Fischer), pp. 26–44.

Rehberg, Karl-Siegbert (1999) 'Hans Freyer (1887–1960), Arnold Gehlen (1904–1976), Helmut Schelsky (1912–1984)' in Dirk Kaesler (ed.) *Klassiker der Soziologie, Vol. 2* (München: Beck), pp. 72–104.

Rehberg, Karl-Siegbert (2000) '"Großexperiment" und Erfahrungsschock. Zu einer Forschungsinitiative über das Zusammenwachsen der Deutschen' in Hartmut Esser (ed.) *Der Wandel nach der Wende. Gesellschaft, Wirtschaft, Politik in Ostdeutschland* (Opladen: Westdeutscher Verlag), pp. 11–27.

Rehberg, Karl-Siegbert (2010) 'Das Unbehagen an der Soziologie. Antisoziologische Motive und die Etablierung einer akademischen Disziplin' in Georg Kneer & Stephan Moebius (eds) *Soziologische Kontroversen. Eine andere Geschichte der Wissenschaft vom Sozialen* (Berlin: Suhrkamp), pp. 217–253.

Reichardt, Sven & Malte Zierenberg (2009) *Damals nach dem Krieg. Eine Geschichte Deutschlands 1945 bis 1949* (München: Goldmann).
Reimann, Horst & Klaus Kiefer (1969) *Soziologie als Beruf. Eine Untersuchung über Herkunft, Studiensituation und Berufsbild von Soziologie-Studenten*, 2nd ed. (Tübingen: Mohr Siebeck).
Riemer, Svend (1932) 'Zur Soziologie des Nationalsozialismus' in *Die Arbeit. Zeitschrift für Gewerkschaftspolitik und Wirtschaftskunde*, 1932 (2), pp. 101–118.
Ringer, Fritz (1990) 'The Intellectual Field, Intellectual History, and the Sociology of Knowledge' *Theory and Society* 19 (3), pp. 269–294.
Ritsert, Jürgen (2010) 'Der Positivismusstreit' in Georg Kneer & Stephan Moebius (eds) *Soziologische Kontroversen. Eine andere Geschichte der Wissenschaft vom Sozialen* (Berlin: Suhrkamp), pp. 102–130.
Roesler, Jörg (2012) *Geschichte der DDR* (Köln: PapyRossa).
Rohstock, Anne (2010) *Von der "Ordinarienuniversität" zur "Revolutionszentrale"? Hochschulreform und Hochschulrevolte in Bayern und Hessen 1957–1976* (München: Oldenbourg).
Römer, Oliver (2018) 'Die Entwicklung der deutschsprachigen Soziologie im Spiegel des wissenschaftlichen Verlagswesens' in Stephan Moebius & Andrea Ploder (eds) *Handbuch Geschichte der deutschsprachigen Soziologie, Vol. 1* (Wiesbaden: VS), pp. 477–502.
Römer, Oliver (2019) 'Soziologische Aufklärung. Über Bücher, Lektoren und Verlage' *Soziopolis*, www.Soziopolis.de/erinnern/jubilaeen/artikel/soziologisiche-aufklaerung/ (accessed September 23, 2019).
Römer, Oliver & Ina Alber-Armenat (eds) (2019) *Erkundungen im Historischen: Soziologie in Göttingen. Geschichte, Entwicklungen, Perspektiven* (Wiesbaden: VS).
Rosa, Hartmut (2013) *Social Acceleration. A New Theory of Modernity* (New York: Columbia University Press).
Rossi, Pietro (1987) *Vom Historismus zur historischen Sozialwissenschaft* (Frankfurt/M.: Suhrkamp).
Ruck, Michael (2003) 'Ein kurzer Sommer der konkreten Utopie – Zur westdeutschen Planungsgeschichte der langen 60er Jahre' in Axel Schildt et al. (eds) *Dynamische Zeiten. Die 60er Jahre in den beiden deutschen Gesellschaften*, 2nd ed. (Hamburg: Christians), pp. 362–401.
Rust, Holger (1973) 'Wissenschaft und Politik. Zur Situation der Gesellschaftswissenschaft in der DDR' *Archiv für Rechts- und Sozialphilosophie/ Archives for Philosophy of Law and Social Philosophy* 59 (1), pp. 139–152.
Rutkoff, Peter M. and William B. Scott (1986) *New School: a history of the New School for Social Research* (New York: Free Press).
Rutkoff, Peter M. and William B. Scott (1988) 'Die Schaffung der 'Universität im Exil", in Ilja Srubar (ed.) *Exil, Wissenschaft, Identität. Die Emigration deutscher Sozialwissenschaftler 1933–1945* (Frankfurt/M.: Suhrkamp), pp. 106–141.

Sahner, Heinz (1982) *Theorie und Forschung. Zur paradigmatischen Struktur der westdeutschen Soziologie und zu ihrem Einfluß auf die Forschung* (Opladen: Westdeutscher Verlag).
Sahner, Heinz (ed.) (2000) *Soziologie als angewandte Aufklärung. Weniger als erwartet, aber mehr als zu befürchten war. Die Entwicklung der Nachkriegssoziologie aus der Sicht der frühen Fachvertreter* (Baden-Baden: Nomos).
Sambale, Jens et al. (eds) (2008) *Das Elend der Universitäten. Neoliberalisierung deutscher Hochschulpolitik* (Münster: Westfälisches Dampfboot).
Sauer, Dieter (2018) 'Geschichte des Instituts für Sozialwissenschaftliche Forschung' in Stephan Moebius & Andrea Ploder (eds) *Handbuch Geschichte der deutschsprachigen Soziologie, Vol. 1* (Wiesbaden: VS), pp. 1025–1044.
Scaff, Lawrence (2011) *Max Weber in America* (Princeton/New Jersey: Princeton University Press).
Schad, Susanne P. (1972) *Empirical Research in Weimar-Germany* (Paris-The Hague: Mouton).
Schäfer, Gerhard (1990) 'Wider die Inszenierung des Vergessens. Hans Freyer und die Soziologie in Leipzig 1925–1945' in Heinz-Jürgen Dahme, Carsten Klingemann, Michael Neumann, Karl-Siegbert Rehberg & Ilja Srubar (eds) *Jahrbuch für Soziologiegeschichte 1990* (Opladen: Leske & Budrich), pp. 121–175.
Schäfer, Gerhard (1996) 'Soziologie auf dem Vulkan – Zur Stellung René Königs in der Dreieckskonstellation der westdeutschen Nachkriegssoziologie' in Frank Deppe et al. (eds) *Antifaschismus* (Heilbronn: Distel), pp. 370–387.
Schäfer, Gerhard (1997) 'Soziologie als politische Tatphilosophie. Helmut Schelskys Leipziger Jahre (1931–1938)' *Das Argument* 222, pp. 645–665.
Schäfer, Gerhard (2000) 'Die nivellierte Mittelstandsgesellschaft – Strategien der Soziologie in den 50er Jahren'. In Georg Bollenbeck & G. Kaiser (eds) *Die janusköpfigen 50er Jahre. Kulturelle Moderne und bildungsbürgerliche Semantik III* (Opladen: Westdeutscher Verlag), pp. 115–142.
Schäfer, Gerhard (2014) 'Der Nationalsozialismus und die soziologischen Akteure der Nachkriegszeit: am Beispiel Helmut Schelskys und Ralf Dahrendorfs' in Michaela Christ & Maja Suderland (eds) *Soziologie und Nationalsozialismus. Positionen, Debatten, Perspektiven* (Berlin: Suhrkamp), pp. 119–161.
Schäfer, Gerhard (2015) *Soziologie ohne Marx. Helmut Schelsky als "Starsoziologe" und Intellektueller im Hamburg der 1950er Jahre* (Hamburg: VSA).
Schäfer, Gerhard (2017) 'Zur Herausbildung des philosophisch-soziologischen Denkens bei Helmut Schelsky in der Ära des Nationalsozialismus', in Thomas Gutmann, Christoph Weischer & Fabian Wittreck (eds) *Helmut Schelsky. Ein deutscher Soziologe im zeitgeschichtlichen, institutionellen und disziplinären Kontext – Interdisziplinärer Workshop zum 100. Geburtstag. Rechtstheorie, Beiheft 22* (Berlin: Duncker & Humblot), pp. 17–56.

Schäfers, Bernhard (1993) 'Zur Lage des Faches nach der Vereinigung' in: ibid. (ed.) *Lebensverhältnisse und soziale Konflikte im neuen Europa. Verhandlungen des 26. Deutschen Soziologentages in Düsseldorf 1992* (Frankfurt/M./New York: Campus), pp. 827–833.

Schäfers, Bernhard (2016) 'DGS und GfS: Die Gesellschaften für Soziologie im Vereinigungsprozess' *Soziologie* 45 (1), pp. 24–32.

Schauer, Alexandra (2018) 'Soziologie in Deutschland zur Zeit des Nationalsozialismus' in Stephan Moebius & Andrea Ploder (eds) *Handbuch Geschichte der deutschsprachigen Soziologie, Vol. 1* (Wiesbaden: VS), pp. 117–148.

Schelsky, Helmut (1957) *Die skeptische Generation. Eine Soziologie der deutschen Jugend* (Düsseldorf/Köln: Diederichs).

Schelsky, Helmut (1959) *Ortsbestimmung der deutschen Soziologie* (Düsseldorf/Köln: Diederichs).

Schelsky, Helmut (1965) *Auf der Suche nach Wirklichkeit. Gesammelte Aufsätze* (Düsseldorf/Köln: Diederichs).

Schelsky, Helmut. (1977 [1975]) *Die Arbeit tun die anderen. Klassenkampf und Priesterherrschaft der Intellektuellen* (München: DTV).

Schelsky, Helmut (1981) *Rückblicke eines "Anti-Soziologen"* (Opladen: Westdeutscher Verlag).

Schildt, Axel (2007) *Die Sozialgeschichte der Bundesrepublik Deutschland bis 1989/1990* (München: Oldenbourg).

Schildt, Axel (2011) 'Zur sogenannten Amerikanisierung in der frühen Bundesrepublik. Einige Differenzierungen' in ibid. *Annäherungen an die Westdeutschen. Sozial- und kulturgeschichtliche Perspektiven auf die Bundesrepublik* (Göttingen: Wallstein), pp. 143–158.

Schildt, Axel & Detlef Siegfried (2009) *Deutsche Kulturgeschichte. Die Bundesrepublik von 1945 bis zur Gegenwart* (München: Hanser).

Schildt et al. (eds) (2003) *Dynamische Zeiten. Die 60er Jahre in den beiden deutschen Gesellschaften*, 2nd edition (Hamburg: Christians).

Schimank, Uwe (2013) *Gesellschaft* (Bielefeld: transcript).

Schimank, Uwe (2015) 'Grundriss einer integrativen Theorie der modernen Gesellschaft' *Zeitschrift für Theoretische Soziologie* 2/2015, pp. 236–268.

Schmid, Michael (1993) 'Der Positivismusstreit in der deutschen Soziologie 30 Jahre danach' *Logos. Zeitschrift für systematische Philosophie* N.F. 1/1993, pp. 35–81.

Schmid, Michael (2004) *Rationales Handeln und soziale Prozesse* (Wiesbaden: VS).

Schmidt, Gert (1980) 'Zur Geschichte der Industriesoziologie in Deutschland' *Soziale Welt* 2/1980, pp. 257–278.

Schmitt, Horst (1997) 'Ein 'typischer Heidelberger im Guten wie im Gefährlichen'. Arnold Bergstraesser und die Ruperto Carola 1923–1936' in Reinhard Blomert et al. (eds) *Heidelberger Sozial- und Staatswissenschaften. Das Institut für Sozial- und Staatswissenschaften zwischen 1918–1958* (Marburg: Metropolis), pp. 167–196.

Schmitz, Andreas, Christian Schmidt-Wellenburg, Daniel Witte & Maria Keil (2019) 'In welcher Gesellschaft forschen wir eigentlich? Struktur und Dynamik des Feldes der deutschen Soziologie' *Zeitschrift für Theoretische Soziologie*, 2/2019, pp. 245–279.

Schnitzler, Sonja (2018) 'Die Deutsche Gesellschaft für Soziologie zur Zeit des Nationalsozialsimus' in Stephan Moebius & Andrea Ploder (eds) *Handbuch Geschichte der deutschsprachigen Soziologie, Vol. 1* (Wiesbaden: VS), pp. 849–866.

Schneikert, Christian et al. (2019) 'The Sociological Canon, Relations between Theories and Methods, and a Latent Political Structure: Findings from a Survey of Sociology Students in Germany and Consequences for Teaching' *Teaching Sociology*, Online First (2019), pp. 1–11, doi:10.1177/0092055X19865301 (accessed August 8, 2019).

Schultheis, Franz et al. (eds) (2008) *Humboldts Alptraum. Der Bologna-Prozess und seine Folgen* (Konstanz: UVK).

Schulze, Gerhard (1995) *Die Erlebnisgesellschaft. Kultursoziologie der Gegenwart* (Frankfurt/M./New York: Campus).

Schulze, Gerhard (1996) 'Der Film des Soziologen. Dieses Fach muß sich von der Naturwissenschaft endgültig verabschieden' in Joachim Fritz-Vannahme (ed.) *Wozu heute noch Soziologie?* (Opladen: Leske & Budrich), pp. 51–57.

Sennett, Richard (1998) *The Corrosion of Character: The Personal Consequences of Work in the New Capitalism* (London/New York: W. W. Norton & Company).

Siefer, Gregor & Frederick Abrahams (1994) 'Studying Sociology in Postwar Germany: A Historical Synopsis of the Development of Academic Degree Programs at German Institutions of Higher Learning' in Bernhard Schäfers (ed.) *Sociology in Germany. Development – Institutionalization – Theoretical Disputes. Special Edition of Soziologie. Journal of the Deutsche Gesellschaft für Soziologie* (Opladen: Leske & Budrich), pp. 284–297.

Siegfried, Detlef (2003) 'Vom Teenager zur Pop-Revolution. Politisierungstendenzen in der westdeutschen Jugendkultur 1959–1968' in Axel Schildt et al. (eds) *Dynamische Zeiten. Die 60er Jahre in den beiden deutschen Gesellschaften*, 2nd ed. (Hamburg: Christians), pp. 582–623.

Siegfried, Detlef (2018) *1968. Protest, Revolte, Gegenkultur* (Stuttgart: Reclam).

Simmel, Georg (1987 [1911]) 'Der Begriff und die Tragödie der Kultur' in ibid. *Das individuelle Gesetz. Philosophische Exkurse* (Frankfurt/M.: Suhrkamp), pp. 116–147.

Simmel, Georg (1989 [1900]) *Die Philosophie des Geldes, Gesamtausgabe Vol. 6* (Frankfurt/M.: Suhrkamp).

Simmel, Georg (1995 [1903]) 'Die Großstädte und das Geistesleben' in ibid. *Aufsätze und Abhandlungen 1901–1908, Gesamtausgabe Vol. 7* (Frankfurt/M.: Suhrkamp), pp. 116–131.

Simmel, Georg (1999 [1914]) 'Der Krieg und die geistigen Entscheidungen' in ibid. *Der Krieg und die geistigen Entscheidungen. Grundfragen der Soziologie. Vom Wesen des historischen Verstehens. Der Konflikt der modernen Kultur. Lebensanschauung, Gesamtausgabe Vol. 16* (Frankfurt/M.: Suhrkamp), pp. 7–58.

Simmel, Georg (2005) *Briefe. 1880–1911. Gesamtausgabe Vol. 22* (Frankfurt/M.: Suhrkamp).

Simmel, Georg (2008 [1908]) 'Beilage: Einladung zur Gründung einer Deutschen Gesellschaft für Soziologie' in ibid. *Briefe 1880–1911, Gesamtausgabe Vol. 22* (Frankfurt/M.: Suhrkamp), pp. 672–678.

Sparschuh, Vera & Ute Koch (1997) *Sozialismus und Soziologie. Die Gründergeneration der DDR-Soziologie. Versuch einer Konturierung* (Opladen: Leske & Budrich).

Srubar, Ilja (2010) 'Der Streit um die Wissenssoziologie' in Georg Kneer & Stephan Moebius (eds) *Soziologische Kontroversen. Beiträge zu einer anderen Wissenschaft vom Sozialen* (Berlin: Suhrkamp), pp. 46–78.

Stäheli, Urs (2000) *Poststrukturalistische Soziologien* (Bielefeld: transcript).

Staritz, Dietrich (1985) *Geschichte der DDR. 1949–1985* (Frankfurt/M.: Suhrkamp).

Stehr, Nico (1994) *Knowledge Societies* (London: Sage).

Steiner, Helmut (1988) 'Zur Soziologie des Neubeginns nach 1945 in der Sowjetischen Besatzungszone Deutschlands', in Christoph Cobet (ed.) *Einführung in Fragen an die Soziologie in Deutschland nach Hitler 1945–1950* (Frankfurt/M.: Cobet), pp. 76–94.

Steiner, Helmut (1997) 'Aufbruch, Defizite und Leistungen der DDR-Soziologie: die 60er Jahre' in Hans Bertram (ed.) *Soziologie und Soziologen im Übergang. Beiträge zur Transformation der außeruniversitären soziologischen Forschung in Ostdeutschland* (Opladen: Leske & Budrich), pp. 223–262.

Steinmetz, George (2007) 'The Historical Sociology of Historical Sociology. Germany and the United States in Twentieth Century' *Sociologica. Italian Journal of Sociology on line* 3/2007, pp. 1–28, https://www.rivisteweb.it/doi/10.2383/25961 (accessed August 8, 2019).

Steinmetz, George (2009) 'Neo-Bourdieusian Theory and the Question of Scientific Autonomy: German Sociologists and Empire, 1890s–1940s' *Political Power and Social Theory* 20, pp. 71–131.

Steinmetz, George (2010) 'Ideas in Exile: Refugees from Nazi Germany and the Failure to Transplant Historical Sociology into the United States' *International Journal of Politics, Culture, and Society* 23 (1), pp. 1–27.

Steinmetz, George (2017) 'Field Theory and Interdisciplinarity: History and Sociology in Germany and France during Twentieth Century' *Comparative Studies in Society and History* 59 (2), pp. 477–514.

Stichweh, Rudolf (2000) *Die Weltgesellschaft. Soziologische Analysen* (Frankfurt/M.: Suhrkamp).

Stockmann, Reinhard (2002) 'Soziologie, die Erfolgsgeschichte eines akademischen Faches' in Reinhard Stockmann et al. (eds) *Soziologie im Wandel. Universitäre Ausbildung und Arbeitsmarktchancen in Deutschland* (Opladen: Leske & Budrich), pp. 239–248.

Stölting, Erhard (1984) 'Kontinuitäten und Brüche in der deutschen Soziologie 1933/34' *Soziale Welt* 35 (1/2), pp. 48–59.

Stölting, Erhard (1986) *Akademische Soziologie in der Weimarer Republik* (Berlin: Duncker & Humblot).

Stölting, Erhard (2006) 'Die Soziologie in den hochschulpolitischen Konflikten der Weimarer Republik' in Bettina Franke & Kurt Hammerich (eds) *Soziologie an deutschen Universitäten: Gestern – heute – morgen* (Wiesbaden: VS), pp. 9–30.

Strubenhoff, Marius (2017) 'The Positivism Dispute in German Sociology, 1954–1970' *History of European Ideas* 2/2017, pp. 260–276.

Sywottek, Arnold (2003) 'Gewalt – Reform – Arrangement. Die DDR in den 60er Jahren' in Axel Schildt et al. (eds) *Dynamische Zeiten. Die 60er Jahre in den beiden deutschen Gesellschaften*, 2nd ed. (Hamburg: Christians), pp. 54–76.

Tegeler, Evelyn (2003) *Frauenfragen sind Männerfragen. Helge Pross als Vorreiterin des Gender-Mainstreaming* (Wiesbaden: VS).

Tenbruck, Friedrich H. (1979) 'Deutsche Soziologie im internationalen Kontext. Ihre Ideengeschichte und ihr Gesellschaftsbezug' in Günther Lüschen (ed.) *Deutsche Soziologie nach 1945. Sonderheft 21/1979 der Kölner Zeitschrift für Soziologie und Sozialpsychologie* (Opladen: Westdeutscher Verlag), pp. 71–107.

Tenbruck, Friedrich H. (1984) *Die unbewältigten Sozialwissenschaften oder Die Abschaffung des Menschen* (Graz/Wien/Köln: Styria).

Tent, James F. (1998) *Academic Proconsul. Havard Sociologist Edward Y. Hartshorne and the Reopening of German Universities, 1945–1946. His Personal Account* (Trier: WVT).

Terhoeven, Petra (2017) *Die Rote Armee Fraktion. Eine Geschichte terroristischer Gewalt* (München: Beck).

Ther, Philipp (2019) *Das andere Ende der Geschichte. Über die Große Transformation* (Berlin: Suhrkamp).

Thomas, Rüdiger (1990) *Zur Geschichte soziologischer Forschung in der DDR*, online: http://ruedigerthomas.eu/?p=189 (cited pages concern the downloaded word-file, accessed September 1, 2019).

Tjaden, Karl Hermann (1969) 'Zur Kritik eines funktional-strukturellen Entwurfs sozialer Systeme' *Kölner Zeitschrift für Soziologie und Sozialpsychologie* 21 (1969), pp. 752–769.

Tjaden, Karl Hermann (ed.) (1971) *Soziale Systeme: Materialien zur Dokumentation und Kritik soziologischer Ideologie* (Neuwied/Berlin: Luchterhand).

Tönnies, Ferdinand (1911) 'Wege und Ziele der Soziologie' in Deutsche Gesellschaft für Soziologie (DGS) (ed.) *Verhandlungen des Ersten Deutschen Soziologentages vom 19.–22. Oktober in Frankfurt a. M. Reden und Vorträge* (Tübingen: Mohr), pp. 17–38.

Tönnies, Ferdinand (2012 [1919]) 'Vorrede der dritten Auflage' in Ferdinand Tönnies (2012) *Studien zu Gemeinschaft und Gesellschaft* (Wiesbaden: VS), pp. 213–219.

Tönnies, Ferdinand (2017 [1887] [1935]) *Gemeinschaft und Gesellschaft. Grundbegriffe der reinen Soziologie*, 8th ed. (Wien: Profil).

Treiber, Hubert (2016) 'Max Weber as reader of Nietzsche – remark on a German discussion' in Ian Bryan, Peter Mangford & John McGarry (eds) The Foundation of the Juridico-Political. Concept Formation in Hans Kelsen and Max Weber Oxon/New York: Routledge), pp. 165–184.

Tuma, René & René Wilke (2018) 'Zur Rezeption des Sozialkonstruktivismus in der deutschsprachigen Soziologie' in Stephan Moebius & Andrea Ploder (eds) *Handbuch Geschichte der deutschsprachigen Soziologie*, Vol. 1 (Wiesbaden: VS), pp. 589–617.

Turner, Stephen P. (1992) 'Sociology and Fascism in the Interwar Period' in ibid. & Dirk Kaesler (eds) *Sociology responds to Fascism* (London/New York: Routledge), pp. 1–13.

Turner, Stephen P. & Regis D. Factor (1984) *Max Weber and the Dispute over Reason and Value: A Study in Philosophy, Ethics, and Politics* (Boston: Routledge & Kegan Paul).

Turner, Stephen P. & Dirk Kaesler (eds) (1992) *Sociology responds to Fascism* (London/New York: Routledge).

Turner, Victor (1969) *The Ritual Process. Structure and Antistructure* (Chicago: Aldine).

Ullrich, Volker (1997) *Die nervöse Großmacht. Aufstieg und Untergang des Deutschen Kaiserreichs 1871–1918* (Frankfurt/M.: Fischer).

Ullrich, Volker (2009) *Die Revolution von 1918/19* (München: Beck).

Villa Brasvlasky, Paula-Irene (2020) 'Heterotopien des Unbehagens' in Texte zur Kunst, online: https://www.textezurkunst.de/articles/heterotopien-des-unbehagens (accessed October 1, 2020).

Vogel, Ulrike (2006) 'Zur Konzeption der Veröffentlichung' in ibid. (ed.) *Wege in die Soziologie und die Frauen- und Geschlechterforschung. Autobiographische Notizen der ersten Generation von Professorinnen an der Universität* (Wiesbaden: VS), pp. 9–15.

Wagner, Wolf (1996) *Kulturschock Deutschland* (Berlin: Rotbuch).

Walther, Andreas (1927) *Soziologie und Staatswissenschaften in Amerika und ihre Bedeutung für die Pädagogik* (Karlsruhe: Braun).

Waßner, Rainer (1986) 'Andreas Walther und das Seminar für Soziologie in Hamburg zwischen 1926 und 1945. Ein wissenschaftsbiographischer Umriss' in Sven Papcke (ed.) *Ordnung und Theorie. Beiträge zur Geschichte der Soziologie in Deutschland* (Darmstadt: WBG), pp. 386–420.

Weber, Max (1988a [1904]) 'Die "Objektivität" sozialwissenschaftlicher und sozialpolitischer Erkenntnis' in ibid. *Gesammelte Aufsätze zur Wissenschaftslehre* (Tübingen: Mohr/UTB), pp. 146–214.

Weber, Max (1988b [1921]) 'Soziologische Grundbegriffe' in ibid. *Gesammelte Aufsätze zur Wissenschaftslehre* (Tübingen: Mohr/UTB), pp. 541–581.

Weber, Max (1994 [1917] [1919]) *Wissenschaft als Beruf 1917/1919. Politik als Beruf 1919, Studienausgabe* (Tübingen: Mohr).

Weber, Max (2016 [1904–1905] [1920]) *Die protestantische Ethik und der "Geist" des Kapitalismus*, ed. and with a preface by Klaus Lichtblau & Johannes Weiß (Wiesbaden: VS).

Wehler, Hans-Ulrich (1977) *Das Deutsche Kaiserreich 1871–1918* (Göttingen: Vandenhoeck & Ruprecht).

Wehler, Hans-Ulrich (2010) *Deutsche Gesellschaftsgeschichte 1914–1949* (Bonn: BPB).

Wehrs, Nikolai (2014) *Protest der Professoren. Der "Bund Freiheit der Wissenschaft" in den 1970er Jahren* (Göttingen: Wallstein).

Weidig, Rudi (1997) *Soziologische Forschung in der DDR. Einige Aspekte der Arbeit des Wissenschaftlichen Rates* (Berlin: WZB), https://bibliothek.wzb.eu/pdf/1997/iii97-407.pdf (accessed October 1, 2019).

Weischer, Christoph (2004) *Das Unternehmen "Empirische Sozialforschung". Strukturen, Praktiken und Leitbilder der Sozialforschung in der Bundesrepublik Deutschland* (München: Oldenbourg).

West, Candace & Don H. Zimmerman (1987) 'Doing Gender' *Gender and Society* 1 (2), pp. 125–151.

Weyer, Johannes (1984a) *Westdeutsche Soziologie 1945–1960. Deutsche Kontinuitäten und nordamerikanischer Einfluss* (Berlin: Duncker & Humblot).

Weyer, Johannes (1984b) '75 Jahre Kapitulation vor der Wirklichkeit: Betrachtungen zu einem Jubiläum der Deutschen Gesellschaft für Soziologie' *Soziologie. Mitteilungsblatt der Deutschen Gesellschaft für Soziologie* 2, pp. 91–101.

Weyer, Johannes (1984c) 'Die Forschungsstelle für das Volkstum im Ruhrgebiet (1935–1941) – Ein Beispiel für Soziologie im Faschismus' *Soziale Welt Heft* 35 (1/2), pp. 124–145.

Weyer, Johannes (1984d) 'Soziologie im Faschismus. Ein Literaturbericht' *Das Argument* 146, pp. 564–576.

Weyer, Johannes (1986) 'Der "Bürgerkrieg in der Soziologie". Die westdeutsche Soziologie zwischen Amerikanisierung und Restauration' in Sven Papcke (ed.) *Ordnung und Theorie. Beiträge zur Geschichte der Soziologie in Deutschland* (Darmstadt: Wissenschaftliche Buchgesellschaft), pp. 280–304.

Wheatland, Thomas (2009) *The Frankfurt School in Exile* (Minneapolis/London: University of Minnesota Press).

Wierzock, Alexander (2017) 'Die Ambivalenzen eines Republikaners. Ferdinand Tönnies und die Weimarer Republik', in: Andreas Braune & Michael Dreyer (eds): *Republikanischer Alltag. Die Weimarer Demokratie und die Suche nach Normalität* (Stuttgart: Steiner), pp. 69–86.

Wiese, Leopold von (1948) 'Die gegenwärtige Situation, soziologisch betrachtet' (inklusive der Diskussion) in Deutsche Gesellschaft für Soziologie (ed.) *Verhandlungen des Achten Deutschen Soziologentages vom 19. bis 21. September 1946 in Frankfurt a. M.* (Tübingen: Mohr), pp. 20–56.

Wiggershaus, Rolf (2001 [1988]) *Die Frankfurter Schule. Geschichte – Theoretische Entwicklung – Politische Bedeutung*, 6th ed. (München: DTV).

Wingens, Matthias (1988) *Soziologisches Wissen und politische Praxis. Neuere theoretische Entwicklungen der Verwendungsforschung* (Frankfurt/M./New York: Campus).

Winkler, Heinrich August (2005) *Weimar 1918–1933. Die Geschichte der ersten deutschen Demokratie*, 4th ed. (München: Beck).

Wittich, Dietmar & Horst Taubert (eds) (1970) *Soziologie im Sozialismus. Die marxistisch-leninistische Soziologie im entwickelten gesellschaftlichen System des Sozialismus* (Berlin: Dietz).

Wobbe, Theresa (1997) *Wahlverwandtschaften. Die Soziologie und die Frauen auf dem Weg zur Wissenschaft* (Frankfurt/New York: Campus).

Wöhrle, Patrick (2015) *Zur Aktualität von Helmut Schelsky. Einleitung in sein Werk* (Wiesbaden: VS).

Wöhrle, Patrick (2019) 'Wirklichkeitskontrolle. Konturen der Münsteraner Soziologie in den 1960er Jahren' in Joachim Fischer & Stephan Moebius (eds) *Soziologische Denkschulen. Zur Archäologie der bunderepublikanischen Soziologie* (Wiesbaden: VS), pp. 249–276.

Wolfrum, Edgar (2006a) *Die 50er Jahre. Kalter Krieg und Wirtschaftswunder* (Darmstadt: WBG).

Wolfrum, Edgar (2006b) *Die 60er Jahre. Eine dynamische Gesellschaft* (Darmstadt: WBG).

Wolfrum, Edgar (2006c) *Die geglückte Demokratie. Geschichte der Bundesrepublik Deutschland von ihren Anfängen bis zur Gegenwart* (Stuttgart: Klett-Cotta).

Wolfrum, Edgar (2007a) *Die 70er Jahre. Republik im Aufbruch* (Darmstadt: WBG).

Wolfrum, Edgar (2007b) *Die 80er Jahre. Globalisierung und Postmoderne* (Darmstadt: WBG).

Wolfrum, Edgar (2008) *Die DDR. Eine Geschichte in Bildern* (Darmstadt: WBG).

Wolfrum, Edgar (2013) *Rot-Grün an der Macht. Deutschland 1998–2005* (München: Beck).

Yos, Roman (2019) *Der junge Habermas. Eine ideengeschichtliche Untersuchung seines frühen Denkens 1952–1962* (Berlin: Suhrkamp).

Zapf, Wolfgang (1991) 'Modernisierung und Modernisierungstheorien' in: ibid. (ed.) *Die Modernisierung moderner Gesellschaften: Verhandlungen des 25. Deutschen Soziologentages in Frankfurt am Main 1990* (Frankfurt/M./New York: Campus), pp. 23–39.

# Index[1]

**A**
Abendroth, Wolfgang, 62, 78, 80, 87, 96
Aßmann, Georg, 131
Academic Exchange Service, 27, 28
Academy for the Social Sciences at the SED CC, 132n2
Academy of Sociology, 105n4, 168–170
Action research, 106
Actor-centered institutionalism, 118
Adenauer, Konrad, 26, 54n3, 57, 62, 64–67, 100
Adler, Frank, 135
Adler, Max, 37, 38
Adorno, Theodor W., 34, 39, 46, 50, 59, 61–64, 66, 67, 70, 72–74, 78, 83, 87–90, 95, 109, 110, 114
Akademie für Gemeinwirtschaft, Hamburg, 53, 58, 77
Albert, Hans, 73, 167
Alexander, Jeffrey C., 115, 117

American Economic Association, 169n24
American Jewish Committee (AJC), 61
American Journal of Sociology (journal), 14n6
American Reading Room, Karlsruhe, 64
American Sociological Association (ASA), 19n8, 32n13, 164
Analysis of institutions, 118
Analytical philosophy, 168
Anarchism, 87
Anderson, Evelyn, 33
Anderson, Nels, 54
Archiv für Sozialwissenschaft und Sozialpolitik (journal), 18, 19
Arendt, Hannah, 38
Aron, Raymond, 83
Association of Persecutees of the Nazi Regime/Federation of Antifascists, 98
Atteslander, Peter, 61
Außerparlamentarische Opposition (APO), 81, 85, 86, 91

---

[1] Note: Page numbers followed by 'n' refer to notes. Only persons mentioned in the main text are listed, no names of literature references.

Austrian School of Economics, 17
Austrian Sociological Association, 136
Austro-Marxism, 34, 37

**B**
Baader, Andreas, 101
Baecker, Dirk, 160n12
Bahrdt, Hans Paul, 64, 68, 69, 76, 77
Barber, William, 169n24, 170n24
Barth, Paul, 20
Basisgruppe Soziologie, Frankfurt, 90
Bataille, Georges, 114
Bauer-Mengelberg, Käthe, 36
Bauman, Zygmunt, 148
Baumgarten, Eduard, 83n19
Bearman, Peter, 118
Beauvoir, Simone de, 108
Beck, Ulrich, 117, 119, 145, 148, 157, 160n12, 165
Becker, Carl Heinrich, 25
Becker, Hellmut, 82n18
Becker, Howard P., 26, 36, 50
Becker-Schmidt, Regina, 61n11, 109–111
Beck-Gernsheim, Elisabeth, 109
Beer, Ursula, 111
Bellah, Robert, 115
Bendix, Reinhard, 83, 83n19
Benjamin, Walter, 34, 39
Benseler, Frank, 80
Berger, Peter L., 69, 107, 145
Bergson, Henri, 14n6
Bergstraesser, Arnold, 27, 28, 46, 57, 58n8, 72, 96
Berliner Ensemble, 124
Berlin Journal of Sociology (journal), 133, 144
Berlin Social Science Center (WZB), 92, 146
Beziehungslehre, 25, 26, 38, 47
Biographical research, 107
Birmingham Centre for Contemporary Cultural Studies (CCCS), 115–116

Bismarck, Otto von, 19
Blair, Tony, 117
Blumer, Herbert, 106
Boehm, Max Hildebert, 46, 162
Bogart, Leo, 54n3
Boltanski, Luc, 155
Borkenau, Franz, 46, 50
Boudon, Raymond, 118
Bouglé, Celestin Charles, 36, 37
Bourdieu, Pierre, 87, 100, 110, 115–117, 136, 149–151
Bracher, Karl Dietrich, 78n16
Brandt, Willy, 80, 101, 102, 126
Braun, Siegfried, 68
Braunreuther, Kurt, 130, 131
Brecht, Bertolt, 124
Brentano, Lujo, 17
Brepohl, Wilhelm, 70
Breuer, Stefan, 83n19
Breysig, Kurt, 30
Briefs, Goetz, 30
Brinkmann, Carl, 29, 36, 56
Bulmahn, Thomas, 147
Büschges, Günter, 118
Butler, Judith, 111, 151–154, 160n12

**C**
Carlé, Wilhelm, 33
Castel, Robert, 156
Center for Surveys, Methods and Analyses (ZUMA), Mannheim, 146
Central Institute for Youth Research (ZIJ), Leipzig, 130
Centre for Interdisciplinary Research (ZIF), Bielefeld, 63
Chiapello, Ève, 155
Chicago School, 14n6, 106
Christ, Michaela, 163
Christian Democratic Union of Germany (CDU), 54n3, 66, 80, 120

Christian Social Union in Bavaria
    (CSU), 80
Cicourel, Aaron, 106–107
Claessens, Dieter, 69, 95
Clausen, Lars, 64
Club of Rome, 102
Colander, David, 169n24
Coleman, James, 118
Collins, Randall, 145n2
Cologne School, 61, 62, 74, 78, 167
Commission for the Study of
    Social and Political Change
    in the New Federal States
    (KSPW), 145
Communist Party of Germany (KPD),
    24, 25, 41, 66, 98, 123
Communist Party of the Soviet Union
    (CPSU), 123
Communitarianism, 12
Community studies, 53
Comte, Auguste, 7, 11, 59
Conflict theory, 77, 79, 82
Congress of Arts and Sciences, St.
    Louis, 14n6
Congress of GDR Sociology,
    132–135, 138, 144
Conservative Revolution, 24
Constructivism, 136, 153
Contract theory, 7
Critchley, Simon, 160n12
Critical rationalism, 73, 98, 118, 167
Critical Theory, 39, 61, 87, 89–91,
    95, 96, 104, 105, 110, 151,
    152, 164
Croner, Fritz Simon, 28
Cultural anthropology, 31
Cultural criticism, 59
Cultural history, 16, 27
Cultural philosophy, 16
Cultural sciences, 15n7, 16
Cultural studies, 4, 116n11
Curtius, Ernst Robert, 38

D
Dahrendorf, Ralf, 30n12, 55, 64, 68,
    69, 72, 73, 76, 77, 81, 88, 89,
    93, 150, 167
Deconstructivism, 151, 168
Deleuze, Gilles, 166
Demirović, Alex, 90, 160n12
Democracy Now, 141
Democratic liberalism, 96
Demography, 134, 136
Depth hermeneutics, 106
Derrida, Jacques, 152
Deutsche Kommunistische Partei
    (DKP), 98
Deutsche Zeitschrift für Philosophie
    (journal), 133
Developmental psychology, 96
Development of personality, 133
Dilthey, Wilhelm, 8n3, 15, 39
Doing gender, 153, 153n6
Dölling, Irene, 110, 136
Dreitzel, Hans Peter, 69
Drucker, Peter, 50
Dunkmann, Karl, 30, 36
Durkheim, Émile, 11n5, 59, 67, 80,
    99, 117, 134, 142, 157n9
Durkheim School, 14n6, 59, 116
Dutschke, Rudi, 86, 91

E
Eichmann, Adolf, 83
Eisenstadt, Shmuel, 115, 148
Elias, Norbert, 20, 29, 33,
    33n14, 46, 116
EMNID, Bielefeld, 54
Empirical social research, 19, 31, 39,
    51, 54, 55, 59, 60, 62, 64, 74,
    76, 79, 92, 103–106, 117, 120,
    128–130, 132, 133, 135, 162,
    166, 167
Empiricism, 11

Engels, Friedrich, 8, 130, 137
Ensslin, Gudrun, 101
Equality-difference debate, 111
Erhard, Ludwig, 66, 80
Esser, Hartmut, 118, 168n23
Ethnography of communication, 106
Ethnomethodology, 106, 165
Ethno-psychoanalysis, 106
Ethnosociology, 76
Ethnotheory, 106
Ettrich, Frank, 128, 132, 133, 137
European Sociological Association (ESA), 164

**F**
Faßhauer, Gertrud, 36
Faculty of Social Sciences, Konstanz, 94
Faculty of Sociology, Bielefeld, 94
Fassbinder, Rainer Werner, 81
Feminist Marxism, 136
Fischer, Joachim, 145
Flowerman, Samuel H., 61
Folk psychology, 13
Foucault, Michel, 115, 116, 151, 152
Fraenkel, Ernst, 50
Francis, Emerich K., 58n8
Franco, Francisco, 43
Frankfurter Beiträge zur Soziologie (journal), 79
Frankfurt School, 51, 61, 62, 72n14, 74, 89, 99, 128, 167
Fraser, Nancy, 151
Free Democratic Party (FDP), 66, 77
Freiburg School of ordoliberalism, 66
Freud, Sigmund, 87
Freudenthal, Margarete, 33
Freund, Gisèle, 33, 33n14
Freyer, Hans, 31, 32, 46, 47, 51, 57, 70, 72, 128, 162, 165
Friedeburg, Ludwig von, 68, 88

Friedmann, Georges, 83
Fromm, Erich, 34, 46, 50
Fukuyama, Francis, 147
Functionalism, 105
Fürstenberg, Friedrich, 80

**G**
Gagarin, Yuri, 126
Garfinkel, Harold, 107, 151, 153
Gay/lesbian studies, 154
Gehlen, Arnold, 31, 46, 53, 57, 58n8, 63, 66, 69, 70, 72, 79, 167
Geiger, Theodor, 35, 35n15, 36, 39, 40, 46, 49, 55
Gender studies, 107–111, 152–154
Genetics, 10
Gennep, Arnold van, 142
Gerhard, Ute, 110
German Academic Exchange Service (DAAD), 27
German Democratic Party (DDP), 22
German Historical School of Economics, 17
German Institute for Surveys of the People (DIVO), Frankfurt, 54
German Peace Society, 98
German Philosophical Association, 73
German Research Foundation (DFG), 146
German Sociological Association (GSA), 19–22, 25, 26, 37, 38, 40, 47, 49–53, 55, 56, 60, 70–72, 76, 77, 78n16, 83, 88, 93, 98, 100, 104, 105n4, 106, 107, 110, 112, 116, 136, 148, 163, 168–170
Gerth, Hans, 28, 33, 46
Gesellschaftswissenschaft (the science of society), 8
Giddens, Anthony, 117, 157

Gieryn, Thomas F., 154
Gildemeister, Regine, 153
Gilligan, Carol, 109
Gini, Corrado, 70
Goethe, Johann Wolfgang von, 13, 169
Goffman, Erving, 69, 107, 153
Goldmann, Lucien, 80
Goldscheid, Rudolf, 17, 36
Gorbachev, Mikhail, 120, 127, 141
Göring, Hermann, 41
Gouldner, Alvin, 98
Governmentality studies, 165
Granovetter, Mike, 118
Grazer Soziologische Gesellschaft, 19n8
Green Party of Germany, 121
Greens, The, 91, 103, 157, 158
Grossmann, Henryk, 34
Group discussion, 62
Group experiment, 62
Grünberg, Carl, 34
Grünwald, Ernst, 38
Guillaume, Günter, 102
Günther, Hans K., 46

# H

Habermas, Jürgen, 61, 73–76, 76n15, 84, 89, 90, 94–97, 102, 109, 113–117, 114n10, 146, 148, 149, 151, 152
Habermas-Luhmann debate, 94–97
Hagemann-White, Carol, 109, 153
Hager, Don, 51n2
Hahn, Erich, 132
Halbwachs, Maurice, 37, 80
Halperin, Natalie, 33
Hamburg Institute for Social Research, 162
Hark, Sabine, 109
Hartshorne, Edward Y., 50, 50n1
Hartz, Peter, 158n10
Haug, Frigga, 69, 109
Hauptmann, Gerhart, 10
Haussig, Frieda, 33
Haverkamp, Anselm, 160n12
Heberle, Rudolf, 36
Hedström, Peter, 118
Hegel, Georg Wilhelm Friedrich, 39
Heidegger, Martin, 96, 114
Heimann, Eduard, 50
Heinemann, Gustav, 100
Heintz, Peter, 60
Heitmeyer, Wilhelm, 157
Hennis, Wilhelm, 83n19
Hermeneutics, 96, 106, 107
Hertz, Friedrich, 36
Higher Academy of Administration, Speyer, 53
Hindenburg, Paul von, 23, 24, 41
Hirschauer, Stefan, 168n23
Historical materialism, 97, 116, 130, 133
Historicism, 11, 16, 27
Historikerstreit, 114, 114n10
Hitler, Adolf, 24, 35, 41–45, 51
Hobbes, Thomas, 7, 11, 14
Hofmann, Werner, 62
Honecker, Erich, 125–127, 133, 135, 142
Honigsheim, Paul, 26, 46
Horkheimer, Max, 34, 38, 39, 46, 50, 52, 57–59, 61–64, 67, 70, 72, 73, 78, 87, 96, 109
Humanities, 15, 40, 62
Humboldt, Wilhelm, 94

# I

Information on Sociological Research in the German Democratic Republic (journal), 133
Infratest, Munich, 54

Institute for Economic Sciences at the
    German Academy of the Sciences,
    Berlin, 131
Institute for Employment Research,
    Nuremberg, 91
Institute for Marxist Studies
    and Research (IMSF),
    Frankfurt, 91
Institute for Opinion Research at the
    SED CC, 135
Institute for Public Opinion Research
    in Allensbach, 54, 54n3, 146
Institute for Social Research
    (IfS), 34, 54, 61, 62, 68,
    88, 90, 95, 96
Institute for Social Science Research
    (ISF), Munich, 91
Institute for Social Sciences and
    Staatswissenschaften,
    Heidelberg, 27
Institute for Social Sciences at the SED
    CC (IfG), 132, 132n2
Institute for Social Sciences,
    Darmstadt, 54
Institute for Sociology and Social
    Policy at the Academy of the
    Sciences, GDR, 135
Institute for Sociology, Marburg, 63
Institute of Economics of the
    Trade Unions (WWI),
    Cologne, 54, 68
Institut International de Sociologie
    (IIS), 19n8, 70, 71
Interactionist phenomenological
    theory, 97
International Sociological Association
    (ISA), 35n15, 59, 60, 70,
    131, 164
Intersectionality, 154
Ipsen, Gunther, 31, 46, 70, 71, 162
ISA World Congress of
    Sociology, 59, 130

J
Jaffé, Edgar, 19
Jahrbuch für Gesetzgebung,
    Verwaltung und Rechtspflege des
    Deutschen Reiches (journal), 18
Jahrbuch für Soziologie
    (journal), 32, 37
Jantke, Carl, 72
Jellinek, Georg, 20
Jerusalem, Wilhelm, 36, 46
Joas, Hans, 69, 113, 116, 147, 165
Jüres, Ernst August, 68

K
Kaesler, Dirk, 1, 40, 83n19, 112, 150
Kant, Immanuel, 74, 115
Katz, Jakob, 33
Kaube, Jürgen, 134, 137, 138
Kelsen, Hans, 36
Kennedy, John F., 101
Kern, Horst, 78, 92
Kessler, Suzanne J., 153
Kesting, Hanno, 68
Khrushchev, Nikita, 129
Kiesinger, Kurt Georg, 80
Kirchheimer, Otto, 34
Klamer, Arjo, 169n24
Klein, Viola, 33
Klingemann, Carsten, 57, 162
Kluge, Alexander, 81
Knapp, Gudrun-Axeli, 109
Knöbl, Wolfgang, 113
Knorr-Cetina, Karin, 94
Kohl, Helmut, 54n3, 120, 142, 154,
    155, 157
Kohli, Martin, 147
Kölner Vierteljahrshefte für
    Sozialwissenschaften
    (journal), 26
Kölner Vierteljahrshefte für Soziologie
    (journal), 26, 36, 55

Kölner Zeitschrift für Soziologie und Sozialpsychologie (KZfSS) (journal), 26, 55, 60, 61, 69, 79, 83, 112, 155
König, Josef, 77
König, René, 34, 50, 57–64, 59n9, 67, 69–73, 71n12, 78, 79, 105, 110, 112, 116, 130, 169
Konstanz School, 107
Kracauer, Siegfried, 34, 39, 40, 46
Krais, Beate, 110
Kreckel, Reinhard, 164n19
Kreps, David M., 169, 170n24
Kretzschmar, Albrecht, 135
Krieck, Ernst, 46
Krüger, Gerhard, 46
Kuczynski, Jürgen, 128, 130

## L
Lamprecht, Karl, 20
Landsberg, Paul Ludwig, 36
Landshut, Siegfried, 30, 77
Latour, Bruno, 166
Lazarsfeld, Paul F., 55, 60, 106
Lazarus, Moritz, 13
Lederer, Emil, 22, 28, 29, 31, 33, 39, 46, 50
The Left, 158
Leipzig sociology, 31
Lepenies, Wolf, 1, 112, 166n20, 170n24
Lepsius, M. Rainer, 83n19, 112, 122
Leviathan (journal), 87, 93
Lewin, Kurt, 62
Lichtblau, Klaus, 83n19
Lindenberg, Siegwart, 118
Lipps, Theodor, 20
Litt, Theodor, 128
Locke, John, 7
Lockwood, David, 77
Logical empiricism, 74

Logical positivism, 72n14
London School of Economics (LSE), 73, 76, 77, 89
Lötsch, Ingrid, 135
Lötsch, Manfred, 131, 133, 135
Lowe, Adolph, 50
Löwenthal, Leo, 34
Lowie, Robert H., 37
Lübbe, Hermann, 67
Luckmann, Thomas, 69, 107, 145
Ludz, Christian, 78n16
Luhmann, Niklas, 64, 75, 76, 76n15, 84, 94–97, 113–117, 148, 149
Lukács, Georg, 29, 39, 52, 61, 67, 80, 87
Lütkens, Charlotte, 33
Lutz, Burkart, 68
Luxemburg, Rosa, 87

## M
Mackenroth, Gerhard, 58n8, 59n8
Macrosociology, 145
Malinowski, Bronislaw, 31, 37
Manchester School of Economics, 17
Manheim, Ernest, 46
Mann, Heinrich, 10
Mannheim, Karl, 2, 26, 29, 33–36, 33n14, 38–40, 46, 50, 56, 73, 116, 118n12
Marburg School, 62
Marcuse, Herbert, 34, 38, 61, 80, 83, 87, 89, 155
Marr, Heinz, 33
Marshall, Thomas H., 77
Martin, Alfred von, 46, 56
Marx, Karl, 8, 30, 39, 67, 68, 76, 79, 87, 90, 100, 104, 116, 117, 130, 137
Marxism, 34, 38–42, 45, 52, 62, 63, 80, 87, 92, 96, 99, 100, 108, 111, 116, 128, 137, 138, 151

Marxism-Leninism, 124, 127–138
Marxist-Leninist philosophy, 3
Materialism, 8
Matthes, Joachim, 97, 106
Maunier, René, 37
Maus, Heinz, 51, 52, 62, 80, 128
Max Planck Institute for Human Development, Berlin, 82n18, 146
Max Planck Institute for the Study of Societies, Cologne, 113n9
Max Planck Institute for the Study of the Scientific-Technical World, Starnberg, 97, 113
Mayer, Carl, 29
Mayer, Jacob Peter, 30
Mayntz, Renate, 61n11, 76, 78n16, 104, 113n9, 118, 145, 150
McKenna, Wendy, 153
Mead, George Herbert, 69, 80
Meier, Artur, 133
Meja, Volker, 167
Menger, Carl, 17
Merton, Robert K., 60, 106, 157n9
Methodological individualism, 105
Methods
  qualitative, 62, 68, 103–107, 117
  quantitative, 60, 78, 105, 106, 117, 118, 151, 168, 169
Meusel, Alfred, 128
Meuter, Hanna, 36
Meyer, Carl, 46
Meyer, Hansgünter, 131, 133
Michels, Robert, 36, 37
Microsociology, 145
Mies, Maria, 107
Mills, C. Wright, 33, 80
Misgeld, Dieter, 167
Modernization theory, 146, 147
Mohl, Robert von, 8, 18
Mommsen, Wolfgang J., 83n19
Monatsschrift für Soziologie (journal), 18

Mosca, Gaetano, 37
Mühlmann, Wilhelm Emil, 72
Müller, Hans-Peter, 83n19, 150
Müller, Karl Valentin, 32, 57, 70, 71
Müller-Armack, Alfred, 66
Münch, Richard, 115, 160n13

N
National Democratic Party of Germany (NPD), 83
National Socialism, 1, 3, 23, 31, 32, 34, 35, 40–42, 45–47, 45n18, 49–52, 51n2, 54n3, 55, 67, 70, 71, 71n12, 83, 112, 162–163
National Socialist German Workers' Party (NSDAP), 24, 25, 33, 35, 41, 50, 58, 59n8, 63, 80
Natural sciences, 15
Nave-Herz, Rosemarie, 61, 61n11
Neo-institutionalism, 118, 164
Neo-Kantianism, 15
Neo-Marxism, 79
Neo-pragmatism, 165
Network research, 118
Neuloh, Otto, 53
Neumann, Erich P., 54, 54n3
Neumann, Franz, 34, 46, 50
Neumann, Sigmund, 50
Neurath, Otto, 38
New Forum, 141
New School for Social Research, 28, 46
Nickel, Hildegard Maria, 136, 146
Nida-Rümelin, Julian, 160n12
Nietzsche, Friedrich, 10, 11, 13, 15
Noelle-Neumann, Elisabeth, 54, 54n3, 72
Nolte, Ernst, 114n10
Nunner-Winkler, Gertrud, 109

## O

Objective hermeneutics, 106
Oelsner, Toni, 33
Oevermann, Ulrich, 106
Ogburn, William F., 37
Ohnesorg, Benno, 86, 101
Ohrnberger, Anny, 26
OMGUS Surveys, 54
Opp, Karl-Dieter, 97, 118, 146
Oppenheimer, Franz, 20, 25, 29, 32, 32n13, 33, 36, 46, 118n12
Organicism, 15
Organization for Economic Co-Ordination and Development (OECD), 81
Ostner, Ilona, 109

## P

Park, Robert E., 14n6, 36
Parsons, Talcott, 28, 67, 69, 80, 83, 94, 115, 116
Party of Democratic Socialism (PDS), 158
Paulitz, Tanja, 109, 151, 153, 153n6
Peter, Lothar, 1, 2, 137, 155
Pfeffer, Karl-Heinz, 32, 46, 71
Phenomenology, 26, 106, 107, 116
Philosophical anthropology, 26, 39, 59, 67, 68, 77, 116, 165
Philosophy of history, 8, 57
Philosophy of language, 96
Philosophy of life, 21
Pirker, Theo, 68
Plenge, Johann, 36
Plessner, Helmuth, 26, 27, 36, 39, 57, 58n8, 69–72, 77, 78, 96
Ploder, Andrea, 106, 167n22
Pollack, Detlef, 146
Pollock, Friedrich, 34, 46
Popitz, Heinrich, 30n12, 64, 68, 69, 76, 77

Popper, Karl, 73, 74, 77, 167
Positivism, 11, 15, 60, 62, 73, 78, 89, 97, 168
Positivism Dispute, 72–75, 97, 103
Postcolonial studies, 116n11, 148
Postmaterialism, 121
Postmodernism, 113, 114, 121, 147, 148
Poststructuralism, 114, 116n11, 152, 165, 166
Pragmatism, 96, 116
Priority Program at the German Research Foundation (DFG), 146
Professional Association of German Sociologists, 104, 163
Programme for International Student Assessment (PISA), 160n13
Pross, Helge, 61n11, 109
Psychoanalysis, 10
Public opinion, 82

## Q

Queer studies, 154, 166

## R

Rammstedt, Otthein, 162
Ransch, Siegfried, 131
Raspe, Jan-Carl, 101
Rational choice theories, 118, 120, 146, 147, 164
Reagan, Ronald, 101, 120
Red Army Faction (RAF), 91, 101
Reemtsma, Jan Philipp, 162
Rehberg, Karl-Siegbert, 145
Reich, Wilhelm, 87
Reichenau, Charlotte von, 36
Religious studies, 10
Research Association for Sociology and Society, GDR, 131

218  INDEX

Research Institute for Social and Administrative Sciences at the University of Cologne, 54
Research Institute for Social Sciences, Cologne, 26
Reza Pahlavi, Mohammed, 86
Rickert, Heinrich, 15, 15n7
Riemer, Svend, 28
Ringer, Fritz, 76
Risk society, 119
Rockefeller Foundation, 35, 60
Role Debate, 69, 75
Role theory, 69, 77, 99
Römer, Oliver, 93
Rothacker, Erich, 95
Rubinstein, Nina, 33
Rucht, Dieter, 146
Rudolph, Günther, 131
Rumpf, Max, 36, 46, 162
Rüschemeyer, Dietrich, 60
Rüstow, Alexander, 56

S
St Antony's College, Oxford, 89n1
Saint-Simon, Henri de, 7, 11
Salomon, Albert, 28, 29
Salomon, Friedrich, 30
Salomon, Gottfried, 29, 32, 33, 37
Sapir, Edward, 37
Schabowski, Günter, 127, 142
Schäfers, Bernhard, 146
Schäffle, Albert, 18
Scharpf, Fritz, 104, 118
Scheler, Hermann, 130, 131
Scheler, Max, 22, 25–27, 36, 39
Schelling, Friedrich Wilhelm Joseph, 95
Schelsky, Helmut, 31, 40, 46, 53, 57–59, 59n8, 63–64, 66, 67, 69–72, 71n12, 74, 75, 78, 79, 93–96, 99, 100, 112, 119n12, 131, 165, 167
Schelting, Alexander von, 38
Scheu, Maria, 26
Scheuch, Erwin K., 60, 61, 76, 78
Schimank, Uwe, 165
Schluchter, Wolfgang, 78n16, 83n19, 146
Schmidt, Gert, 68
Schmidt, Helmut, 102
Schmoller, Gustav, 17, 18
Schmollers Jahrbuch (journal), 18
Schopenhauer, Arthur, 14
Schröder, Gerhard, 117, 157–159
Schubert, Rainer, 131
Schulz, Robert, 130
Schulze, Gerhard, 150
Schumann, Michael, 78, 92
Schumpeter, Joseph A., 50
Schütz, Alfred, 39, 46, 107, 116
Schütze, Fritz, 106
Science studies, 166
Scientific Council for Sociological Research in the German Democratic Republic, 125, 131–133
Scientism, 73
Section for Sociology of the Association of the Philosophical Institutions of the GDR, 131
Sennett, Richard, 155
Shils, Edward, 115
Siebeck, Paul, 22
Siegfried, Detlef, 87
Simmel, Georg, 8, 10–15, 14n6, 18, 20, 21, 25, 29, 29n11, 39, 69, 99, 108, 116
Small, Albion, 14n6
Social and Political Change in the Course of the Integration of the GDR Society
Social Democratic Party in the GDR, 141

Social Democratic Party of Germany
    (SPD), 24–25, 66, 80, 86, 91,
    101, 120, 123, 157, 158
Social
  history, 60n10
  indicators, 104
  inequality, 82, 109, 111, 117, 136,
    147, 155, 156n8, 157
  mobility, 60n10, 82
  philosophy, 59
  planning, 82
  policy, 60n10, 82, 104
  policy research, 134
  problems, 37, 40, 47, 59, 64, 104,
    117, 137, 142, 143,
    150, 154–157
  question, 7–9, 7n1, 17–19
  stratification, 35, 39, 49, 60n10,
    67, 77, 82
Socialist German Student Union
    (SDS), 86, 87, 91
Socialist Unity Party of Germany
    (SED), 123–126, 131, 132, 134,
    135, 141, 142, 158
Social Research (journal), 28
Social Research Centre at the
    University of Münster in
    Dortmund, 53, 57, 64, 68,
    71, 77, 95
Social Science Student Association, 18
Social structure, 27, 35, 40,
    49, 65, 136
  research on, 117, 131,
    134–136, 147
Society for Sociology of the GDR
    (GfS), 133, 138, 144
Sociobiology, 116
Sociolinguistics, 134
Sociological Research Institute
    Göttingen (SOFI), 77, 91, 92
Sociological theory, 67, 83, 95, 114,
    116, 117, 119, 152
Sociologus (journal), 37, 79
Sociology
  of age and aging, 148
  of agriculture, 133
  agricultural, 47
  analytical, 118
  applied, 19, 40, 45, 47, 51, 54, 59,
    60, 104, 105, 121, 129, 135
  of art, 28, 60n10
  of bureaucracy, 77
  of business, 68
  community, 60
  of companies, 39
  of consumption, 82
  of crime, 136
  cultural, 16, 27, 30, 39, 77, 99,
    100, 116, 117, 149n4
  of culture, 117, 133, 149, 159
  of developing countries, 104
  of development, 60n10, 134
  dialectical, 89
  of Eastern Europe, 76, 91, 104
  economic, 39, 149, 159
  of education, 64, 76, 78, 82, 91,
    103, 104, 117, 133
  of election, 60n10
  of emotions, 147, 164
  empirical, 59, 60, 168
  empirical-analytical, 105, 168
  of employment, 28
  English, 15
  of the environment, 77, 136
  of ethnicity, 39
  of everyday life, 60n10, 77
  explanatory, 118, 151
  of the family, 60, 60n10, 63, 64, 67,
    68, 76, 77, 104, 136
  of fashion, 60
  feminist, 108n5, 111, 151–154, 165
  formal, 25, 30, 32, 39, 47
  French, 15, 130
  of the GDR, 60n10

Sociology (*cont.*)
 of gender, 117, 146, 152
 of generations, 63
 group, 53
 historical, 27, 31, 32, 39, 56, 57, 116, 118n12, 165
 industrial, 53, 67, 68, 76–78, 80, 82, 83, 91, 92, 103, 104, 120, 130, 131, 133
 of institutions, 146
 of intellectuals, 39, 117
 of juvenile delinquency, 60n10
 of knowledge, 26, 28, 29, 32, 34, 38, 39, 73, 107, 149
 of labor, 39, 53, 91, 103, 131, 133
 of language, 39, 60n10, 104, 107, 117
 of law, 39, 60n10, 95, 104, 114, 128, 146, 148
 of leisure, 82, 136
 of literature, 39
 of mass communication, 76, 134
 of masses, 39
 of medicine, 60n10, 104, 134
 of the military, 60n10
 municipal, 53, 60n10, 67, 68
 of music, 39
 of organizations, 53, 64, 76, 94, 131, 133
 of the people, 55
 phenomenological, 39
 political, 39, 78n16, 83, 149
 of population, 39, 47
 public, 121, 149, 164
 of public opinion, 28
 of religion, 60n10, 76, 104, 117, 134, 158
 of revolutions, 28
 of school, 60n10
 of science, 60n10, 77, 104, 134
 of sexuality, 63
 of social mechanisms, 118
 of social movements, 146
 of sport, 60n10, 134
 of technology, 39
 urban, 47, 53, 77, 82, 103, 104, 134, 136
 US-American, 30, 31, 35, 55, 59, 62, 74, 130, 167
 of violence, 28
 völkisch, 45, 46, 71
 of war and peace, 91, 136
 of work, 53, 78, 120, 136, 149, 159
 of youth, 63, 64, 67, 68, 76, 82, 104, 130, 133, 136
Sociology of Knowledge Dispute, 37–40
Soeffner, Hans-Georg, 107
Solms, Max Graf zu, 36
Sombart, Werner, 13, 17, 19, 20, 28, 30, 36, 38, 118n12, 162
Sorokin, Pitirim A., 36, 37
Soziale Welt (journal), 55, 64, 79
Soziologentag, 20, 26, 37–40, 49, 50, 52, 76, 83, 88, 89, 95, 97, 98, 104, 136
Soziologie (journal), 93
Soziologische Revue (journal), 87, 93
Soziologische Texte (journal), 80
Spann, Othmar, 36, 162
Speier, Hans, 28, 29, 31, 33, 46
Spencer, Herbert, 7, 11, 15
Spranger, Eduard, 17
Staatliches Berufspädagogisches Institut, 31
Staatswissenschaft (science of the state), 8, 18, 25
Stalin, Josef, 124, 129
Stammer, Otto, 58n8, 72, 78, 78n16
Stegmann, Kurt, 70
Stehr, Nico, 167
Stein, Lorenz von, 8
Steiner, Helmut, 131
Steinhoff, Maria, 36

Steinmetz, Sebald Rudolf, 36, 37
Steinthal, Heyman, 13
Sternberg, Fritz, 32, 50
Strauss, Anselm, 107
Strauß, Franz Josef, 80
Strübing, Jörg, 168n23
Structural functionalism, 59, 69, 79, 99
Structuralism, 136
Suderland, Maja, 163
Swiss Sociological Association, 136
Symbolic interactionism, 116, 136
Systems theory, 95–97, 95n2, 113–115, 146, 151, 156n8, 164

T

Takata, Yasama, 37
Tenbruck, Friedrich, 69, 83n19, 99, 100, 116, 149n4, 167, 168
Teschner, Manfred, 68
Thatcher, Margaret, 150
Theoretical-behavioral approach, 97
Theory comparison debate, 75, 97–98
Theory of communicative action, 96, 97, 113
Theory of multiple modernities, 148
Theory of practice, 165
Theory of reflexive modernization, 119, 148, 151, 165
Theory of the civilizing process, 116
Thiel, Manfred, 131
Thurnwald, Richard, 30, 35–37, 56, 79, 128
Tjaden, Karl Hermann, 95n2, 97
Tönnies, Ferdinand, 8, 11–14, 14n6, 18, 20, 22, 25, 35–37, 46, 51, 128, 131
Topitsch, Ernst, 83, 167
Transformations, sociological research on, 145–147
Treiber, Hubert, 83n19
Treitschke, Heinrich von, 8n3

Troeltsch, Ernst, 13, 20, 22
Trotsky, Leon, 87
Truhel, Käthe, 33
Turner, Victor, 142
Tyrell, Hartmann, 83n19

U

Ulbricht, Walter, 124–127, 133
UNESCO Institute for Social Sciences, Cologne, 54
United Nations Educational, Scientific and Cultural Organization (UNESCO), 56
University of Labor, Politics, and Economics, Wilhelmshaven, 53
Utilitarianism, 11

V

Verein für Socialpolitik, 17, 19
Vienna Circle, 72n14
Vierkandt, Alfred, 20, 30, 35–37, 39, 46, 56, 59, 128
Vierteljahrsschrift für wissenschaftliche Philosophie und Soziologie (journal), 18
Vitalism, 21
Voigt, Peter, 133
von Wiese, Leopold, 131

W

Wagner, Peter, 150
Walther, Andreas, 31, 35, 36, 46, 51, 162
Ward, Lester F., 14n6
Weber, Alfred, 20, 22, 27, 29, 33, 34, 38, 46, 51, 56, 116, 118n12
Weber, Max, 8, 11–20, 14n6, 22, 25, 28, 29n11, 31, 33, 39, 60n10, 67, 68, 83, 83n19, 99, 115–118, 167, 169

Weiß, Johannes, 83n19
Weidig, Rudi, 132, 135
Weigel, Helene, 124
Weingart, Peter, 78n16
Weischer, Christoph, 104, 105, 120
Weizsäcker, Carl Friedrich von, 113n9
Weltz, Friedrich, 68
Wenders, Wim, 81
Werturteilsfreiheit, 17, 19, 21, 22, 73, 168
Werturteilsstreit, 16–17, 19, 20, 167
West, Candace, 153
Wetterer, Angelika, 153
White, Harrison, 118
Wiener Soziologische Gesellschaft, 19n8
Wiese, Leopold von, 25, 26, 36–40, 46, 47, 50–52, 54–56, 58, 60, 162
Wilhelm II., 22
Winckelmann, Johannes, 83n19
Windelband, Wilhelm, 15, 15n7
Winkler, Gunnar, 135
Wissenschaftszentrum Berlin (WZB), 91
Wittvogel, Karl August, 38, 39
Wolf, Herbert Franz, 130, 131, 133
Wolff, Kurt H., 33
Women
  issues, research on, 107–111
  studies, 104, 107, 109, 136, 152
Working Group of Bielefeld Sociologists, 106
Worms, René, 14n6, 70
Wunderlich, Frieda, 29, 31, 33

**Z**

Zapf, Wolfgang, 146
Zeitschrift für die gesamte Staatswissenschaft (journal), 18
Zeitschrift für Sozialforschung (journal), 34
Zeitschrift für Sozialwissenschaft (journal), 18
Zeitschrift für Soziologie (journal), 93, 94
Zeitschrift für Völkerpsychologie und Soziologie (journal), 31, 37
Ziegellaub, Ilse, 33
Ziegler, Rolf, 118
Zimmerman, Don H., 153
Zuckmayer, Carl, 28

The manufacturer's authorised representative in the EU is Springer Nature Customer Service Centre GmbH, Europaplatz 3, 69115 Heidelberg, Germany. If you have any concerns regarding our products, please contact ProductSafety@springernature.com

Printed and bound by CPI Group (UK) Ltd, Croydon, CR0 4YY
23/03/2026
02076663-0002